NORTHWEST
kid trips

| PORTLAND | SEATTLE |
| VANCOUVER | VICTORIA |

LORA SHINN

PARENT MAP

Printed in the United States of America
Published by ParentMap
Distributed by Ingram Publisher Services
04 01 10 MAL 01 40 00 19 95
First Edition

Cover design: Emily Johnson
Interior design and composition: Emily Johnson
Illustrations by Alli Arnold
Front cover photos (left to right): iStock (Cosmonaught Creative Media, LLC), Lora Shinn, iStock (Natalia Bratslavsky), Chris Karges
Back cover photos (left to right): iStock (Jeanne Hatch), Lora Shinn, Lora Shinn, iStock (Frank Leung Birdimages Photography)

Library of Congress Cataloging-in-Publication Data is available.

ISBN-13: 978-0-9823454-3-6
ISBN-10: 0-9823454-3-7

ParentMap dba Gracie Enterprises
4742 Forty-second Ave. S.W., #399
Seattle, WA 98116-4553
206-709-9026

ParentMap books are available at special discounts when purchased in bulk for premiums and sales promotions, as well as for fundraisers or educational use. Place book orders at *parentmap.com* or 206-709-9026.

For Bill, Isabelle, and Emmett:
You make every trip memorable.

contents

acknowledgments

Thank you to the well-traveled, smart, and savvy women who helped me double-check every restaurant, shop, and activity listed in this book. They are, in alphabetical order: Leah Adams, Jen Betterley, Kristin French, Morgan Gilhespy, Sarah Pugh, Julia Rudden, Tera Schreiber, Amy Scott, Marie Wallas, and Melanie Willson.

I appreciate the background and research assistance provided by visitor bureaus, specifically, Deborah Wakefield and Tin Bui at Travel Portland, Emily Armstrong and Amber Zoe Sessions at Tourism Vancouver, Cathy Ray and Holly Lenk at Tourism Victoria, Robin Jacobson at San Juan Islands Visitors Bureau, Marsha Fuzia at the City of Cannon Beach, and Lauren Curtin at Seattle's Convention & Visitors Bureau. Thank you for your insights into the cities you love.

I deeply appreciate my ParentMap team: my fearless and funny editor, Kristen Russell Dobson, who pried the manuscript out of my hands and made it better; my publisher, Alayne Sulkin, who brought a joyful enthusiasm to this project; and art director Emily Johnson, who took this sloppy pile of text and made it look organized and appealing. Thanks, too, to Sunny Parsons, who profred my copee proofread my copy. If not for you all, this book would still be a coffee-stained pile of notebooks.

Thanks to Christina Katz, Northwest-based author of *Writer Mama: How to Raise a Writing Career Alongside Your Kids*. Your book kick-started my writing journey several years ago; I'm pleased with the results. I also appreciate the advice of Amanda Castleman, who taught my first travel-writing course. I loved the professional advice of travel writers Kris Collingridge, Michelle Duffy, Debbie Abrams Kaplan, Jen Miller, and Diane Selkirk.

And my deepest appreciation goes to my patient children and husband, who accompanied me on twelve-hour research days, enduring many bad restaurants and numerous blah activities. Despite all these travails during our travels, they helped me find the gems. They are my inspiration to keep traveling and writing, and to inspire other families to do the same.

After all, we can't keep all this fun to ourselves. Thanks again to everyone who made this book possible.

introduction

THE PACIFIC NORTHWEST: THE PERFECT FAMILY-FRIENDLY DESTINATION

The words "Pacific Northwest" conjure up images of coffee and computers, gray skies and aerospace. But this rain-drenched region has a playful side, too, and a laid-back attitude that makes it a great fit for family adventures. The dress code? Casual. The skies? Nowhere near as gray as you think. The fun? Quirky, smart, and outdoorsy.

This book focuses on family-friendly, locally owned, independent hotels, restaurants, and shops that give a true flavor of the regional spirit — but if there's a chain hotel or restaurant that provides an exceptional experience, I'll let you know.

So you won't find McDonald's in here, but you will find a homegrown alternative (Burgerville). Some restaurants are decked out with toys and play spaces, while others simply have a welcoming attitude towards children; the same is true for hotels — some come with kids' backpacks stuffed with great toys, while others just represent the best of the Northwest, and may be more suitable for older children or teens.

Each city has its own unique vibe; one of the best ways to really know a city is to visit the neighborhoods, away from the tourist crowds. I've incorporated the best and biggest hits of each city (the Space Needle and the Oregon Museum of Science and Industry), and turned up lots of little out-of-the-way treasures that make family travel so memorable.

This book is organized around neighborhoods, with hotels, restaurants, shops, and attractions laid out neighborhood by neighborhood. I've tried to make everything as walkable as possible, so you can hit a museum, have lunch, play in a nearby park, and maybe sample a shop or two. I encourage you to break away from traditional tourist attractions and head instead for children's theater, sports events, and playgrounds. You might be the only out-of-town family in attendance, but it's a great way to forge quick friendships with (and get great tips from) local families.

In my research, I never accepted free stays, gifts, or meals — and just know that for every great restaurant I found, I ate at two awful ones.

Remember that admission prices and times may change with the season, economic conditions, and inflation. I can guarantee that some prices and hours have changed by the time this book gets published — they'll change within the days or weeks after I write this sentence. **Always call ahead to ensure that a business is open.**

WHEN TO GO WHERE

Spring: Spring in the Northwest brings forth the flowers as early as March, without the heavy crowds. The weather can be touch-and-go (rain alternating with sun — every half-hour!), but that keeps everything fresh and clean. Spring school breaks offer nice weather coupled with affordable shoulder-season rates. I especially love Victoria, British Columbia, in spring — because of the flowers — but try to visit when the weather's nice, because it's a walking town.

Summer: Summer is spectacular in the Northwest. Most cities have flower baskets on every lamppost, mild temperatures, and warm city streets, and nature sparkles with green and blue hues. All that beauty comes at a price, though — sky-high rates at most hotels, at attractions, and even in restaurants. Portland is often a good choice during summer — it's warmer than northern neighbors, less afflicted by summer peak pricing, and there's great outdoor dining *everywhere.*

Fall: After older kids go back to school, attractions aren't quite as busy and restaurants aren't quite as full. Fall's mild weather often seems less rainy than spring or winter — great if you've got a baby or toddler in a stroller. It's one of my favorite seasons to travel in the Pacific Northwest. Consider heading to Vancouver, B.C.; the lodging rates are on their way down, the heavy crowds have thinned, and the indoor/outdoor options are still plentiful.

Winter: Locals have more time to chat, and there's nothing quite as nice as tea (or a pint) next to a roaring fireplace. That said, kids don't always love the cold and wet of wintry weather, so pack very warm layers (think woolens), rain-proof gear, and the umbrella. Be aware that some restaurants close or have limited hours in deep winter, due to the slowdown in visitors. Despite this, I love Seattle in winter — and so many Seattle attractions are indoors (The Children's Museum, Pacific Science Center, Experience Music Project (EMP), and the Seattle Aquarium, among others).

SAVING MONEY

I've tried to point out value options throughout the book, and each sleeping and eating option is rated on a price scale, from $ (cheapest) to $$$$ (most expensive). For restaurants, the rule of thumb is, per adult entrée:

$	**$10 and under**
$$	**$11–$20**
$$$	**$21–$30**

For hotels, a room that accommodates four people (two queen beds), during the high season (typically June–August):

$	**$75 and under**
$$	**$80–$150**
$$$	**$155–$200**
$$$$	**over $200**

Rates can go up and down depending on season, events, and popularity. Always ask about AAA traveler and other discounts, and check the hotel's Web site for special online rates.

Here are my top tips for traveling the Northwest affordably and comfortably:

1. Go during the off-season. It's quieter, lodging is far less expensive (sometimes up to 50 percent less), and many child-friendly attractions wisely offer both indoor and outdoor options. Besides, it's the Northwest; put on your waterproof shell and brave the rain!

2. Learn to use Priceline (*priceline.com*). Go to Bidding for Travel (*bidding fortravel.com*) and spend a few minutes learning bidding strategies. You can save hundreds of dollars if you're flexible about your dates, sleep options, and accommodations. My family of four has slept in Portland for just $35/night and Vancouver for $50/night, in three- or four-star hotels. Priceline options in Victoria and Seattle can be more difficult to secure.

3. Eat in. Find accommodations that allow you to cook in the room, saving plenty on eating expenses — even if that just means you've got a fridge for your pizza leftovers. When staying in a hotel, eat one meal per day in-room: oatmeal packets in the morning, or a picnic lunch at noon.

4. Be picky about purchases. Cut down on souvenirs and only buy items that are truly unique — things you can't get at home. You'll find that the kinds of shops listed here carry unusual or region-specific items. Try giving the kids a little money of their own (perhaps $5 for younger children, $10 for older) to mellow out the gimme-gimmes.

5. Buy a membership. Many regional attractions have reciprocity agreements with other attractions — if you buy a membership at Portland's Oregon Museum of Science and Industry (OMSI), you'll get in free to the Pacific Science Center (Seattle) and Telus World of Science (Vancouver), through the ASTC Passport Program. Read more at *astc.org*. The Oregon Zoo in Portland and Seattle's Woodland Park Zoo offer a similar reciprocal arrangement; check your local memberships to see if you can benefit from such an agreement.

SAMPLE NORTHWEST ROUTES: 3 DAYS, 5 DAYS, 7 DAYS, AND 14 DAYS

When thinking about traveling with kids, remember this: Less is far, far more. While parents often have great dreams of hitting four attractions per day, the perfect toddler schedule runs more like: breakfast, attraction, lunch, nap, park or pool, dinner. Older kids aren't much different — just take out the nap. Try spending a week or even two in just one city. My family does, and we never tire of discovering new neighborhoods, parks, and hidden gems.

Three days: Don't spread your family too thin. Stay in just one city for three days, which works out to just two nights. You won't see it all; cut yourself some slack and make plans to come back.

Five days: See a city and a nearby locale. A few examples: Portland–Cannon Beach; Seattle-Bainbridge; Victoria–San Juan Islands; Vancouver-Whistler.

Seven days: This is a serious vacation. You can combine two large cities without too much stress; just make sure they're near one another. Examples: Portland-Seattle; Seattle-Victoria; Victoria-Vancouver; Seattle-Vancouver. If you're flying in, use the "open-jaw" strategy (fly into Portland, out of Seattle).

Fourteen days: Lucky you (and lucky kids!). You can run the Northwest loop (Portland-Seattle-Victoria-Vancouver) if you want — but definitely fly open-jaw if arriving by plane.

CHILD-FRIENDLY CHAIN HOTELS

Throughout this book I've tried to focus on local and independent standouts, but you might have earned a free night's stay at a chain hotel, with points or miles. Maybe you just yearn for a four-star getaway with kids. My two favorite child-friendly chains:

Westin Resorts. Kids checking in receive a small backpack full of games, treats, and a movie coupon. Can't beat that. In most cities, Westin is located in a prime area, central to the action.

Kimpton Hotels. This San Francisco–based chain offers quirky bennies at many of its hotels, including a free fish to baby-sit during your stay, radio-controlled cars, and a cookie hour.

A VERY IMPORTANT NOTE

In the Pacific Northwest (as everywhere!), hours change, stores come and go, and restaurants are bought and sold. The information in this book was accurate when it went off to the presses, but could have changed the very next day! **Avoid disappointment — always call or look up attractions, restaurants, and stores before heading out.**

FACTS AT A GLANCE

U.S. holidays

This is a list of federal holidays in the U.S., when most banks will be closed and kids will be out of school. Generally, stores and restaurants will observe regular hours during these holidays, with the exception of Christmas Day, Christmas Eve (day before Christmas), New Year's Eve, and New Year's Day. Columbus Day is generally not observed in Washington state or Oregon. The day after Thanksgiving is a heavy shopping day in the U.S. If a holiday falls on the weekend, banks and other federal entities will observe the holiday on the preceding Friday. Long weekends (Saturday–Monday) can bring long lines at Canadian-U.S. border crossings; pack patience or go early.

January 1: New Year's Day
Third Monday in January: Martin Luther King Jr. Day
Third Monday in February: Presidents Day
Last Monday in May: Memorial Day
July 4: Independence Day
First Monday in September: Labor Day
October 12: Columbus Day

November 11: Veterans Day
Fourth Thursday in November: Thanksgiving Day
December 25: Christmas Day

Canadian holidays

Banks will be closed on the following holidays, and employees are entitled to New Year's Day, Good Friday, Canada Day, Labour Day, and Christmas Day off or must receive overtime.

January 1: New Year's Day
Friday before Easter: Good Friday
Monday after Easter: Easter Monday
Monday on or before May 24: Victoria Day
July 1: Canada Day
First Monday in August: B.C. Day
First Monday in September: Labour Day
Second Monday in October: Thanksgiving Day
November 11: Remembrance Day
December 25: Christmas Day
December 26: Boxing Day

Measurements

Canada uses the metric system; the U.S. uses the imperial system.
1 Canadian gallon = 4.5 liters
1 American gallon = 3.8 liters
Miles x 1.6 = kilometers
Kilometers x 0.6 = miles
20° C = 68°F
0° C = 32°F

Phones

When calling between the U.S. and Canada, there's no need to do anything special other than dial the area code, but international call rates will apply. Your cell phone will likely automatically convert to a new carrier when entering the neighboring country, but check with your cell phone company beforehand about international call rates or data rates.

Currency and spending money

Debit and credit cards are accepted everywhere. Tell your bank before you leave that you'll be visiting — vigilant credit card companies may "turn off" your card, fearing that it's been stolen and used at charming, child-friendly restaurants.

You may also be surprised with a small gift when returning home: Card companies may charge between 1 percent and 5 percent of the total in fees when purchasing in a foreign currency. Cards vary, so compare rates before you leave and call your credit card company to verify the fees it will charge.

The fees are still better than fees you'll incur when exchanging money, so your best bet is to take out cash from an ATM to use as spending money, despite the card fee.

The exchange rates between U.S. and Canadian dollars fluctuate wildly. I've used local currencies when writing the book; compare today's rates at *xe.com*.

Taxes

Purchases made in British Columbia are subject to a 12 percent sales tax — a combination of the federal sales tax (GST) of 5 percent and the provincial sales tax (PST) of 7 percent — which applies to retail purchases. The exception is the purchase of liquor, which is taxed at 10 percent. Groceries, restaurant meals, children's clothing, and books are PST exempt, unless taxed by the city. As of mid-2010, the new 12 percent Harmonized Sales Tax will be in effect, which will combine the GST and PST. Read more at *gov.bc.ca/hst*. Hotel stays and rentals incur additional taxes.

Washington state purchases are subject to 6.5 percent sales tax, in addition to municipal taxes that may be charged.

Oregon state purchases are not subject to tax, with the exception of a 1 percent lodging tax and any additional municipal taxes.

Tipping

Tipping is the same as anywhere: 15 percent for adequate service, 20 percent for great service. Consider being generous when leaving a tip — we families tend to make a bigger mess than the average visitor!

Child car seats

British Columbia and Washington state all impose stiff fines for going without seatbelts and require rear-facing infant car seat use, but rules vary on booster seats:

B.C.: Infants up to one year of age and weighing less than 9 kilograms (20 pounds) must use a rear-facing car seat. Children younger than age five must use an approved safety seat.

Washington: Infants who are younger than one year of age and weigh less than 20 pounds must ride in a rear-facing car seat. Children younger than eight must be secured in child-restraint systems (car seat or booster seat), unless the child is 4 feet 9 inches or taller. Children younger than thirteen years old must be transported in rear seats where it is practical to do so.

Oregon: Children must ride in a federally approved car seat until they weigh at least 40 pounds, measure 4 feet 9 inches tall, or are eight years old. Infants must ride in rear-facing car seats until they reach both one year of age and 20 pounds.

Entry into the U.S.

Anyone sixteen years of age or older (including U.S. citizens) entering the United States by land or sea must have a current passport or other document accepted by the Western Hemisphere Travel Initiative (WHTI) or Customs and Border Patrol (CBP). At present, children under age sixteen can generally enter with proof of citizenship, such as a birth certificate.

If entering the U.S. by air, all travelers, regardless of age (including newborns and infants), must have their own passport.

This information — and more — is available at the Western Hemisphere Travel Initiative's Web site (*getyouhome.gov*) and CBP (*cbp.gov*). **Please read the site carefully and closely before you cross any land, sea, or air border into the United States; requirements may change or could depend upon your family's unique situation.**

At this time, United States citizens don't need a passport to enter Canada by land or sea, but you will need one to re-enter the U.S., so U.S. travelers must bring the documents required by WHTI. Entering Canada by air does require a valid passport or equivalent.

Read more about entry into Canada on the Canada Border Services Agency's Web site (*cbsa.gc.ca*). **Please read the site carefully and closely before you cross any land, sea, or air border into Canada; requirements could change or depend on your family's situation.**

Regarding customs, your personal exemption is the total value of merchandise you're bringing back to your home country (United States or Canada) without having to pay duty and fees. The exemption depends upon how long you've been gone and what you're bringing back.

Some items, such as fruits and vegetables, are frowned upon for cross-border transport. Check current regulations carefully before luggage gets searched and items get confiscated: the Canadian Border Services Agency site at *cbsa.gc.ca* and U.S. Customs at *cbp.gov/xp/cgov/travel.*

Crossing borders with kids

Children traveling with one divorced parent, a married parent alone, or grandparents or other non-custodial individuals may raise special concerns when crossing borders. Because of heightened sensitivity about cross-border child abduction, you'll want to make it clear that you have official permission of the other parent(s) to travel with children. Read up on current rules on the sites above. To play it safe, many individuals traveling solo with kids bring legal custody documents and/or a dated, notarized letter of authorization to travel from the non-traveling parent (or in the case of grandparents, both parents). This letter includes the dates of travel, location of travel, and contact information (address, phone, cell phone, etc.). Border officials may call the non-traveling parent to verify the letter's accuracy, whether you're going by car, plane, train, or ferry.

INTRODUCTION

portland

portland

All those rumors you've heard about Portland are true. Is Portland a little weird? Definitely. An über-crunchy city filled with vegan restaurants and Birkenstock shops? Yup. Clean and wholesome? Uh-huh. Does Portland pull out all the stops for kids and families? Without a doubt.

In many a metropolis, families are relegated to the noise 'n' cheese chain restaurants, with few other alternatives. But Portland offers first-class dining options, public transportation, and places to sleep. And Portland has no problem with kids coming along to enjoy all three; everyone's friendly and informal here.

Portland still takes pride in its counterculture roots, even as it grows into a mature metropolitan mecca of urban planning, green living, and affordable diversions.

SUGGESTED ITINERARIES

If you're staying for two days: Visit the Oregon Museum of Science and Industry (OMSI), walk through the Pearl District (fondly referred to as simply "The Pearl") or downtown, and head for the Portland Children's Museum.

If you're staying for three days: Visit the places listed above, plus the Oregon Zoo, Portland Saturday Market (also open on Sundays), and an additional neighborhood, such as Alberta or Sellwood.

If you're staying for five days: Visit the places already mentioned, plus two neighborhoods, and take a day or overnight trip to either Mount Hood or the Oregon coast.

If you're staying for a week: Visit all of the above and spend a few days on the coast.

MATCH YOUR TRAVEL ITINERARY TO YOUR FAMILY STYLE

Active families: Hike through Washington Park, catch an inexpensive ballgame at PGE Park, head for Mount Hood's slopes, or watch wipeouts at Burnside Skate Park. Stay at the Embassy Suites, which offers a pool.

Artsy families: Gawk at Portland Art Museum's modern masterpieces, catch a play, create clay or 3-D sculpture at the Portland Children's Museum. Stay at the Hollywood-inspired Hotel deLuxe.

Foodie families: Eat your way through the Alberta neighborhood, and visit Portland's Farmers' Market for locally sourced goodies. Stay downtown or at McMenamins Kennedy School.

Retro families: Visit Sellwood's 1950s-style streets for antiques, books, and old-fashioned playthings; hit high scores at Ground Kontrol; and see ancient dolls and fire trucks at Kidd's Toy Museum. Stay at the Ace Hotel, with turntables in family-style rooms.

SIX THINGS YOU MUST DO IN PORTLAND

1. Build your brain — without pain — at OMSI. Undoubtedly one of the nation's finest science museums, with continually changing exhibits, innovative displays, and edu-tainment for every age (page 28).

2. Watch a movie. Portland offers unique, old-fashioned movie options for parents and kids alike. We check out a movie at McMenamins every time we visit (page 26).

3. Drink from a Benson Bubbler. These petite, four-headed water fountains flow throughout Portland's downtown.

4. Go to Powell's City of Books. If you've been looking high and low for a favorite book from your own childhood, check the towering stacks here. Or just browse the board or chapter books with your kids and seek out a new classic (page 22).

5. Dine outside. The town's warmer climate lends itself to al fresco dining, and Portland's restaurants dish up some of the best kid-friendly outdoor eats in the Northwest. Eat on the Hopworks Urban Brewery's outdoor patio (page 29) or at Laughing Planet in the Pearl neighborhood (page 21).

6. Ride the Portland Aerial Tram. It's a quick, two-minute swoop from ground to sky, but the view and experience are incredible (page 13).

Shopping families: Head for the Pearl District and the Portland Saturday Market. Stay at the Inn at Northrup, close to Northwest Portland's shopping action.

WHAT KIDS LIKE BEST, AGE BY AGE

Babies: A quiet stroll in the Japanese Gardens or some play time in the baby garden at Portland Children's Museum, and shopping in the Pearl's kid boutiques.

Toddlers and preschoolers: OMSI, the Children's Museum, and the Oregon Zoo.

Elementary-school-age kids: OMSI, the Oregon Zoo, and either Oaks Amusement Park or the Portland Art Museum; going for a dip in the Kennedy School's pool.

Middle-school-age kids: Old-school video games at Wunderland or Ground Kontrol, picking through the Portland Saturday Market, browsing at Powell's City of Books, and a family movie at a McMenamins establishment.

Teens: Shopping downtown and in the Pearl District for clothing, music, and books; checking out the downtown area's teen attractions (such as putt-putt golf with glow-in-the-dark pirates), and a side trip for skiing on Mount Hood.

TRAVEL INFORMATION

Travel Portland provides travel deals and promotional materials. For more information: *travelportland.com* or 503-275-9750. Make hotel reservations through Travel Portland at 87-Portland (877-678-5263).

"The Compendium of Small Museums and Obscure Collections" lists all the cool and weird museums that may intrigue preteens and teens (BMX museum, anyone? How about the bathtub art museum?). See more at *hiddenportland.com*.

PORTLAND IN THE MEDIA

Author Beverly Cleary of "Ramona" series fame hails from nearby McMinnville. Fans will want to check out the Beverly Cleary Children's Room on the first floor of the Multnomah County Library, or the Beverly Cleary Sculpture Garden at Portland's Grant Park. Read more at *multcolib.org /kids/cleary.*

Matt Groening, creator of *The Simpsons*, also lived here. You'll see multiple Portland references in every episode, including Mayor Quimby (Quimby Street) and Reverend Lovejoy (Lovejoy Street). See a map of Groening's Portland references at *movingtoportland.net/matt_groening_map.htm*.

The chapter-book series "Minerva Clark" is set in Portland. Middle-schoolers might want to pick up *Minerva Clark Gives Up the Ghost, Minerva Clark Goes to the Dogs*, and *Minerva Clark Gets a Clue* by Karen Karbo.

CALENDAR

February

CHINESE NEW YEAR. Not the largest Chinese New Year festival in the Northwest, but the Lan Su Chinese Garden knows how to put on a show, which includes lion dances, folktales, paper cutting and calligraphy, and lantern-making activities for the annual lantern parade. More info: *portlandchinese garden.org.*

CHOCOLATEFEST. Held at the World Forestry Center, this fest lets you check out dozens of chocolate vendors, win raffle prizes, learn about chocolate's rich history, and watch chefs cook with chocolate. Willy Wonka would be here. Shouldn't you be?

April

PORTLAND ROSE FESTIVAL. This is Portland's showcase festival, stretching from April through August, with clown shows, parades, dragon boat races, park concerts, movies, fireworks, and foot runs. More info: *rosefestival.org.*

May

CINCO DE MAYO FIESTA. Portland is home to one of the largest Hispanic populations along the I-5 corridor, so Cinco de Mayo is a full-on five-day festival, featuring music, vendors, great food, and a children's stage with piñatas. More info: *cincodemayo.org.*

July

WATERFRONT BLUES FESTIVAL. Workshops, live tunes, and cruises. Usually coinciding with July 4's waterfront fireworks; arrive early to get a good spot. More info: *waterfrontbluesfest.com*.

SAND IN THE CITY. Sand — 450 tons of it! — and 4,500 gallons of water are trucked into Pioneer Courthouse Square, where sand architects create sculptures. There are also root-beer floats, face painting, and crafts for kids. More info: *powerfulpuppetry.org /SandintheCity.php*.

August

BITE OF OREGON. Sample from Oregon eateries, watch live cooking demos, listen to music, and drink some beer (well, adults, anyway). Kids are free. More info: *biteoforegon.com*.

MULTIPLE FREE CULTURAL FESTIVALS occur this month in Pioneer Courthouse Square, including Festa Italiana (*festa-italiana.org*) and India Festival (*icaportland.org /events/india-festival*).

September

ALBERTA STREET FAIR. Arts, crafts, foods, live music, and a parade are among the fair festivities taking place along one of Portland's most kid-friendly streets. More info: *albertastreet fair.com*.

PORTLAND PIRATE FESTIVAL. Aaaarr! Nobody does pirates like Portland! This carnival for scallywags offers grub, grog, and great merriment. Just for kids: jugglers, exotic birds, inflatable rides, and puppet shows. More info: *portlandpiratefestival.com*.

October/November

GREEK FESTIVAL. Watch folk dancers, enjoy traditional music, play in the children's corner, and gorge yourself on baklava and gyros at the Greek Festival (my favorite fest as a kid). More info: *goholytrinity.org /cGreekFest.html*.

SAUVIE ISLAND. Head to Sauvie Island in the weeks before Halloween to enjoy animal rides, a corn maze designed with GPS technology, tractor rides, and a barbecue. More info: *sauvieislandfarms.com/fall _activities.htm*.

TREE LIGHTING. On the day after Thanksgiving, join residents for the lighting of a 75-foot-tall tree at Pioneer Courthouse Square. More info: *pioneercourt housesquare.org*.

WORDSTOCK. This annual book fair hosts hundreds of author readings, plus a children's stage with storytelling workshops and puppet shows. Kids can make bookmarks and get their favorite author's autograph. More info: *wordstockfestival.com*.

December

ZOOLIGHTS. At the end of November, the Oregon Zoo is transformed by thousands of tiny lights taking the shapes of more than 200 animated monkeys, penguins, frogs, and bats through-out the zoo. Locals flock in droves to the zoo's touring train ride, so dress warmly for waiting in line. More info: *oregon zoo.org/Events/ZooLights*.

PORTLAND

Those interested in Oregon's history may enjoy *A Heart for Any Fate: Westward to Oregon, 1845* by Linda Crew.

PORTLAND NICKNAMES

Stumptown
PDX (after the airport code)
Rose City
Bridgetown
Beertown

SAFETY

Portland is a relatively safe city. However, you should know that the downtown core empties out dramatically after work, as businesses (including restaurants) shutter for the night. It's safe, but in winter, it can feel eerie. Pioneer Place (700 S.W. Fifth Avenue; *pioneerplace.com*) is one reliable anchor that stays open — food court and all — until 9 p.m. The restaurants listed in this book for downtown will be open at night, but call ahead, particularly on holidays.

The Chinatown area can be hit or miss. I feel confident walking around during the day, but might avoid it at night with kids. The area isn't known to be particularly dangerous, but multiple social-service agencies in the area serve at-risk populations because . . . well, some people have it tough.

One of the most frequent issues in Portland (in fact, the entire Northwest) is car crime. Never leave valuables in vehicles where they can be seen through the windows.

GETTING THERE

Plane: Flights to Portland arrive at Portland International Airport (PDX). From the airport, make your way into town by Airport (Red Line) MAX, a 35-minute light-rail ride that costs just a couple of bucks. Do not stay at an airport hotel unless it can't be avoided; they tend to offer marginal accommodations at high prices. Find more information about the Portland airport at *portland airportpdx.com* or call 877-739-4636.

Amtrak: Amtrak Cascades trains (*amtrakcascades.com*) leave Seattle for Portland five times a day, with the cost of a one-way trip starting around $30, and the actual trip taking about three hours. Amtrak Cascades trains leaving from Vancouver (connecting through Seattle; #516) depart once a day and take roughly eight hours. Arriving at Portland's gorgeous brick Union Station (800 N.W. Sixth Avenue), you'll need to take a bus, walk, or grab a taxi. Families may want to opt for the taxi — to walk or take a bus into downtown (particularly with luggage) would be an ambitious undertaking.

The "Starlight Express" train leaves Seattle once daily for Los Angeles, stopping in Portland along the way. This train, which often runs late, does offer an upstairs glass-covered observation dome, which can be fun for kids. Read more about Amtrak and book tickets at *amtrak.com*.

FUN FACTS

- Portland was almost named Boston. Portland, Oregon, was founded by Asa Lovejoy of Boston, Massachusetts, and Francis Pettygrove of Portland, Maine. Each wanted to name the city after his own hometown and agreed to settle it on a coin toss. Pettygrove won.

- You can't pump your own gas in Oregon. It's illegal.

- The world's smallest dedicated park is the 24-inch Mill Ends Park at S.W. Naito Parkway and Taylor Street.

- Powell's City of Books is the largest independent bookstore in the world.

- Portlandia, a 36-foot-tall copper statue, reaches down to the masses at 1120 S.W. Fifth Avenue. Only the Statue of Liberty is bigger than Portlandia, as far as copper statues go.

Greyhound Bus: This takes a very long time. It's cheap but distinctly lacking in the fun department. I did it for almost a year without kids and found it miserable. Save your pennies and go by train.

Car: You'll drive toward Portland along I-5 from points either north or south. Coming from the north (Seattle), it's roughly a three- to three-and-a-half-hour drive to Portland on a good day; on a bad day, all bets are off. It's taken us as long as six hours on holiday weekends or when there were road accidents. We've had more success with leaving early in the morning, before rush hour starts. Leaving midday or late afternoon can be a sure recipe for frustration all the way. Listen to radio station 530 AM in Seattle for traffic advisories.

En route, there are several nice places to stop off of Centralia's Exit 82. Try Burgerville (818 Harrison Avenue, 360-736-5212) or McMenamins Olympic Club Hotel and Theater's Club Pub (112 N. Tower Avenue, 866-736-5164). Burgerville has great locally sourced foods, children's meals, and indoor and outdoor seating. The Olympic Club offers sit-down pub grub at decent prices and is located right next to some train tracks — fun for those train-obsessed toddlers.

GETTING AROUND

Navigating Portland: Burnside Street divides north and south Portland, and the Willamette River divides east and west Portland. Streets north of Burnside are also known as "Alphabet Soup," because they proceed in alphabetical order: Burnside, Couch (pronounced "kooch"; hey, I didn't make it up!), Davis, Everett, and so forth.

Portland is set out in a grid format, with streets proceeding in an incredibly orderly fashion. Avenues run north-south, and streets run east-west. An example: 407 N.W. Seventeenth Avenue is approximately four blocks north of Burnside; 408 N.W. Couch Street is four blocks west of the Willamette River.

ESSENTIALS

Area code: 503

Baby accessories: Babies-on-the-Go Rentals has a three-day minimum charge for strollers, cribs, car seats, and baby-holders (playpens). See *rent4baby.com* or call 888-677-BABY (2229).

Emergencies: Call 911. Oregon Health Sciences University offers pediatric emergency care at 3181 S.W. Sam Jackson Park Road in Portland; 503-494-7551.

Mail a postcard: Head to the University Post Office at 1505 S.W. Sixth Avenue in Portland. It's open Monday–Friday, 7 a.m.–6 p.m.; Saturdays, 10 a.m.–3 p.m.

News: *The Oregonian* (*oregonlive.com/Oregonian*) is Portland's newspaper of record; to find out what's going on with Portland parents, check out *NWkids* (*nwkids.com*), *Metro-Parent* (*metro-parent.com*), or subscribe to *ParentMap*'s weekly e-newsletter (*parentmap.com*).

Parks: Find all of Portland's parks at *portlandonline.com/parks*.

Pharmacy: The Walgreens at 2103 W. Burnside Street in Portland is open 8 a.m.–10 p.m. daily.

Taxes: There is a 12.5 percent hotel tax. There is no sales tax in Oregon on goods and services. For real!

Car: Buy a road map at one of the local supermarkets or grocery stores, or map out your drive online. Portland is a compact city and easy to navigate, but newcomers often find the city's one-way streets, multiple bridges (there are eight crossing the Willamette), and on-ramps confusing. However, once you figure it out, you'll discover how easy Portland driving is, with ample roadways that aren't too crowded, and multiple methods for getting from here to there.

Street parking is often available in the Pearl and in most neighborhoods, but can be scarce downtown during weekdays. Parking in public lots is the least expensive option downtown — look for the "Smart Park" garages. Weekends and evenings tend to be less crowded in the downtown area.

Public transportation: Portland offers several options for getting around town, including bus, light rail, and streetcar. Kids love the Metropolitan Area Express (MAX) and streetcars (*portlandstreetcar.org*), which glide silently down the streets, open doors for passengers, then move along again. The easiest way to figure out routes and times is on the Tri-Met Web site (*trimet.org*); you can also call Tri-Met at 503-238-7433.

The Max and streetcars are free within the "free rail zone" in Portland's compact downtown. Outside of that zone, tickets are good for two hours;

adults pay about $2; children between seven and seventeen pay about $1.50, and kids six and younger are free with a paying adult. Most visitors to Portland will stay within two zones.

Bicycle: Portland has the highest percentage of commuter cyclists in the United States, according to the U.S. Census. And with more than 200 miles of bike lanes, you'll see plenty of parents pulling their kids along in Xtracycles and bike trailers. It's no big deal to bring a bike to Portland via Amtrak and get around by pedal power alone. For detailed bike routes, either buy a bike map at Powell's City of Books (*powells.com*) or view and print the free maps available at *portlandonline.com/transportation*. Choose "Bicyclist" under the "Select a profile" heading in the left column.

Traffic notes: Gridlock in Portland is particularly notorious along I-5 heading south in the morning (7–9 a.m.) or heading north in the evening (4–6 p.m.), and I-84 westbound in the morning and eastbound in the evening. Try to avoid going into or out of the city when everyone else is doing the same thing.

MAX lines can be packed; if there's no room for you and the family, just wait for the next train — you may find it to be much less crowded.

DOWNTOWN/CHINATOWN

Chinatown and downtown offer the most to do per Portland square mile. While downtown, visit the Portland Art Museum on Saturdays and Sundays for family tours and projects, go shopping and listen to live music at the Saturday Farmers' Market, watch a baseball or soccer game in PGE Park's family suite, or connect to the Aerial Tram. Many hotels are located in the city's center, and it's a great central location for travel by MAX, streetcar, bike, or bus. But affordable, family-friendly eats here are limited compared to other neighborhoods; ethnic restaurants are your best bets downtown.

Chinatown isn't as vibrant as Seattle's International District or Vancouver's Chinatown; for a long time, it was known as the place to go for the down and out. But today, you'll find several great spots for older children and teens, such as the Lan Su Chinese Garden, Ground Kontrol Classic Arcade, and Backspace; downtown, you'll find pirate putt-putt golf, shopping options, and a skate bowl.

SLEEP

Ace Hotel Portland $$–$$$$

1022 S.W. Stark Street; 503-228-2277; *acehotel.com/portland*

It's a hipster hotel! If you're so retro you'd rather listen to records than an iPod, this is the way to introduce your kids to the cool life. Only a few blocks to the Pearl and Powell's City of Books, it's also well situated. The 550-square-foot family-size rooms feature a queen-size bed, wall-size art, an old-school phonograph and records, and an L-shaped couch that transforms into two twin beds. This is Portland, so Ace offers bike rentals. Take your teens here and feel your cool quotient rise. Ask for a quiet room off the street if you'd like the kids to pass out by 9 or so, as this can be a happening neighborhood at night.

Embassy Suites Hotel Portland Downtown $$-$$$

319 S.W. Pine Street; 503-279-9000 or 800-EMBASSY; *embassyportland.com*
Built at the turn of the twentieth century, this hotel is a great mix of family-friendly basics (pool, microwave, fridge, separate one-bedroom sleeping quarters) and old-fashioned fun. It is a chain hotel, but doesn't feel like one because of the vintage surroundings and high ceilings. It's a short few blocks to the Portland Saturday Market, Voodoo Doughnut, and other downtown attractions; farther to the Pearl District. Breakfast is included in the nightly rate.

Hotel deLuxe $$$-$$$$

729 S.W. Fifteenth Avenue; 866-986-8085 or 866-895-2094;
hoteldeluxeportland.com
Glamour with a "u," this hotel is decked out in 1930s film-style décor. Practically next door to PGE Park and sandwiched between the MAX lines, it's a little farther from the Pearl and downtown attractions. But it's a good value, because Hotel deLuxe is also one of the most unusual hotels in the area, offering iPod docking stations and a pillow-choice menu. And you can teach World Religions 101 right in the room, as Hotel deLuxe also offers a "spiritual menu," so families can take a look at the Bhagavad Gita, Bible or Qur'an (among others).

Hotel Monaco Portland $$-$$$

506 S.W. Washington Street; 503-222-0001 or 888-207-2201;
monaco-portland.com
Gee willikers! If Little Orphan Annie visited Portland, she'd stay here. She'd love the lush velvet elevator walls and high-ceilinged rooms. With advance notice, families can baby-sit a goldfish, paint a masterpiece during afternoon tea time, and play with the stuffed dog available in each room. Monaco provides a blue kid's backpack, stuffed with a coloring book, crayons, and a yo-yo, among other toys. Queen or king deluxe rooms offer a separate bedroom, plus a pull-out couch, microwave, and mini-bar.

Mark Spencer Hotel $-$$

409 S.W. Eleventh Avenue; 800-548-3934 or 503-224-3293; *markspencer.com*
This friendly hotel has a very European and jumbly feeling, but it's close to all of the Pearl District's amenities — and offers Old World prices. It's an easy two-minute stroll to Powell's City of Books and the Pearl. Full (but dated) kitchens are available in some rooms, along with thin doors, cramped space, and budget-style décor. This isn't a luxe hotel; if you're comfortable with about two stars, you'll be fine here.

DO

Backspace

115 N.W. Fifth Avenue; 503-248-2900; *backspace.bz*
Backspace is like your teen's friend's basement, if that friend's mom had lots of networked computers, coffee, cool music, vegan food, Voodoo doughnuts, and chess. She probably doesn't. So here you are, with the cool kids. Open Monday–Wednesday, 7 a.m.–11 p.m.; Thursday and Friday, 7 a.m.–midnight; Saturday, 10 a.m.–midnight; Sunday, 10 a.m.–11 p.m. Cost: $6 per hour for non-members with a $3 half-hour minimum; $5 more for music shows.

Burnside Skatepark

Under the east end of the Burnside Bridge; *burnsideskatepark.blogspot.com*
This is one of the most famous skate spots in the world. Chances are that if you've got a preteen or teen into skating, they already know all about the Burnside Skatepark and have it scheduled into your itinerary. After all, it's where national pros and local amateurs skate side by side. If the weather's too miserable on your trip to Portland or your child isn't ready for the aggro-style skating, try the Department of Skateboarding's (*departmentofskateboarding.com*) indoor bowl, which has a fourteen-or-younger session between 10 a.m. and 1 p.m. on Saturdays.

Glowing Greens Black Light Adventures Miniature Golf (Pirate Adventure)

509 S.W. Taylor Street; 503-222-5554; *glowinggreens.com*
The Pirates of the Caribbean could never hold their own against the Pirates of the Putt-Putt. This blacklighted golf adventure offers ska-style music, mildly scary skeletons, a rockin' and rollin' jukebox, and the typical ups and downs of a putt-putt course. Add 3-D glasses to make the fish and shells come alive. A good spot for tweens and teens; with younger children, assess the appropriateness in advance, or pay for a short half-course. No food or drink allowed inside, so get your grog beforehand. Open Sunday, noon–10 p.m.; Monday–Thursday, 3–10 p.m.; Friday, 3 p.m.–midnight; Saturday, noon–midnight. Adults (ages 13 and older)/$7; youth 7–12/$6; second game and half-round/$4.

Ground Kontrol Classic Arcade

511 N.W. Couch Street; 503-796-9364; *groundkontrol.com*
Kids nowadays! They just don't appreciate rudimentary graphics, joysticks, and the satisfying "clink" of a quarter dropping in the slot. Take kids (elementary-school age or older) down memory lane at Ground Kontrol, where a bag of quarters will still buy you time with Frogger, Qwerty, Ms. Pac-Man, and the Simpsons. Drive race cars really fast or play a mean game of pinball upstairs. It's deliciously dark and grimy, like the pizza parlors of our youth. Kids are allowed in until 5 p.m., when the game show goes twenty-one and older. Open daily, noon–2:30 a.m.; children not admitted after 5 p.m. Free admission; most games cost one or two quarters per play.

Independent Publishing Resource Center

917 S.W. Oak Street, #218; 503-827-0249; *iprc.org*
If your teen authors are into cutting, pasting, and stapling their own 'zines, steer them here. On Sunday afternoons, the IPRC opens the door to a drop-off 'zine session especially for kids younger than eighteen. The staff members provide help upon request. Teens and younger are welcome at other open times as well, but staff can't give as much assistance. Open Monday, noon–10 p.m.; Tuesday–Thursday, 4–10 p.m.; Friday and Saturday, noon–6 p.m.; special youth-only sessions Sunday, noon–5 p.m. Cost: $5/hour for workspace and equipment, free for youth on Sundays, noon–5 p.m.

Lan Su Chinese Garden (formerly Portland Classical Chinese Garden)
239 N.W. Everett Street; 503-228-8131; *portlandchinesegarden.org*
Modeled on a Ming dynasty garden, the Lan Su Chinese Garden is a graceful
mosaic of textures: smooth bamboo, rippling creeks, hand-carved wood, and
roughhewn tile. Like all classical Chinese gardens, it consists of five elements:
plants, stone, water, architecture, and poetry. The garden is great for curious
older children who can respect the 40,000-square-foot garden's decorum and
stay on the paths that lead through a model scholar's house, over footbridges,
and around artificial ponds. Print out the museum's guide for children and
play a game of "I spy," looking for the ferocious lion protectors or double
rainbows. On rainy days, enjoy a cup of expensive but exquisite tea in the
Tower of Cosmic Reflections (also known as the teahouse). Summer hours
(April 1–October 31): 9 a.m.–6 p.m.; winter hours (November 1–March 31):
10 a.m.–5 p.m. Adults/$8.50; children 6–18/$6.50; children 5 and
younger/free.

Oregon Children's Theatre
Antoinette Hatfield Hall, 1111 S.W. Broadway; 503-228-9571; *octc.org*
Plays for kids age four and older are staged at this downtown venue; many are
based on classic children's books. Performed throughout the school year, these
productions are dress-up occasions that kids will remember. After the show,
stay awhile — the cast will come out to sign autographs, answer questions, and
pose for photos. Times and dates vary, check the Web site for details.
Adults/$16–$24; children/$13–$20.

PGE Park
1844 S.W. Morrison Street; 503-553-5400; *pgepark.com*
Just between home plate and first base lies one of Portland's sweetest deals:
PGE Park's Suite 8 is the free kids' suite. Open to families with children
younger than two, the suite's available during baseball and soccer seasons. A
sign outside asks you to limit your stay if it's busy inside, but that's not often
the case. Inside the suite, you'll find art supplies, toy trucks, playthings, a
couch, and a changing table. Go out on the balcony for two rows of seating.
With older kids, check out the Fred Meyer Family Deck in left field, which
offers shaded picnic tables, inexpensive bouncy castles, and batting cages.
Times and dates vary; see Web site for details. General admission: $8–$11.

Pioneer Courthouse Square
701 S.W. Sixth Avenue; 503-223-1613; *pioneercourthousesquare.org*
Pioneer Courthouse Square is the large brick heart of the city, sandwiched
between two MAX lines and bordered by upscale stores like Nordstrom.
Starbucks can provide quick meals, as can the vendors open at midday. Listen
to free music on summer afternoons, spot the statues, count the miles to
Guadalajara at the milepost sign, or watch the weather machine's antics at
noon. Ask the kids if they'd like to belt out a tune from the echo chamber (the
area next to Starbucks that resembles an amphitheater), which provides a natural microphone — just stand on the metal circle. Free; open 24 hours.

Portland Aerial Tram
Lower Tram Terminal at 3303 S.W. Bond Avenue; *portlandtram.org*
Although it costs $4 per person for the quick two-minute ride, you may find that the novelty is worth it. Originally built as a commuter link for employees of the Oregon Health Science University, the enclosed tram also serves as a 490-foot thrill ride, safe and enjoyable for toddlers through teens. Ride on clear days for a view of Mount Hood and Portland, or go weekday nights in winter, when an early sunset presents thousands of twinkling city lights. There's ample parking on weekends, but it's easy to get turned around en route. Take the Portland Streetcar, which drops you off right at the station. Open weekdays, 5:30 a.m.–9:30 p.m.; Saturday, 9 a.m.–5 p.m.; Sunday, 1–5 p.m. (from mid-May through mid-September). Adults/$4; 6 and younger/free.

Portland Art Museum
1219 S.W. Park Avenue; 503-226-2811; *portlandartmuseum.org*
Kids love modern art in a way that few adults can. It has texture, shape, color, and most of all, a sense of absurdity that speaks to them. So at the Portland Art Museum, head for the Belluschi Building, which hosts all of PAM's modern paintings, sculptures, and . . . a toddler-size icebag that puffs up and deflates. Over and over. Yes, it will be your two-year-old child's favorite art, forever. For older children, the museum's European Art area is a quick intro to Van Gogh and friends. Sunday is Family Day, when tours, story times, and drop-in art projects take the spotlight. The museum's bookstore offers a great little children's section, including books, toys, and even a coloring book about the museum. Open Sunday, noon–5 p.m.; closed Monday; Tuesday and Wednesday, 10a.m.–5 p.m.; Thursday and Friday, 10 a.m.–8 p.m.; Saturday, 10 a.m.–5 p.m. Adults/$12; children 17 and younger/free.

Portland Living Room Theaters
341 S.W. Tenth Avenue; 971-222-2010; *livingroomtheaters.com*
Popular with teens, this velvet-seated theater offers an intimate movie-viewing experience, with only a few dozen seats per room. Black-and-white, classic, and PG-rated movies flicker on the screen, but kids under twenty-one can only stay until 3:30 p.m. The front area slings wine, Toblerone chocolate, and paprika-spiked popcorn, or you can order lunch and eat in your seat. Dates and times vary; check Web site for details. Screenings before 5 p.m. are $7; all movies on Monday and Tuesday are $5, excluding holidays and 3-D films.

Washington Park
washingtonparkpdx.org
More than 400 acres of trees, roses, gardens, and family fun lie deep within Washington Park. Stroll through the free International Rose Test Garden (7:30 a.m.–9 p.m. in summer; 10 a.m.–6 p.m. in spring and fall; 10 a.m.–5 p.m. in winter), clamber up and over the peaked-gable playground, or hike through twelve miles of trails at the free Hoyt Arboretum (*hoytarboretum.org*).

In summer, the Portland Japanese Garden and Rose Test Garden connect by either train (fee) or shuttle to the Oregon Zoo, the Children's Museum, and World Forestry Center Discovery Museum.

Bring food. The pickings are slimmer than slim here, and may even be nearly inedible at some locations. Pack a picnic, eat well before you arrive, or plan to eat once you leave. No matter how you do it, don't plan on eating here.

To reach the park, just hop on the MAX line and get off in the second-deepest transit station in the world, Washington Park Station.

WASHINGTON PARK

Oregon Zoo

4001 S.W. Canyon Road; 503-226-1561; *oregonzoo.org*

Pass through the world's geographic areas, discovering animals native to each. On hot days, hang a left toward the cool "Great Northwest" forest, which gradually slopes down into a ravine as you pass black bears and eagles; on cooler days, try out the open-air African savanna and rainforest, or the farm, where kids can pretend to drive an adult-sized tractor and pat goats.

From mid-May through Labor Day, don't miss the zoo's 1950s-era steam train ($5/general), which winds through forest and field en route to Washington Park. There, you can disembark and walk through the free rose gardens or climb on the enormous playground structure. In late November, the train reopens for ZooLights, a local family favorite. Rides take about half an hour to cover four miles. Zoo hours: April 15–September 15, open 9 a.m.–6 p.m.; the grounds close at 7 p.m. September 16–April 14, open 9 a.m.–4 p.m.; the grounds close at 5 p.m. Adults /$10, children (3–11)/$7.50, 2 and younger free. Train: $5 ages 3 and older; show your Tri-Met stub and save $1.50 off admission.

Portland Children's Museum

4015 S.W. Canyon Road; 503-223-6500; *portlandcm.org*

Inspired by the cutting-edge Reggio Emilia philosophy (imported from Italy), the Children's Museum wants kids to touch, build, and experiment. Younger children splash and pour in the water-based play area, while older kids construct dams. Younger kids can create with clay, while older children (older than six) work in the Garage, hammering, taping, and drilling pieces of recycled scraps into works of art.

Children of all ages can put on a play, steer a ship, dig with construction vehicles in the foam-rock chips, or walk through a slightly spooky dark forest. They can shop for realistic-feeling apples and bread at the Grasshopper Grocery and Butterfly Bistro (cloth sacks only, of course — this is Portland!), or stack hundreds of Kapla blocks into new configurations. A new, popular deli/café inside serves healthy quick foods. The only downside: The attached store doesn't reflect the imaginative toys inside.

PLAY
South Park Blocks
S.W. Park Avenue from Salmon Street to Jackson Street
While mom (or dad) shops the farmers' market or enjoys art inside the Portland Art Museum, the other parent can take the kids to explore the park blocks. You'll find enormous statues, picturesque fountains, and a little fenced-in playground (south end of the blocks, keep going uphill). It's right next to Portland State University, so during the school year, you'll see students studying among the trees.

WASHINGTON PARK *continued*
March–Labor Day: open daily, 9 a.m.–5 p.m. September–February 28: open Tuesday–Sunday, 9 a.m.–5 p.m. Ages 1–54/$8; with military ID/$7; younger than age 1/free.

Portland Japanese Garden
611 S.W. Kingston Avenue; 503-223-1321; *japanesegarden.com*
The Portland Japanese Garden is five and a half acres of carefully manicured beauty, serene and pristine, on Washington Park's hill. Gardens composed of pebbles, moss, sculptured shrubs, and koi ponds are set upon a variety of levels. Catch great views of surrounding mountains next to the ceremonial teahouse. Extremely cool and shady, the garden is the place to seek refuge on blazing-hot days or when shrouds of clouds descend on the city, providing just the right touch of mystery.

The ponds and pathways might make parents of no-holds-barred toddlers nervous, but babies in carriers will probably be content, as will older children if given the ability to hike around the area. Note: Access is either by shuttle, which runs every 15 minutes, or up a steep dirt path (followed by dozens of steps). No food or drink is allowed in the park. Hours: April 1–September 30: Tuesday–Sunday, 10 a.m.–7 p.m.; Monday, noon–7 p.m. October 1–March 31: Tuesday–Sunday, 10 a.m.–4 p.m.; Monday, noon–4 p.m. Adults/$8; children (6–17)/$5.25; children younger than 6/free.

World Forestry Center Discovery Museum
4033 S.W. Canyon Road; 503-228-1367; *worldforestry.org*
The museum's displays can come across as an apologist's treatise on logging, with pointed arguments for the need for felling trees. At the same time, it's hard not to come away without a healthy respect for wood's role in the world; after all, tree fibers even make their way into our toothpaste and tires (the giving tree, indeed!). The museum's gift store is nice, with Paul Bunyan coloring books, puzzles from eco-friendly woods, and bamboo bowls. Open daily, 10 a.m.–5 p.m. Adults/$8; children 3–18/$5; children 2 and younger free; $4/person for the Take Me to the Top Canopy Lift (optional).

EAT

Food carts

Cities around the world do the food cart, but Portland has taken it to new levels; you'll find a veritable United Nations of mobile food trucks serving ethnic foods (Thai, German, Turkish, Lebanese, Vietnamese). Find pay-and-carry dishes along Third Avenue and Washington Street, and Tenth Avenue and Alder Street, among many other locations. But just wander through Portland — you'll find a food cart or two through serendipity. Most trucks in the downtown core are dependably open on weekdays during the lunch rush; on weekends they may be closed or hold irregular hours. For a more in-depth look at various carts and their epicurean options, see the blog *foodcartsportland.com*.

Hush Hush Cafe $

433 S.W. Fourth Avenue; 503-274-1888; *hushhushcafe.com*
Follow the long, long lines to Hush Hush, where the kids will love the name, the informal dining, and the vibrant atmosphere. There's five-napkin (read: messy) falafel, doughy pita, meat on bamboo skewers (don't give them to the baby), and grilled chicken at affordable prices. You'll be full all afternoon. The café is only open on weekdays and caters to a business crowd. Know your order when you approach the counter or be prepared for angry "suit wrath" behind you. Wait and watch for an open table, then jump at the opportunity. Open Monday–Friday, 10 a.m.–7 p.m.

Karam Lebanese Cuisine $$

316 S.W. Stark Street; 503-223-0830; *karamrestaurant.com*
Karam can give you something that's hard to find anywhere else in the Northwest — great falafel. Portland has a large expat community of Lebanese and Palestinian families, and its Middle Eastern dining scene puts Seattle and Vancouver to shame. Falafel sandwiches are convenient to eat in the hotel room, and these monsters are easy to share between child and parent. Open Monday–Saturday, 11 a.m.–10 p.m.

McMenamins Ringler Pub $-$$

1332 W. Burnside Street; 503-225-0627; *mcmenamins.com*
Nothing particularly special about the décor, nor is it particularly child friendly. But it is wallet-friendly: Eating here between 11:30 a.m. and 6 p.m. may set you back as little as $2 per menu item on the "Happy Hour" menu. The menu is restricted to four or five entrées, and you'll need to order a beverage costing more than $2 to make the $2/item deal kick in after 3 p.m.; but even with those caveats, it's easy for a family to eat well for less than $20. Tip well!

Mother's Bistro and Bar $$

212 S.W. Stark Street; 503-464-1122; *mothersbistro.com*
Look at you, wasting away in Portland! Here, have another bite. Mother's presents hefty breakfast plates in a cheerfully Regency-period environment. Kids are as plentiful here as the dozens of mirrors adorning the walls. Crayons and a kids' menu come automatically — order the mouse-shaped pancake with banana-and-chocolate-chip eyes. But don't come with low blood sugar, unless

you've made reservations. Long waits are typical after 9 a.m. at this top-rated breakfast/brunch spot; the self-serve coffee helps take the edge off. Open Tuesday–Thursday, 7 a.m. –2:30 p.m. and 5:30–9 p.m.; Friday, 7 a.m.–2:30 p.m. and 5–10 p.m.; Saturday, 9 a.m.–2:30 p.m. and 5–10 p.m.; Sunday, 9 a.m.–2:30 p.m.; closed Monday.

Safeway $
1030 S.W. Jefferson Street; 503-205-1849; *safeway.com*
Safeway is downtown Portland's only traditional grocery store, and it's a bit of a haul, located on the fringes of downtown. However, you can get your necessities here, along with food for cooking in-room meals. Open Sunday–Thursday, 5 a.m.–midnight; Friday and Saturday, 5 a.m.–1 a.m.

Tandoor Indian Kitchen $
406 S.W. Oak Street; 503-243-7777; *portlandtandoor.com*
See the cook in back? He's cooking everything fresh for you, so be patient. You'll be rewarded with light-as-air, piping hot naan. There's no kids' menu here, but if you have spice-adventurous children, there's no need for one — a single, mild curry can easily be shared. You won't find toys or crayons either, but a large-screen TV plays entrancing Bollywood videos. Buffet, Monday–Friday, 11:30 a.m.–2 p.m.; dinner, Monday–Saturday, 5:30–9 p.m.

Typhoon! On Broadway $$
410 S.W. Broadway; 503-224-8285; *typhoonrestaurants.com*
Upscale Thai food in downtown Portland, offering classics like pad Thai to eat at booths or take back to your hotel room. For delicate taste buds, request a no-star meal. Open Monday–Thursday, 6 a.m.–2 p.m. and 3–9:30 p.m.; Friday, 6 a.m.–2 p.m. and 3–10:30 p.m.; Saturday, 6 a.m.–10:30 p.m.; Sunday, 6 a.m.–9:30 p.m.

Voodoo Doughnut $
22 S.W. Third Avenue; 503-241-4704; *voodoodoughnut.com*
Punk-rock doughnuts with classic kid toppings! I'm talking about doughnuts with Fruit Loops layered on frosting and supersweet fillings. The storefront looks more like an over-twenty-one venue, however, and there are plenty of doughnut names that might provide more sex ed than you're ready to explain. Go with kids too young to get it or too old to care, if you're concerned. Open 24 hours (more or less), but on Sunday, only open until 2 p.m.

SHOP

Compound Gallery
107 N.W. Fifth Avenue; 503-796-2733; *compoundgallery.com*
Tokidoki toys, foot-tall figures, plush dolls, compelling (and odd) art, tees, super old-school shoes (parents who grew up in the '80s will be torn between nostalgia and nausea, depending upon your memories of that decade). It's the place to go to see where contemporary culture will be in five years or so; right now, it's for cutting-edge mature teens. Open Monday–Saturday, noon– 8 p.m.; Sunday, noon–6 p.m.

Finnegan's Toys

922 S.W. Yamhill Street; 503-221-0306; *finneganstoys.com*
Finnegan's isn't just another toy store, it's a destination. It's a Toys R Us for the rest of us. Example: Finnegan's has not one type of construction kit (you know, hammers, saws, and the like), but twelve, including all-wood varieties. It's also got baby toys, science toys, bath toys, learning toys, Thomas toys, Playmobil toys, big toys, small toys, cheap toys, spendy toys, doll toys, puppet and plush toys, digger toys, and . . . Mr. Bill. Also, board games. For play, there's the requisite train table (no shortage of Thomas and friends here). Open Monday–Saturday, 10 a.m.–6 p.m.; Sunday, 11 a.m.–5 p.m.

Pioneer Place

700 S.W. Fifth Avenue; 503-228-5800; *pioneerplace.com*
On rainy days, when there's not much else to do and everything else is closed, or if you're traveling with testy teens uninterested in anything other than shopping mainstream stores, Pioneer Place may have just what you need. You'll find retailers like Saks Fifth Avenue, Betsey Johnson, and Juicy Couture in this light-filled indoor mall, along with a fountain-decorated food court, kids' clothing stores like Gymboree, and first-run movies. Sure, this mall could be found anywhere else in the country, but it's an OK spot in a pinch. Open Monday–Saturday, 10 a.m.–8 p.m.; Sunday, 11 a.m.–6 p.m.

Portland Saturday Market

Downtown in Governor Tom McCall Waterfront Park (north end of the park: 108 W. Burnside); 503-222-6072; *saturdaymarket.org*
A favorite with tourists and locals alike, the Portland Saturday Market is now open on Sundays, too. Many stalls feature traditional Pacific Northwest wear (wool, tie-dye, and polar fleece) along with those special finds (handcrafted jewelry and art). Great for kids of all ages: wooden boats, tops, and cars for toddlers; duct-tape wallets and purses for teens; and the incredibly odd spoony goodness for everyone at The Spoonman's stall: eyeglasses made out of spoons, and hats made out of knives. Look for gold-lame-attired street mimes and guitar-strumming cowboys. Open March through December 24: Saturday, 10 a.m.–5 p.m.; Sunday, 11 a.m.–4:30 p.m.

Reading Frenzy

921 S.W. Oak Street; 503-274-1449; *readingfrenzy.com*
Reading Frenzy, an indie-press shop, carries offbeat publications like *The Believer* alongside homemade 'zines put out by kids. There's a small children's book selection, but prints from Washington art-star mama Nikki McClure make this a great stop for parents of young kids, and teens may be inspired to create their own 'zine. Adult-themed magazines fill the shelves; keep an eye out if you're concerned. Open Monday–Saturday, 11a.m.–7 p.m.; Sunday, noon–6 p.m.

Saturday Portland Farmers' Market

South Park blocks between S.W. Harrison and Montgomery at Portland State University; 503-241-0032; *portlandfarmersmarket.org*
Want just-picked tiny strawberries, straight from the organic farm? Earthy mushrooms plucked from surrounding forests? The Portland Farmers' Market

provides fresh produce, handmade breads, delectable chocolates, and even a meal or two (check out the biscuits and gravy). Listen to bands while chowing down, or take your bountiful basket back to your room's kitchen. On Wednesdays, you can visit the market downtown on the South Park blocks between S.W. Main and Salmon streets; Thursday's market is at the Ecotrust Building, N.W. Tenth Avenue between Johnson and Irving streets. Check the Web site for times. With babies and toddlers, a baby carrier or compact stroller is a must; the crowds here are thick and voracious. A children's playground is located two blocks south, so a parent can head there with bored little ones. If you don't have cash, the information booth provides $5 wooden tokens, charging them against your credit or debit card. The tokens can be used like cash at vendor stalls. Open Saturdays: April–October, 8:30 a.m.–2 p.m.; November and December, 9 a.m.–2 p.m.

PEARL/NORTHWEST PORTLAND

The Pearl District was once a maze of abandoned buildings, but city planners have transformed the neighborhood into a dense, upscale area perfect for exploration. Shop for books at Powell's City of Books, browse racks at the numerous kids' clothing boutiques, grab a snack (this isn't the neighborhood for great kid-friendly restaurants), and be sure to visit the play-perfect Jamison Square Park.

Then, either walk or ride the tram uphill from the Pearl, past small apartment buildings and houses before hitting N.W. Twenty-first and Twenty-third avenues. N.W. Twenty-first is quiet and residential, while N.W. Twenty-third is home to chain stores like Pottery Barn, alongside a few locally grown boutiques. Northwest is also called "Trendy-third" and "Nob Hill," if those monikers give you a sense of the neighborhood. There are good, family-friendly food and lodging options here.

SLEEP

Inn @ Northrup Station $$-$$$
2025 N.W. Northrup Street; 1-800-224-1180 or 503-224-0543; *northrupstation.com*

OK, any hotel that puts out enormous, overflowing bowls of candy is at the top of my kids' list. The Inn has studio-style rooms with kitchenettes, a fold-out couch, and a pop-art retro décor bursting with purple, orange, and red. Locally owned and located in a quiet neighborhood, it's a short walk to the N.W. Twenty-third Avenue shopping area, or a tram ride to the Pearl and downtown. Check out the rooftop terrace.

DO

3D Center of Art and Photography
1928 N.W. Lovejoy Street; 503-227-6667; *3dcenter.us*

Spectacularly strange, this tiny stop is kitschy-kitschy cool. The only museum in the United States devoted solely to stereo image "artistry," it features 3-D devices dating from the late 1800s, a rotating exhibition, and 3-D movies to watch. Don't miss the Viewfinder cards focusing on Portland and the Columbia Gorge. Open Thursday–Saturday, 11 a.m.–5 p.m.; Sunday, 1–5 p.m.; first

Thursday of the month, open until 9 p.m. Adults (older than 12)/$5; families/$7; first Thursday is free.

Northwest Children's Theater and School

1819 N.W. Everett Street; 503-222-2190; *nwcts.org*
Like Oregon Children's Theatre, this theater focuses on musical and dramatic adaptations of children's stories. But one show per run is designated as a "family date night," with a theme-related dinner served before the play. For example, *The Hobbit* is accompanied by Gandalf's Magical Feast (no word on whether troll stew is served!). Times and dates vary; check the Web site for details. Tickets: Prices change according to performance.

PLAY

Jamison Square Park

810 N.W. Eleventh Avenue
Portland has plenty of fountains, but few are as fun as the one at Jamison Square. This fountain bounds down a set of steps, filling a miniature swimming hole. Then, the water disappears down the drain. A few minutes pass before the water springs forth again. Wash, rinse, repeat. You can wade here or go for the full splash, but it's wise to bring a towel and change of clothes along — few kids can resist sitting under a stepped waterfall. Once dried off, check out the enormous Lego-style statues grinning and grimacing street-side. Big caveat: There is no place to change into bathing suits. Buy something at Cool Moon or another neighboring coffee shop and plead to use their facilities.

EAT

Cool Moon $

1105 N.W. Johnson Street; 503-224-2021; *coolmoonicecream.com*
This newish ice cream shop will blow your taste buds away with innovative flavors — or just keep them happy with traditional standards. Experiment with a kid's cone ($2.50) of kulfi or peanut butter cookie; or stay the course with Oregon blueberry or Indonesian vanilla. Local ingredients are tops here; the milk comes from nearby Alpenrose Dairy. Open Monday–Thursday, 11:30 a.m.–10 p.m.; Friday and Saturday, 11:30 a.m.–11 p.m.; Sunday, 11:30 a.m.–9:30 p.m.

Cupcake Jones $

307 N.W. Tenth Avenue; 503-222-4404; *cupcakejones.net*
Move over, chocolate and vanilla. Cupcake Jones offers quirky flavors like strawberry lemonade, banana split, and Boston cream. The cupcake menu changes daily; it can be hard to choose just one, so the mini-cakes provide a two-bite sample of each variety. Open Monday–Saturday, 10 a.m.–8 p.m.; Sunday, noon–6 p.m.

Hot Lips Pizza — Ecotrust $ (slice)

Ecotrust Building, N.W. Tenth Avenue at Irving Street; 503-595-2342; *hotlipspizza.com*
Pizza so good, it makes you want to kiss someone! Each 13- or 18-inch pie is loaded with locally sourced, zingy ingredients, such as 100 percent whole-milk

mozzarella, delicata squash, hazelnuts, and barbecued pork (thankfully, not all on the same pie!). Pizza by the slice is also perfectly acceptable — look for the rotating menu with pizzas like The Waldorf (olive oil, apples, walnuts, Gorgonzola). On nice days, grab your slice and eat outside on the patio. Try Hot Lips' own brand of pop (or "soda," if you insist) in Northwest flavors like blackberry and apple. Open Sunday–Thursday, 11 a.m.–9 p.m.; Friday and Saturday, 11 a.m.–10 p.m.

Laughing Planet — Ecotrust $

Ecotrust Building, 721 N.W. Ninth Avenue, #175; 503-505-5020; *laughingplanetcafe.com*

A chain unlike any other! The kids' menu offers kid-pleasing plates like organic mashed potatoes and cheese or mini quesadillas ($2.95). The adults get inventively named platters like Soylent Green (shiitake pilaf, greens, broccoli, tempeh, and cilantro pesto) or Sasquatch Salad (organic spinach, apples, almonds, and strawberry vinaigrette dressing). Plenty of reasonably priced organic meats and unmeats (tofu, tempeh) available here, along with plastic dinosaurs for play. Open daily, 11 a.m.–9 p.m.

Laurelwood Public House and Brewery $$

2327 N.W. Kearney Street; 503-228-5553; *laurelwoodbrewpub.com*

One of three Laurelwoods in Portland, but the most accessible for families staying downtown. Right next door to a toy store, this brew-and-bistro-style pub provides plenty of kid favorites on the menu, along with extensive choices for adults. Ask to sit upstairs — that's where the playroom is. The only caveat: Wait times can be very long between ordering and eating, and it can be a mob scene on unlucky evenings. Call ahead to ask about the wait if you're short on time. Open Tuesday–Thursday, 11 a.m.–10 p.m.; Friday, 11 a.m.–11 p.m.; Saturday, 10 a.m.–11 p.m.; and Sunday, 10 a.m.–10 p.m.

Mio Gelato $

25 N.W. Eleventh Avenue; 503-226-8002; *mio-gelato.com*

Ah, Mio Gelato. The Pearl offers multiple ice cream and gelato shops, but this is my family's favorite. It's located right across the street from Powell's City of Books and offers more than a dozen gelato flavors. To save money and taste-test multiple flavors, try ordering a multi-scoop bowl and sharing it. Open summer hours: Monday–Friday, 8 a.m.–11 p.m.; Saturday, 10 a.m.–midnight; Sunday, 11 a.m.–11 p.m. Winter hours: Monday–Wednesday, 11 a.m.–9 p.m.; Thursday, 11 a.m.–10 p.m.; Friday and Saturday, 11 a.m.–11 p.m.; Sunday, 11 a.m.–9 p.m.

Papa Hadyn West $$$, desserts $–$$

701 N.W. Twenty-third Avenue; 503-228-7317; *papahaydn.com*

Make no mistake: Papa Hadyn is best for couples and canoodlers, with a price tag to match. But the Papa serves some of Portland's very best desserts — and Portland really knows how to do dessert. Skip eating a meal here and bring older children for a tasteful experience they won't forget for a very long time. Open Monday–Thursday, 11:30 a.m.–10 p.m.; Friday and Saturday, 11:30 a.m.–midnight; Sunday, 10 a.m.–10 p.m.

Whole Foods $

1210 N.W. Couch Street; 503-525-4343;
wholefoodsmarket.com/stores/portland
This Whole Foods is right next door to Powell's City of Books, making it a great stop for refreshments after your rendezvous with Waugh or Poe (or Seuss). You'll find sandwiches, breakfast goodies, and other grab-and-go necessities. It's also the only organic grocery within walking distance of downtown. Open 7 a.m.–10 p.m. daily.

SHOP

Green Frog Toys

1031 N.W. Eleventh Avenue; 503-222-2646; *greenfrogtoys.com*
The sister store to Child's Play on N.W. Twenty-third, Green Frog provides a colorful array of playthings: art supplies, Calico Critters, travel games, Thomas the Tank Engine, and more. Open Monday–Saturday, 10 a.m.–7 p.m.

Hanna Andersson

327 N.W. Tenth Avenue; 503-321-5275; *hannaandersson.com*
Perhaps you've looked longingly over Hanna's brightly colored catalogs (which seem to arrive biweekly). Maybe you've coveted thy neighbor's knits. You'll find every Hanna and then some at the flagship store, which stocks apparel for babies through adults. Open Monday–Friday, 10 a.m.–6 p.m.; Saturday, 10 a.m.–5 p.m.; Sunday, noon–5 p.m.

Little Urbanites

916 N.W. Tenth Avenue; 503-227-8729; *littleurbanites.com*
Located next to Jamison Park, Little Urbanites offers eco-shampoos, clothing, great wall art, and functional yet fun furniture. Open Monday–Saturday, 10 a.m.–6 p.m.; Sunday, noon–5 p.m.

Posh Maternity

809 N.W. Eleventh Avenue; 503-478-7674; *poshbaby.com*
It's a "mom and me" shopping experience here, with chic clothes for kids alongside women's boutique apparel, plus BPA-free bottles, and natural teethers and toys for the younger set. Open Monday–Friday, 10 a.m.–6:30 p.m.; Saturday, 10 a.m.–6 p.m.; Sunday, 10 a.m.–5 p.m.

Powell's City of Books

1005 W. Burnside Street; 503-228-4651; *powells.com*
If your kids love reading — and even if they don't — Powell's is a must-do in Portland. Stocking more than a million titles in 68,000 square feet, Powell's offers an awesome array of used and new books. The children's area has small tables for reading, and shelf after shelf of classic picture books, early readers, chapter books, manga, and more. Powell's will also buy your used picture or board books and provide cash or store credit. The café inside serves small treats, sandwiches, and coffee. Open daily, 9 a.m.–11 p.m., 365 days a year.

SELLWOOD

Sellwood takes you back to grandma's day; a kind of horn-rimmed-glasses-meets-soda-fountain sensibility. Only a quick five-minute drive from downtown, the wide avenues and '50s-era signs provide a glimpse into the past, along with a vintage movie theater, amusement park, and bookstore-in-a-caboose.

But the whimsical children's shoe store (remember, no tax!), stellar toy shop, organic grocery, and diverse eats take you back to the future. Plan to spend one to three hours here, depending upon whether you watch a flick, roller-skate in an old-fashioned rink, or jump on Oaks Amusement Park's Lewis and Clark ride. No hotels in this area.

DO

Moreland Theatre

6712 S.E. Milwaukie Avenue; 503-236-5257

The Moreland Theatre is an aging — but still glamorous — dame. The theater's fabrics are worn down, a bare red light bulb shines eerily on the upstairs bathroom area, and Neil Diamond's "Solitary Man" might play ten times in a row, but this cavernous 1920s theater (with box seats still in place near the red-velvet-shrouded screen) feels like a real-life history museum. And a large popcorn's only $3.75! Frequently shows family-friendly first-run movies, but it's a single-screen theater, so your evening's entertainment is hit or miss. The doors open about 15 minutes before show time. Hours vary. Admission: $5 before 5:30 p.m.; adults/$6.75; ages 11 and younger/$5.

Oaks Amusement Park

7805 S.E. Oaks Park Way; 503-233-5777; *oakspark.com*

All the carnival rides of your past — and your great-grandma's! — are here, because Oaks Amusement Park has been in operation since 1905. At only forty-four acres, it's like a low-key county fair, offering spills and thrills on bumper cars, a Ferris wheel, the Zipper, and Lewis and Clark's Big Adventure ride. And there's also a sweet, old-fashioned roller rink and a carousel. Preschool kids (ages six and younger) have special roller hours on Tuesday and Wednesday mornings; adults skate or walk on the rink for free. Pack a picnic (or stop at New Seasons on the way in) and eat on the grassy lawn. Frequent discounts on weekdays. Hours vary; check the Web site for more information. Ride bracelets $11.75 (limited), $14.50 (deluxe).

PLAY

Sellwood Parks

Beginning at S.E. Seventh Avenue and Miller Street;
portlandonline.com/parks/finder **(type in "sellwood")**

Five different park and recreation facilities are interconnected along the Willamette River's waterfront, including Sellwood Riverfront Park, Sellwood Park, and Oaks Bottom Wildlife Refuge. All are located next to Oaks Amusement Park, so once the funhouse atmosphere there gets to be too much for you, wander out and along hiking trails to playgrounds, picnic facilities, an outdoor swimming pool, and bird-watching vantage points. Oaks Bottom

Wildlife Refuge is a 140-mile floodplain containing a diversity of fowl, including hawks, quail, mallards, coots, woodpeckers, and the great blue heron, the City of Portland's official bird. Look for summer concerts, which typically draw family crowds.

EAT

Cha Cha Cha Mexican Taqueria $

1605 S.E. Bybee Boulevard; 503-232-0437

Cha Cha Cha is a local Mexican chain serving straightforward Mexican fare like burritos and enchiladas, but this location stands out because of its proximity to the Moreland Theatre, along with its outdoor seating and creaky vintage-home setting. It's new Portland meets old Portland. Options on the kids' menu are cheap and very filling: One dish will probably fill two kids. Monday–Sunday, 10 a.m.–10 p.m.

New Seasons Market $

1214 S.E. Tacoma Street; 503-230-4949; *newseasonsmarket.com*

New Seasons is Portland's locally grown organic answer to Whole Foods. However, they also stock traditional goods (yes, you will find Coca-Cola here!), so if dad needs his pop, he won't go without. There's a great produce selection in case you're cooking in your room, as well as deli options for a quick lunch on the go. Open daily, 8 a.m.–10 p.m.

Papa Haydn East $$$ meals; $–$$ desserts

5829 S.E. Milwaukie Avenue; 503-232-9440; *papahaydn.com*

One of Portland's first high-class dessert spots, Papa Haydn East is more low-key than Papa Haydn West. Many families eat here nightly, and there are highchairs and menus for kids. Still, dessert's the thing — stop for a slice of banana cream pie or Georgian peanut butter mousse after catching a movie. Open Monday–Thursday, 11:30 a.m.–10 p.m.; Friday and Saturday, 11:30 a.m.–midnight; Sunday, 10 a.m.–9 p.m.

Staccato Gelato $

1540 S.E. Bybee Boulevard; 503-517-8957; *staccatogelato.com*

Excellent panini (including PB and banana for the kids), doughnuts, coffee, and rBST-free gelato in wacky flavors like Girl Scout Thin Mint, strawberry mojito, and blood orange. Eat at long, wooden, daylight-soaked benches, then jump up and play in the kids' corner (check out the fantasy-style city woodcut overhead). This is my favorite kid-friendly dining choice in Sellwood. Open Monday–Friday, 11a.m.–10 p.m.; Saturday, 8 a.m.–10 p.m.; Sunday, 8 a.m.–9 p.m.

Ugly Mug $

8017 S.E. Thirteenth Avenue; 503-230-2010; *uglymugpdx.com*

Sellwood's neighborhood coffee shop, where Wi-Fi and wee ones can coexist. The kids' corner has stuffies, a little table, picture books, and games donated by SpielWerk (down the street), plus crayons, checkers, and a basket of toys. In summer, ask for lavender lemonade; in winter, try the hot chocolate. Open Monday–Friday, 6:30 a.m.–10 p.m.; Saturday and Sunday, 7 a.m.–10 p.m.

SHOP
Haggis McBaggis
6802 S.E. Milwaukie Avenue; 503-234-0849; *haggismcbaggis.com*
If kids knew they were going shoe shopping at this store, they wouldn't complain! Stairs, slides, a Robeez Shoe Tree, fantastic paintings on the walls, shooting hoops with balls, a boat, and cookies . . . what's to complain about? Sizes newborn through adult (women) by Geox, Merrell, Aster and See Kai Run, among others. Open Monday–Saturday, 10 a.m.–6 p.m.; Sunday, noon–5 p.m.

Looking Glass Bookstore
7983 S.E. Thirteenth Avenue; 503-227-4760; *lookingglassbook.qwestoffice.net*
Hop aboard the Reading Railroad at this quaint little bookstore, which you'll recognize by the red caboose in the front. Open the caboose's door and a cozy warren of children's books awaits inside. Farther in, the store offers fiction and nonfiction for adults. Open Tuesday–Saturday, 9 a.m.–6 p.m.; Sunday, 10 a.m.–5 p.m.; closed Mondays.

SpielWerk Toys
7956 S.E. Thirteenth Street; 503-736-3000; *spielwerk.net*
Fittingly for Sellwood, SpielWerk sells toys of a handcrafted, vintage nature — but often with a Waldorf spin. From playsilks to pirate gear, cooperative games to a coffee grinder, wax-based art materials to wooden replicas of toys from the '50s, this store has a little bit of everything. It's obvious that the owner spends a lot of time hand-selecting each piece; you'll see items here you won't see anywhere else in the Northwest. Don't miss the locally made doll clothes or purse-size, handmade wooden puzzles. For play, there's a small kitchen and nursery-style setup in front, and a coloring table in back. The only caveat: This place is incredibly small. On busy days, prepare to park strollers outside. Open Monday–Saturday, 10 a.m.–6 p.m.; Sunday, 11 a.m.–5 p.m.

ALBERTA
Alberta is a fine and funky neighborhood, with shops packed into the blocks. And with so many kids in the area, you'll find toy stores, a stellar natural-mama shop, a craft store packed with great art stuff for school-age children, and a pizza-and-movie pub. Eating options range from cheap to midpoint.

Budget about two hours for Alberta shopping and dining, more if you'd like to catch a movie or take a dunk in the Kennedy School soaking pool. It's a good street for browsing with babies through elementary-school-age kids, but Alberta's shops cover more than 15 blocks, so bring that baby carrier. There's one hotel in the neighborhood, the fabulous (but without TV) McMenamins Kennedy School.

SLEEP
McMenamins Kennedy School $$–$$$
5736 N.E. Thirty-third Avenue; 503-249-3983 or 888-249-3983;
kennedyschool.com
Who else snoozed through Mr. Copeland's fourth-quarter biology class? Yeah, me, too. But at McMenamins, nodding off won't get you kicked out of class. After

all, Kennedy is housed in a 1915 school and retains many of the turn-of-the-century charms. No television sets, but who needs one? There's a movie theater, where you can catch a flick while eating pizza and downing beer (or root beer), a 102-degree soaking pool (popular with locals in winter), kid-friendly pub grub, chalkboards in every well-appointed room, and once the kids go to bed, mom and dad can take turns visiting the Detention Bar. Best of all, Kennedy is a short walk to Alberta's kid-friendly picks, plus a park. Only a 15-minute drive to downtown.

DO
McMenamins Kennedy School Movies and Soaking Pool
5736 N.E. Thirty-third Avenue; 888-249-3983; *kennedyschool.com*
Pizza and pub! Kids and flicks! All in one location, believe it or not. For its movies, Kennedy School welcomes families for the first nightly showing, one weekend daytime showing, and also provides "mommy matinees" during selected weekdays. Sit back in a funky chair or couch, eat your food, and enjoy the show. If you're not up for the movies, try the soaking pool — it'll take the chill right out of your bones. Family matinees before 7 p.m.; mommy matinees weekly, check Web site for details; pool open to minors between 10 a.m. and 8 p.m. $3/general admission ticket for movies, $5 per person/per hour soaking pool (pool free for hotel guests).

PLAY
Wilshire Park
N.E. Thirty-third Avenue & Skidmore Street
My choice in the Alberta/Concordia neighborhood is Wilshire Park's fourteen acres of landscaped and symmetrical beauty. Well-shaded grassy areas stay cool on hot summer days, and the park offers a wonderful playground with enough equipment for everyone, including jungle gyms, an airplane, and swings.

EAT
Tin Shed Garden Cafe $
1438 N.E. Alberta Street; 503-288-6966; *tinshedgardencafe.com*
Appropriately named, Tin Shed is a little shack serving up simple, tasty vittles. Eat outside in the garden on nice days, or inside — either way, the kids get a tumbler stuffed with crayons. It's a good spot to get breakfast before exploring the Alberta neighborhood. Your meat options include bacon, or apple link, veggie, or vegan sausages. Older kids will get a kick out of the menu's names, like Rosemary's Gravy Baby (buttermilk biscuits with mushroom-rosemary gravy). For lunch, dig into sandwiches, soups, and salads, including old standbys like tuna salad. Daily, 7 a.m.–10 p.m.

Vita Café $$
3023 N.E. Alberta Street; 503-335-8233; *vita-cafe.com*
Whether you sit on the meat lover's side of the fence, the veggies-only side, or somewhere in between, Vita has your order. The cooks take scary things like quinoa and tempeh and make them taste . . . bad for you. (Don't worry — there are hormone-free meats for the carnivores, too.) Great greasy grits — I love it!

Crayons are available, along with books and a few toys. Open Monday–Friday, 9 a.m.–10 p.m.; Saturday and Sunday, 8 a.m.–10 p.m. Kids' menu items are only $1 on weekday nights between 5 and 7 p.m.

SHOP

Collage Art Materials and Workroom
1639 N.E. Alberta Street; 503-249-2190; *collageonalberta.com*
It's like a tiny, indie Michael's craft store. Stuffed with everything from how-to-draw-manga kits to placemat activity kits, this shop has everything for little artists or crafty kids. Stamps, stencils, and stickers with retro and modern themes line the walls; you'll see artists stopping by to pick up their paints. Open Monday–Friday, 10 a.m.–8 p.m.; Saturday and Sunday, 10 a.m.–6 p.m.

Grasshopper
1816 N.E. Alberta Street; 503-335-3131; *grasshopperstore.com*
Supersweet store with a focus on books, Portland-made T-shirts, wooden toys, organic outfits, crafty kits, and a fun area for play. The staff is helpful and doesn't bat an eye when kids test the toys — even the ones with wheels. Open Tuesday–Saturday, 10 a.m.–6 p.m.; Sunday and Monday, 10 a.m.–5 p.m.

Green Bean Books
1600 N.E. Alberta Street; 503-954-2354; *greenbeanbookspdx.com*
If Powell's overwhelms your family, you'll find solace here, in a living-room-size book nook with small surprises around each corner. You'll find a limited number of very well-selected children's books; many offer a delightful sense of humor. But don't miss the eccentric fun: Select a cute finger puppet out of an automatic dispenser ($3), buy a fake moustache (and try it on in the mirror), and seek out the mini dollhouse hidden among the books (hint: you have to open a door). Open Monday–Saturday, 11 a.m.–6 p.m.; Sunday, 10 a.m.–5 p.m.

Milagros Boutique
5433 N.E. Thirtieth Avenue; 503-493-4141; *milagrosboutique.com*
We love our green boutiques here in the Northwest, and there are few places as quintessentially green as Milagros Boutique. Among the green goods: a wall of cloth diapers in a variety of styles, American-made wooden baby toys, breast-feeding (or pumping) supplies, consigned clothes, infant carriers, fair-trade tees, and swank baby bags. And, because this is Portland, pirate- and ninja-themed T-shirts. Right in front, kids can pretend to cook in the play kitchen or hide out in a compact cave. Open Sunday–Friday, 11 a.m.–5 p.m.; Saturday, 11 a.m.–6 p.m.

AROUND PORTLAND

DO

Electric Castle's Wunderland
3451 S.E. Belmont Street; 503-238-1617; *wunderlandgames.com*
Clowns on the building's exterior provide the first clue: This is campy fun for arcade-game champs. Off-brand arcade games, skee ball, zooming motorcycles, revving race cars, and Dance! Dance! Revolution make this an inexpensive stop

for tweens and teens. Not a good choice for younger kids — the two blinking, whirring rooms could disturb a Zen master. Pay the entrance fee and most games are a nickel (or four) apiece. Adults/$2.50; children/$2. Open Sunday–Friday, noon–midnight; Saturday, 11 a.m.–midnight.

Kidd's Toy Museum
1300 S.E. Grand Avenue; 503-233-7807; *kiddstoymuseum.com*
Enter the fluorescent-lit room packed with thousands of unmarked toys (no historical notes or placards here), and you'll see how children played long ago. Before little boys played with metal cars, they raced toy horse-drawn buggies. The floor-to-ceiling shelves are stacked with dolls, banks, figurines, trains, and more. A caveat: America's history isn't particularly sensitive to non-whites, and neither are some of these toys. You will see stereotypes and epithets directed at non-whites and women (the militant suffragette caught my attention, along with "Jolly N-word" banks). Be prepared to have some important discussions after coming to this museum. This place is notoriously hard to find — there's no tourist-friendly sign outside — so look for the street address, find the brown door with a paper sign taped on it, and knock loudly. Open Monday–Thursday, noon–6 p.m.; Friday, 1–6 p.m. Admission is free (donations welcome).

Oregon Museum of Science and Industry (OMSI)
1945 S.E. Water Avenue; 503-797-4000; *omsi.edu*
Play with light in the laser and holography lab, climb inside a cochlea (ouch!), or feel the earth move in the Earthquake House, with settings for a medium-size earthquake or a more severe one. The ball room is an engineering spectacle; kids use tubes, siphons, funnels, ramps, and a maze to send blue balls bouncing, spinning, and flying. Toddlers and preschoolers love the upstairs — that's where they'll find the Science Playground's sand, dress-up, water, and art explorations.

In addition to the fun stuff already mentioned, OMSI presents spectacular exhibits from across the country on a temporary basis; an OMNIMAX movie theater; and laser light shows on weekends. If you're a member of any of the ASTC (*astc.com*) museums, you'll get in free. Regular hours: Tuesday–Sunday, 9:30 a.m.–5:30 p.m. Summer hours: 9:30 a.m.–7 p.m. Adults/$11; children (ages 3–13)/$9.

Rose Quarter sports and events
One N. Center Court; 503-235-8771; *rosequarter.com*
Five large venues await sports fans: the 20,000-seat Rose Garden, the 12,000-seat Memorial Coliseum, the 6,500-seat Theater of the Clouds, the 40,000-square-foot Exhibit Hall, and the Rose Quarter Commons. This is where you'll come to catch a variety of kid-friendly concerts, plus basketball (NBA Portland Trail Blazers, *nba.com/blazers*), lacrosse (Portland LumberJax), and hockey (Winterhawks). Some Rose Quarter events offer a parent room (which will be noted on the above Web site), which also provides popcorn, pop, and water. Ticket prices and times depend on the game or performance; check Web site for details.

SCRAP

2915 N.E. M.L.K. Jr. Boulevard; 503-294-0769; *scrapaction.org*
If the kids enjoyed their experience at the Children's Museum and want to collect additional scrap materials for further art projects, this is the place to go. Fabric, office supplies, art materials, paper, yarn, and other castoffs from modern life are yours for the up-cycling. Open Monday and Tuesday, 11 a.m.–6 p.m.; Wednesday, 11 a.m.–7 p.m.; Thursday–Saturday, 11 a.m.–6 p.m.; Sunday, 11 a.m.–5 p.m.

PLAY

Mount Tabor Park

Sixtieth and Salmon streets
Atop Portland's only, long-dormant volcano, you'll find a tiny but complete playground, surrounded by towering firs. And Portland hasn't banned all seesaws (like many municipalities), so you'll see old-fashioned bump-yer-butt ones here, along with swings, a zipline, climbing structures, and a play jeep (probably powered by pretend biofuel!). The castle-style bathrooms are unusual, and potty-humor-loving kids can tell their friends they went to the bathroom on a volcano.

EAT

Hopworks Urban Brewery (HUB) $$

2944 S.E. Powell Boulevard; 503-232-HOPS (4677); *hopworksbeer.com*
It's a little out of the way, but this organically focused brewpub is worth a side trip. HUB offers bike-inspired décor and pizza pies with topping options such as organic Roma tomato sauce, free-range chicken, and Rogue River blue cheese. Ask to be seated in the family-friendly area, where you'll find a train table, chalkboard, and toy wooden pizzas. The friendly staff provides crayons, kids' menus, and pizza dough for play. The prices can be a little higher than typically found in Portland, but one large pizza can easily feed a family of four. Open Sunday–Thursday, 11 a.m.–11 p.m.; Friday and Saturday, 11 a.m.–midnight.

The Mississippi Pizza Pub $

3552 N. Mississippi Avenue; 503-288-3231; *mississippipizza.com*
Eat slices and pies in a large, rambling location. There's plenty of seating for everyone during the day, but the music shows (check the Web site for times and days) are popular evening events. Once a month, a special kids' live show really draws crowds; plan accordingly. Older kids may delight in watching a favorite adult misspell "vociferous" at the Monday Night Spelling Bee. In summer, the staff sells Hawaiian-style shave ice from a streetfront window. Wheat-free pizzas are also available. Open Sunday–Thursday, 11:30 a.m.–midnight; Friday and Saturday, 11:30 a.m.–1 a.m.

Old Wives' Tales $$

1300 E. Burnside Street; 503-238-0470; *oldwivestalesrestaurant.com*
Wholly granola! Your kids will call you Best Parent of the Year if you bring them to this restaurant's playroom — a fantasy underwater scene complete with a boat-style loft. And they'll probably love the kids' menu, too — an à la

carte feast of dozens of healthy yet kid-friendly sides, like one slice of toast, half a waffle, and vanilla yogurt for breakfast; steamed veggies, a turkey frank, and a mug of chicken broth for lunch. It's definitely the most complete kids' menu I've ever seen. The restaurant's grown-up food offers plenty of healthy meat and veggie choices. I recommend going for breakfast or brunch. Open Sunday–Thursday, 8 a.m.–9 p.m.; Friday and Saturday, 8 a.m.–10 p.m.

¿Por Qué No? Taqueria $

3524 N. Mississippi Avenue; 503-467-4149; *porquenotacos.com*

Crazy, loud, and hot — but delicious. ¿Por Qué No? (which means "why not?") dishes up tasty, sustainably harvested meats on sloppy soft tacos next to '70s thrift-store wall art. Say "si" to the fresh, pink watermelon drink. Crayons and paper for the kids make the short wait OK, as does Por Qué's slightly spicy guacamole and kid-sized $2 quesadillas. Seating is scarce, though; hungry eaters put in an order and wait until a spot opens up. You'll eventually get a table. But the best option is to come before or between the lunch and dinner crushes. Open Sunday–Thursday, 11 a.m.–9:30 p.m.; Friday and Saturday, 11 a.m.–10 p.m.; Sunday, 11 a.m.–3 p.m.

Waffle Window $

S.E. Thirty-sixth Avenue and Hawthorne Boulevard; 503-239-4756; *wafflewindow.com*

Mmm, waffles! A kid food we all love. Right outside Bread and Ink restaurant, a maroon awning protects dedicated waffle fans from the elements, as cooks inside whip up fresh fruit and granola waffles, pumpkin pie waffles, and other exotic squares. Eat outside at the tables and chairs, or head inside to dig in at Bread and Ink's long, oilcloth-covered table (bus your own dishes, of course). Open Sunday–Thursday, 8 a.m.–5 p.m.; Friday and Saturday, 8 a.m.–9 p.m.

SHOP

Black Wagon

3964 N. Mississippi Avenue; 866-916-0004; *blackwagon.com*

Black Wagon doesn't focus on filling the store's every nook and cranny, but on hand-selecting high-quality products for children from newborn to age six. Retro tees for babies and toddlers, handmade wooden toys, funky stuffed animals, and lovely books abound. The helpful owner is a fount of knowledge about the Mississippi Avenue area. Open Monday–Friday, 11 a.m.–7 p.m.; Saturday, 10 a.m.–7 p.m.; Sunday, 10 a.m.–5 p.m.

Kids at Heart

3445 S.E. Hawthorne Boulevard; 503-231-2954; *kidsathearttoys.com*

German construction toys and quirky science kits, a wall of stuffed animals, plenty of games and inexpensive plastic playthings, check. But Kids at Heart is also notable for its selection of local toys: heirloom-quality wooden cars and trucks handmade in Ashland, Oregon; Edith's Aprons, sewn by a local 100-year-old grandma; and Mary's Soft Dough — a more natural alternative to Play-Doh. Open Monday–Saturday, 10 a.m.–7 p.m.; Sunday, 10 a.m.–6 p.m.

Missing Link

3562 S.E. Hawthorne Boulevard; 503-235-0032; *missinglinktoys.com*
This toy store doesn't carry cuddly stuffed animals; the toys (like the prickly
Cactus Pups) very much fall at the collector-art end and may appeal more to
teens. Here, you'll find backpacks, bags, T-shirts, stuffed animals, and a small
collection of upscale design and art books. There's also mature content inside,
so if you have little ones, scope it out first. If your teens are into Kid Robot,
they'll get this store — and they'll love browsing Hawthorne Boulevard,
chock-a-block with independent stores. Open Tuesday–Friday, noon–7 p.m.;
Saturday, 11 a.m.–7 p.m.; Sunday, 11 p.m.–6 p.m.; closed Monday.

getaway
MOUNT HOOD LOOP

One of the most accessible peaks in the Northwest, the 11,249-foot-high,
glacier-blanketed Mount Hood is a mere 50 miles east of Portland. The mountain is Oregon's tallest, and a wonderful place to visit year-round. The peak's
proximity and number of activities make it a unique destination.

In winter, Mount Hood provides cross-country and alpine skiing. Enjoy all the
winter sports you can handle — or just play in the snow. Popular spots include
Skibowl, Mount Hood Meadows Ski Resort, and Timberline Lodge. The mountain gathers families and teens by the busload on winter weekends and evenings.

In summer, wildflowers bloom alongside patches of snow and ice. Mount
Hood often offers snow year-round (it's not always prime snow, though).

During spring, summer, and fall, try taking the 105-mile loop via the Mount
Hood Scenic Byway (*mthoodterritory.com/byway.htm*). Head east down the
Columbia Gorge along I-84, and stop at Multnomah Falls for a few photos. Then
make your way to Hood River and visit an old-timey frontier town making its
peace with windsurfers. If you have toddlers, ride the Mount Hood Railroad.

Eat lunch in town, or head up Highway 35 to Timberline Lodge and pick
up a cheese-laden pizza at the Blue Ox Bar. I love the café's stained-glass presentation of Paul Bunyan and best friend, plus the heavy wood seating that feels
like it's just been removed from the ground.

For a longer day or an overnight excursion, squeeze in hikes, summer fun at
the Skibowl's Adventure Zone, or a local festival. Otherwise, you can easily leave
Portland at 8 a.m., eat breakfast, do the loop, and be back in Portland by 3 p.m.

Sobering fact: Since 1896, more than 130 mountain climbers have died on
Mount Hood.

SLEEP

Timberline Lodge $$$$

Timberline Road, Mount Hood; 503-272-3311 or 800-547-1406;
timberlinelodge.com
Don't miss visiting or staying at Timberline Lodge, a testament to 1930s-era
craftsmanship in the midst of the Great Depression. Handcrafted by skilled

artisans employed by the WPA, the lodge features a variety of pioneer, Native American, and animal motifs; challenge the kids to see who can find the most animals. You're up at 6,000 feet, so don't be surprised to find yourself feeling a bit light-headed, even if you didn't have a drink at one of the lodge's five restaurants (including the **Blue Ox Bar**). There's a guided tour (which may be slow paced for kids), handouts, and lots of history here for older children; young kids will just love the lodge's stone-and-beam architecture, reminiscent of a fairy tale. Year-round snow sports and lift operation; check the Web site for seasonal hours and pricing.

DO

Mount Hood Meadows Ski Resort

Mount Hood Meadows Road, Mount Hood; 1-800-SKI-HOOD; *skihood.com*

Enjoy skiing through April, alpine or snowboard lessons for kids, ski-in restaurants, and a state-certified day-care facility for children between six weeks and six years old — everything the snow-loving family needs. Warning: The day care offers room for just forty-six children (hourly, half-day, or full-day options available), so call beforehand to make a reservation.

Mount Hood Railroad

110 Railroad Avenue, Hood River; 800-872-4661; *mthoodrr.com*

Hit the rails on Mount Hood Railroad's old-fashioned steam locomotive. Nestled at the base of Mount Hood in Hood River, Oregon, the train takes passengers down tree-lined tracks, through tunnels, and past the gorge's spectacular scenery. The cars are treats in themselves; choose from bench-style seating or keeping your balance in an open-air car. Excursion trains (to Odell's fruit orchards) offer a dome car. Special family-focused rides include a Day Out with Thomas, the Pumpkin Patch Express, science-themed trips with OMSI, plus the Polar Express. Tickets: $15–$90.

Mount Hood Skibowl

87000 E. Highway 26; 1-800-SKI-BOWL; *skibowl.com*

Teens will enjoy skiing in one of America's largest night-ski destinations, as well as hitting the snow-tubing and snow-skating park. Kids too young to ski will love the 2,400-square-foot Super Fun Zone, an indoor play area filled with balls, nets, and slides for kids under 60 inches tall. Skibowl's value-oriented park provides a solid winter option for snow-loving families. In summer, the Adventure Park offers kiddy canoes, kiddy and Indy karts, a rock wall, a sky chair, and more, either à la carte or in package deals.

Multnomah Falls

E. Columbia River Highway; 503-695-2372; *fs.fed.us/r6/columbia/recreation/waterfalls.shtml*

The 620-foot-tall Multnomah Falls crashes past a bridge and into a deep (and very cold) pool below. A 1.2-mile trail leads viewers up 600 feet to the 45-foot-long bridge that crosses the falls' span; hardier hikers can continue up the six miles to the Larch Mountain Lookout. More than 2 million visitors per year come to visit the falls; expect parking nightmares if you come midday on summer weekends. The day-use-only Multnomah Falls Lodge (*multnomah fallslodge.com*) offers breakfast, lunch, dinner, and deluxe Sunday brunches ($1 per year old for children younger than age eight). The visitor center is open daily, 9 a.m.–5 p.m.

EAT

McMenamins Edgefield $-$$
2126 S.W. Halsey Street, Troutdale; 503-669-8610; *mcmenamins.com/edgefield*
If you're seeking an affordable breakfast en route, this McMenamins might be a good choice, with breakfast and pub grub, landscaped grounds for wandering while waiting for food or after the meal, and a rocking-chair-on-the-porch atmosphere. Black Rabbit Restaurant, open daily, 7 a.m.–10 p.m.

getaway
OREGON COAST/CANNON BEACH

Of all the little towns accessible from Portland, Cannon Beach is one of my favorites. It's just the right mix of artsy and touristy. It's got fine seafood and hotels, but it's also got all the junky stuff kids love, from plastic sand toys to saltwater taffy. And in my opinion, Cannon Beach offers some of the very best beaches and sunsets in the Northwest.

On your way there or back, stop in downtown Astoria (page 37). It's got a great funky vibe, and the little city makes sure you won't miss your coffee, comics, toys, or organic goodies. And on gloomy days, go to Astoria's water center and the Fort Clatsop National Memorial.

Or visit Seaside — play pinball and video games at the Fun Center, watch teens flirt on the sidewalk, eat subpar meals, and get saltwater taffy stuck between your teeth as you sit atop sand dunes. Whether you enjoy this scene very much depends upon your tastes, but it's not a bad way to spend a few hours with preteens or teens who are too "bored" with mellower areas like Cannon Beach.

GETTING THERE

Take the easy two-lane roads — Highway 26 west from Portland, or Highway 30 from the north. Or do both, creating a loop with an overnight in Portland. From Portland, Cannon Beach is a short 90-minute drive with no traffic, but can take as long as three hours on heavily trafficked (and wreck-intensive) summer weekends. Use the bathroom before you get in the car, because there aren't many stops on the way out (particularly on Highway 26 connecting Longview and Astoria). As always, go early, and don't travel during evening hours unless you're really comfortable with nighttime rural driving; year-round, these roads are pitch-black at night.

Tip: Don't miss "Bedtime Stories," a half-hour of stories, poetry, and songs for kids, if you can pick up Coast Community Radio at 8 p.m. between Sunday and Thursday. Tune your dial to KMUN (91.9 FM), KTCB (89.5 FM), or KCPB (90.9 FM).

SLEEP

Many of the hotels in Cannon Beach look well-loved and frayed at the edges (and on the doors and windows and everywhere else, too). In the summer, you may not notice because you'll be outside. Below are some standouts that are unusually well kept, distinctive, or otherwise notable. If you can't stay at one of these, take your chances elsewhere and plan to spend lots of time on the beach.

The Courtyard $$–$$$

1116 S. Hemlock Street; 503-436-1392 or 800-238-4107; *thecourtyardcannonbeach.com*

This classical-style inn contains tasteful, modern furnishings and is only a few blocks from the beach. Blinds provide some privacy; families will want to ensure that their room contains a microwave, two-burner stovetop, and fridge (available in some suites, but not all). Only some rooms are big enough for a family of four, with two in a bed, and two on the fold-out couch.

Ecola Creek Lodge $–$$

208 E. Fifth Street; 503-436-2776 or 800-873-2749; *cannonbeachlodge.com*

Large families will appreciate the supersized rooms; little girls into the "princess" craze may want to stay in the Turret Suite, where a sunlit, turret-shaped room holds a dining table. Another unusual perk: The property is over-run with "wild" rabbits that are happy to be fed or patted by children. The hotel has a distinctive Christian aesthetic and is a favorite with church groups, which may or may not be your style.

McBee Cottages $$–$$$

888 S. Hemlock Street; 503-249-3983 or 800-238-4107; *mcbeecottages.com*

Want the Cannon Beach experience, but don't want to take out a second mortgage to get it? McBee Cottages might work for you. A converted motor inn, McBee's clean white interiors put a clever twist on the '50s aesthetic. All rooms come with a microwave, toaster, fridge, and oven. Because the cottages are perched right on a heavily trafficked road, the noise may bother some, and very tight quarters may frustrate others. But hey, you're not here to spend time in your motel room, right?

Surfsand Resort $$$–$$$$

148 W. Gower Avenue; 503-436-2274 or 800-547-6100; *surfsand.com*

If you're going to come all the way out to Cannon Beach, you might as well make a big splash. The Surfsand Resort is luxury in a Northwest setting, offering oceanfront rooms with balconies, kitchenettes, a deep soak tub, and TV/DVD combos (the hotel has a long list of DVDs you can borrow). Sit in your living room and watch families play on the sand, take sunset photos of the pictur-esque rock formations, including the iconic Haystack Rock, or warm up next to your roaring (gas) fireplace. Children's activities include crafts, ice cream socials, and weenie roasts. I want to live here.

DO

Cannon Beach Library

131 N. Hemlock Street; 503-436-1391; *cannonbeachlibrary.com*

Unlike many libraries, this one's completely privately run by a local nonprofit group. Join for only $5 per year, donate your already-read tomes, and dig through the library's collection for a gem to take back to your hotel or condo. The well-loved children's area contains easy readers, a video (not DVD) library, and a rocking chair. Monday, Tuesday, and Friday, 1–5 p.m.; Wednesday and Thursday, 1–7 p.m.; Saturday, 10 a.m.–5 p.m. $5/year membership.

Family Fun Cycles

1170 S. Hemlock Street; 503-436-2247

Call or stop in to rent a bike or trail-a-bike for tooling along the beach during low tide or through Cannon Beach's streets.

PLAY

City Park

Second and Spruce; 503-436-1581; *ci.cannon-beach.or.us*

Take little ones to play on the small playground or your teens to the skate park. Open dawn to dusk.

Ecola State Park

Ecola Road, two miles north of Cannon Beach; 800-551-6949; *oregonstateparks.org/park_188.php*

A breathtaking mix of moss-drenched Sitka spruces, wide-open skies, and smooth-stone beaches, Ecola is picture perfect. Take an easy hike down to the ocean's shore (lots of steps though — don't bring a jogger) and watch surfers catch mammoth waves, look for sealife in tide pools, or spot the unusual obelisk-shaped rocks. Better yet, pack up a lunch in town and chow down at one of Ecola's 20 picnic tables. Open dawn to dusk; day use/$3.

Tolovana State Wayside

U.S. 101, one mile south of Cannon Beach; 800-551-6949; *oregonstateparks.org/park_199.php*

Bring all your beach toys for Cannon Beach's double hit: fine-grained sand mixed with sunny, warm days in summer; dramatic, gloomy days in winter. Creature-filled tide pools often dot the way out to the stoic Haystack Rock during low tide (check the tide schedules). A slow-flow stream provides gentle water for sandcastle construction. On windy days, the flat, wide expanse is great for flying a kite brought from home or one picked up in town. Open dawn to dusk.

EAT

Bruce's Candy Kitchen $

256 N. Hemlock Street; 503-436-2641; *brucescandy.com*

Since 1963, Bruce's has offered traditional saltwater taffy made fresh on site. Go with the expected (peppermint) or unexpected (pomegranate). There's even sugar-free taffy, cheese corn, and caramel corn. Monday–Friday, 10 a.m.–5:30 p.m.; Saturday and Sunday, 10 a.m.–6 p.m.; open until around 9 p.m. during the summer.

Cannon Beach Bakery $

240 N. Hemlock Street; 503-436-0399; *cannonbeachbakery.com*
Some families make an annual pilgrimage to this historic bakery, which stocks beach-ready pastries in a glass case. Try a "Sailor Jack" (spice cake with raisins), the Haystack cake (coconut, dates, and walnuts), buttermilk cruller, or a variety of cookies. Pick up a sandwich inside, or buy in-house baked breads to make your own. Open Wednesday–Monday, 6:30 a.m.–5 p.m.; closed on Tuesday.

Ecola Seafood $$

208 N. Spruce Street; 503-436-9130; *ecolaseafoods.com*
Vinyl tablecloths cover the tables, the TV blares overhead, and you put in your order ($10–$22 per entrée) at a counter. You'll get your bountiful order delivered, without fanfare, in a plastic basket. But then you'll take a bite of your calamari, salmon 'n' chips, or razor clams, and you'll know why this one made the list. I'm talking about really fresh, flaky seafood (the owner catches much of it himself), perfectly prepared in trans-fat-free oil. It's one of the very best seafood meals in the Northwest. Kids' meals come with a lollipop and an obviously inedible plastic fish. Summer: open 9 a.m.–9 p.m. daily. Off-season: open 10 a.m.–7 p.m. daily.

Picnic Basket $

144 N. Hemlock Street; 503-436-1470; *picnicbasketnw.com*
Check out this shop's 95 (more or less) exotic taffy flavors, including pomegranate, papaya, root beer float, and strawberry cheesecake. Pick up a mix to bring home for grandma or play "guess that flavor" in the car on the way home. Summer: usually open daily, 10 a.m.–10 p.m.; fall, 10 a.m.–7 p.m.; winter, 11 a.m.–4 p.m.

Pizza A' Fetta $$$

231 N. Hemlock Street, Suite 109; 877-436-0333; *pizza-a-fetta.com*
Pizza A' Fetta's dense crust and heavy toppings make for the perfect carboholic snack after a hike or an all-day beach venture. However, seating's tight inside; during peak hours, order ahead and pick up your meat, veggie, or seafood pie to go. They'll half-bake it, so you can finish cooking it in your room oven. Family-sized pizzas range from $25 to $34. Summer: open Sunday–Thursday, 11 a.m.–9 p.m.; Friday and Saturday, 11 a.m.–10 p.m. Winter: open Sunday–Thursday, 11 a.m.–8 p.m.; Friday and Saturday, 11 a.m.–9 p.m.

Sweet Basil's Café $

271 N. Hemlock Street, #4; 503-436-1539; *cafesweetbasils.com*
Once you've eaten your fill of greasy, carbo-loaded beach food, you'll start craving fresh vegetables and fruits. When that craving kicks in, head to Sweet Basil's, where you can order wraps (uncooked), cold sandwiches, or a roasted chicken salad. Of course, they've got your carby goodness, too, but with a healthful twist: Try the apple and cheddar panini. Kids can choose from a short menu offering PB&J, tuna salad, or grilled cheese. Summer: open daily, 11 a.m.–4:30 p.m. Winter: open Thursday–Monday, 11 a.m.–4:30 p.m.; closed Tuesday and Wednesday.

Wayfarer Restaurant $$–$$$

1190 Pacific Drive; 503-436-1108; *wayfarer-restaurant.com*
As the restaurant attached to Surfsand, the Wayfarer serves a well-heeled set, but don't let the pricing set you back. Go for breakfast, when the children's menu is reasonable and adult portions generous. Huge picture windows look out over Haystack Rock and all the beachy goings-on. Sit back and eat slowly, coffee (or warm milk) in hand. Summer: open 8 a.m.–10 p.m. Winter: 8 a.m.–9 p.m.

SHOP

Cannon Beach Book Company

130 N. Hemlock Street, #2; 800-436-0906; *cannonbeachbooks.com*
A petite children's section includes pop-ups, readers, picture books, and Klutz's crafty titles. It's the only bookstore in town, so it's a good place to go on a rainy day. Opens at 10 a.m. most days; hours vary by season.

Cannon Beach Farmers' Market

Intersection of Gower and Hemlock streets, in the city's lower parking lot; 503-436-8044; *cannonbeachmarket.org/Home.html*
Head here for live music, freshly baked pies, and just-picked seasonal berries and veggies. Open Tuesdays, 2–6 p.m., mid-June through September.

Gepetto's Toy Shoppe

200 N. Hemlock Street; 503-436-2467
A well-located toy store right on the main drag with all the classic, low-key toys, including Legos, travel games, puppets, and bath toys. Winter: open 10 a.m.–5 p.m. Summer: open 10 a.m.–6 p.m.

Kite Factory

339 Fir Street; 503-436-0839
Don't have a kite? Get one here and take it right down to the beach a few blocks away. Colorful kites for the dabbler or the ambitious (make sure you've got muscles of steel for those big suckers!). Hours vary; call ahead.

getaway
ASTORIA

At the junction of the Columbia River and the Pacific Ocean, this quaint little town awaits curious families. Astoria offers a cool, low-key, artistic vibe, and a great rainy-day escape. Check out historic artifacts (Astoria is the oldest U.S. settlement west of the Rocky Mountains, and Lewis and Clark ended their adventures here), an indoor splash pool, or just walk along Astoria's vintage (and somewhat forlorn) streets. Look high up on the hills for Victorian-era homes, or gaze out to sea, where there have been more than 200 shipwrecks in the area's chilly waters.

DO

Astoria Aquatic Center

1997 Marine Drive; 503-325-7027; *astoriaswim.com*
With pool temps from 86 to 89 degrees, head here for warm-water swimming even when the skies are dark and the ocean is frigid. This indoor water center

offers slides, sprinklers, and toys in two large pools. Open Monday–Friday, 5–7 p.m.; Saturday and Sunday, 11 a.m.–5 p.m. Open swim: Monday–Friday, 1–7 p.m.; Saturday and Sunday, 11 a.m.–5 p.m. Adults/$6; families/$12; children/$4; 2 and younger/free.

Fort Clatsop National Memorial
92343 Fort Clatsop Road; 503-861-2471 ext. 214; *nps.gov/lewi/planyourvisit/fortclatsop.htm*
History from a century ago comes alive at this state park, where, in a small museum, you can learn about Lewis and Clark's expedition, pick up an educational activity guide that leads to honorary park ranger status, and look for bear tracks. The fort replica — a set of adjoining cabins — is the standout exhibit; with its knickknacks and explanatory placards, you can almost smell those burly pioneer men living together in cramped conditions. Makes the car trip home seem not so bad. Open mid-June to Labor Day: 9 a.m.–6 p.m. After Labor Day to mid-June: 9 a.m.–5 p.m.

Columbia River Maritime Museum
1792 Marine Drive; 503-325-2323; *crmm.org*
Boat buffs will want to stop here, but young children may not be so entertained. Noteworthy features include life-size replicas of a boat capsize and rescue, fishermen and a fishing boat, and a steering wheel for pint-size pretend captains. Open 9:30 a.m.–5 p.m. daily. Adults/$10; children ages 6–17/$5; children younger than 6/free.

EAT

Astoria Coffeehouse $
243 Eleventh Street; 503-325-1787; *astoriacoffeehouse.com*
The tropics-themed décor will wake you before the caffeine even kicks in. A coffee shop for the see-and-be-seen crowd visiting Astoria. Open Sunday and Monday, 7 a.m.–5 p.m.; Tuesday and Wednesday, 7 a.m.–9 p.m.; Thursday–Saturday, 7 a.m.–11 p.m.

Blue Scorcher Bakery and Café $
1493 Duane Street; 503-338-7473; *bluescorcher.com*
Playsilks, books, and a tiny toy corner make Blue Scorcher a hot hit with parents. Enjoy the big, open, and airy space on rainy days. Open daily, 8 a.m.–5 p.m.

Fort George Brewery + Public House $–$$
1483 Duane Street, Astoria; 503-325-7468; *fortgeorgebrewery.com*
The combo of excellent beer, burgers, house-made sausage, and great views should put Fort George on your list. The books and small toys (when we were there, a felt play set) and children's menu — served with fresh apple slices and carrots — make it an ideal stop for kids. And although this sounds a bit odd, check out the quirky, mural-painted bathrooms. Your kids will love them. Open Monday–Thursday, 11 a.m.–11 p.m.; Friday and Saturday, 11 a.m.–midnight; Sunday, noon–11 p.m.

SHOP

Amazing Stories Astoria

1405 Commercial Street; 503-325-5518; *amazingstoriesastoria.com*

A store full of graphic novels, comics, superhero gear, Pokémon cards, and collectible action figures. Smartly, this store separates the children's comics from those more appropriate for older children. Open daily, 11a.m.–6 p.m.

Lunar Boy Gallery

1133 Commercial Street; 866-395-1566; *lunarboygallery.com*

Find your *Goonies* memorabilia here (parts of the movie were filmed nearby), cute kids' books, and Matthew Porter art, among other hand-selected items for funky families. In the rear, you'll find art that you may not want your kids to see; scope it out first. Open Monday, Wednesday, Friday, Saturday, 10 a.m.–5 p.m.; Tuesday and Thursday, 10 a.m.–2 p.m.; Sunday, 11a.m.–3 p.m.

Purple Cow Toys

1380 Commercial Street; 503-325-2996; *purplecowtoysastoria.com*

Playmobil, puzzles, games, and a variety of well-made wooden and plastic toys, great for indoor days or the long drive home. Open Monday–Friday, 10 a.m.–6 p.m.; Saturday, 10 a.m.–5 p.m.; Sunday, noon–4 p.m.

seattle

seattle

Seattle presents more kid-friendly attractions and museums per square mile than most cities in the Northwest. Even the city's art museum dedicates a space to entertaining children.

Education and the arts are central themes in Seattle, so you'll see plenty of bookstores, museums (too many to include in this book!), and art galleries throughout downtown and in the neighborhoods. These interior spaces foil rainy and overcast days, as do the welcoming coffee shops and community centers.

Walking through downtown Seattle's hypermodern library amuses even the most jaded kids, as does kissing Rachel the Pig in the Pike Place Market And don't forget to enjoy the city's maritime history and waterfront walks — with ferries, cruises, and boat locks ready to entertain.

SUGGESTED ITINERARIES

If you're staying for two days: Head for the Pike Place Market for a solid four-hour visit. Then check out the nearby Seattle Aquarium or visit the wildlife at Woodland Park Zoo. Spend your second day at Seattle Center; choose from arts, science, or play options.

If you're staying for three days: Take in all of the above, then visit the Ballard, Fremont, or West Seattle neighborhoods.

If you're staying for five days: Visit all of the above, plus two neighborhoods and take a trip to Bainbridge Island.

If you're staying for a week: Experience all of the above, plus a trip to Portland, Victoria, or Vancouver.

MATCH YOUR TRAVEL ITINERARY TO YOUR FAMILY STYLE

Active families: Rent a bike at Recycled Cycles and go for a spin along Seattle's Burke-Gilman Trail, or climb the walls at Stone Gardens. Go to Green Lake and rent paddle boats, take a walk, or ride bikes around the popular lake. Catch a pro baseball or basketball game. Stay at the Inn at Queen Anne, so you'll be centrally located.

Artsy families: Visit Seattle Art Museum's famous "Hammering Man" sculpture, watch a play at the Seattle Children's Theatre, and catch a concert by the Seattle Symphony at Benaroya Hall. Take in a music show or movie at Seattle Center or the Fremont Outdoor Cinema. Stay at the Hotel Monaco, so you're near all the art action downtown.

Foodie families: Dine at Vios, which offers a play area for toddlers and preschoolers. Visit the Pike Place Market for foods from local farms, or the Ballard Sunday Farmers' Market for more of a neighborhood feel. Stay at the MarQueen Hotel, which offers decent-size kitchens for cooking.

FIVE THINGS YOU MUST DO IN SEATTLE

1. Pick up a fish at the Pike Place Market. Seattle's year-round public market has been in operation since 1907. Watch as vendors sell food, handmade crafts, desserts, and produce. Don't miss the fish-flingers tossing salmon to locals and travelers alike (page 56).

2. Boat it. Seattle is in love with boats, and it shows. Ride a water taxi to West Seattle or Vashon Island or a ferry to Bainbridge Island; check out the million-dollar yachts and one-ton tugboats plying Ballard's Hiram M. Chittenden Locks (page 65).

3. Eat fish 'n' chips. Because fishermen park their boats at Seattle's piers, the fish 'n' chip shops are plentiful and plenty good. From the big-name Ivar's (serving its famous chowder; page 53) to the smaller Spud Fish & Chips at Alki Beach (page 72), you'll have the pick of fresh catch.

4. Roam the Woodland Park Zoo. Although not as centrally located as other Seattle attractions, this zoo is one of the best in the Pacific Northwest. Enjoy the indoor play area year-round, see animals in their natural habitats, and visit the deluxe petting zoo (page 61).

5. Visit the Museum of Flight. A little off the beaten path but worth the effort, this soaring air and space museum exemplifies Seattle's dedication to technology (Boeing happens to be just down the street), with many interactive features throughout (page 74).

Retro families: Trace the history of rock 'n' roll at the Experience Music Project | Science Fiction Museum (EMP | SFM), dive deep into antiquated Seattle in the Pike Place Market's maze of neon lights, alleyways, and stalls, and experience sweet mid-twentieth-century modern architecture via an elevator ride to the top of the Seattle Space Needle. Sleep at the Mayflower Park Hotel, a vintage downtown hotel with old-fashioned personal service.

Shopping families: Shop your hearts out in Seattle's downtown core, pick up one-of-a-kind items at the Pike Place Market, and troll the funky flea market in Fremont on Sundays. Stay at the Inn at Pike Place Market, so you won't miss a minute of the action.

WHAT KIDS LIKE BEST, AGE BY AGE

Babies: A quick trip into the Seattle Children's Museum, where babes can splash in water, crawl on foam-covered pads, and go down a baby slide. Beyond that, little ones are portable, so go where you like! Babies love the colors and crowds at the Pike Place Market (but wear your baby in a sling or other carrier; the crowds are thick) and the Seattle Aquarium.

SEATTLE

Toddlers and preschoolers: Woodland Park Zoo may bring out your child's wild side, but the Seattle Aquarium's underwater dome calms most kids. Seattle Children's Museum is geared specifically to this age group; they can shop in the pretend grocery store or visit Japan. Run through the Olympic Sculpture Park and visit the enormous traffic cones, just for a giggle (and a great photo).

Elementary-school-age kids: The Pacific Science Center makes science exciting, and this is the perfect age for a ride on the Monorail to Seattle Center, then an elevator ride up the Space Needle. Don't forget a change of clothes, just in case the kids want to run around in the International Fountain. Go to the Woodland Park Zoo, then out to Green Lake — or a neighborhood toy store — to top off a perfect day. Kids will love the historical and contemporary aircraft on display at the Museum of Flight.

Middle-school-age kids: Watch a pro sports game, shop at Archie McPhee, and visit the Fremont Troll. Go to the underground arcades at the Pike Place Market, where there are lots of stores for this age group — think magic, comics, music, and more. Take advantage of an older child's increased attention span by catching a ferry ride to West Seattle, Bainbridge Island, or another island destination.

Teens: Rock-loving teens will enjoy EMP | SFM, attending one of Seattle's fabulous summertime weekend festivals, shopping the quirky streets of Fremont and Ballard, and people-watching from a perch in the Pike Place Market. Follow your teen's interests, whether art (Seattle Art Museum), skating (Seattle Center Skatepark), or adventure (a ferry ride).

TRAVEL INFORMATION

Seattle Visitor and Concierge Service provides guides, lodging options, and more. Find more information at *visitseattle.org*. Get information in person at the Washington State Trade & Convention Center at Pike and Seventh streets in downtown Seattle, and at the Market Information Center at First and Pike.

Multiple venues throughout town sell the Go Seattle Card (*smart destinations.com*; 800-887-9103), which provides admission to more than 35 attractions, including many of Seattle's favorites (the Space Needle, Pacific Science Center, Woodland Park Zoo, bike rentals, and more). Not a bad deal, if you're in town for a few days. One-day passes start at around $50/adult, $38/child; seven-day passes start at around $150/adult, $90/child.

SEATTLE IN THE MEDIA

Most of Seattle's claim to celebrity fame comes from technology (Bill Gates and Microsoft), and grunge and indie musical acts, including Jimi Hendrix, Pearl Jam, Death Cab for Cutie, and Nirvana. Kids may recognize Seattle-shot movies like the Elvis classic *It Happened at the World's Fair*, or *Harry and the Hendersons* and *The Last Mimzy*. Teens may (or may not) want to watch *Ten Things I Hate About You*, *Sleepless in Seattle*, and the horror flick *The Ring*.

For a walking tour of Seattle's recognizable movie locations, see the City of Seattle's Film Office map: *seattle.gov/filmoffice/docs/map.pdf*.

Tween readers will recognize famous Seattle landmarks from the "Hannah West" mystery series; tween Nickelodeon fans will know that *iCarly* is set in Seattle. Kids will enjoy *Wheedle on the Needle* by Stephen Cosgrove, *E Is for Evergreen: A Washington State Alphabet* by Roland Smith, *A Day at the Market* by Sara Anderson, and the wonderful *Larry Gets Lost in Seattle* and *Seattle ABC*, both by John Skewes. Mature teens might get the giggles from the scatological *Bigfoot: I Not Dead* by Graham Roumieu.

SEATTLE NICKNAMES

Emerald City
Jet City
The Rainy City

SAFETY

Do not leave any valuables in your car anywhere in Seattle. If you must, pack them in your trunk where they aren't visible. Car crime is an ongoing problem in Seattle.

Seattle's downtown core is generally safe, but keep a watchful eye on your purse and your kids. The least-savory elements of downtown generally come out after stores close; avoid wandering most areas after dark when walking with kids (except in winter, when businesses may still be open). Seattle has a visible homeless, panhandling population, which is predominantly harmless.

GETTING THERE

Plane: Flights to Seattle arrive at the Seattle-Tacoma International Airport. From the airport, make your way into town by the new Link Light Rail, a forty-five-minute ride to downtown. You can also take a taxi or rent a car. See all of your options at Sea-Tac's Web site: *portseattle.org/seatac*.

Amtrak: Amtrak Cascades trains (*amtrakcascades.com*) leave from Portland five times a day, with one-way trips starting from $28 and lasting three hours or longer. The trains leave from Vancouver, B.C., twice per day, with one-way trips starting from $35; the trip one way runs a little more than four hours (ask for a seat on the western side of the train, which faces shores, shorebirds, and the sunset). Arriving at the King Street Station, catch a bus into the downtown core or grab a taxi. I would not walk into the downtown area because of safety and distance concerns. This area can be one of the dodgiest parts of Seattle.

The Starlight Express train leaves once daily for Seattle from points south. This train (often not on schedule) offers an upstairs glass-covered observation dome, which can be fun for kids. Read about Amtrak, book tickets, and find out more at *amtrak.com*.

Greyhound Bus: This takes a very long time. It's inexpensive, but very time-consuming and boring. It's well worth it to pay a little extra and go by train. *greyhound.com*

SEATTLE

Car: You'll drive toward Seattle along I-5 from points either north or south. Coming from the north (Vancouver, B.C.) it's roughly a two- to three-and-a-half-hour drive, depending on delays at the border. From the south (Portland), it takes three and a half to five hours, depending on traffic trouble spots in and around Seattle, Tacoma, and Olympia. One bad accident can shut down or slow traffic for hours. Listen to radio station 530 AM for traffic advisories.

We've had more success when leaving early in the morning (before rush hour starts). Leaving midday or late afternoon can be a surefire recipe for frustration all the way.

From points south, a nice stop en route is to take exit 82 in Centralia and grab a bite at either Burgerville (818 Harrison Avenue, 360-736-5212) or McMenamins Olympic Club Hotel and Theater's Club Pub (112 N. Tower Avenue, 866-736-5164). Burgerville offers great locally grown foods in fast-food wrappers, children's meals, and indoor and outdoor seating. The Olympic Club offers sit-down pub grub at decent prices, and is located right next to some train tracks, so toddlers can watch trains come and go.

From points north: A nice stop en route is off exit 256 in Bellingham. Take a left on Meridian Street to find the Barnes & Noble bookstore (4099 Meridian

SEATTLE

FUN FACTS

- The name "Seattle" comes from the Native American Suquamish tribal leader Chief Sealth.

- Seattle was settled after Portland. The first settlers landed at Alki Point in West Seattle on November 13, 1851. Today you can go there for ice cream and fish 'n' chips.

- Seattle's city bird is the great blue heron. Watch for herons at the Ballard locks. Which bird was the second runner-up for the title? The not-so-fancy crow.

- The Space Needle is not Seattle's tallest building. Instead, it's the 937-foot-tall Columbia Center.

- Seattle is consistently ranked among the top three most literate cities in the U.S.

- Seattle's houseboat population is the country's largest.

- The Farmers' Market at the Pike Place Market is the longest continuously operating farmers' market in the U.S.

- The Washington state ferry system is the largest in the country and the third largest in the world, carrying more than 25 million passengers annually.

  - Hot tip: While Seattle isn't the only city in the country to celebrate First Thursday, the number of museums open to the public (for FREE!) in Seattle is spectacular. For a complete listing of museums open for free to families on the first Thursday of the month, visit *nwkidtrips.com*.

CALENDAR

January
FESTÁL. Festál celebrations are a series of free cultural events that happen almost every weekend throughout the year, each celebrating a unique Seattle immigrant culture (e.g., Filipino, Italian, Chinese). *seattlecenter.com/events /festivals/festal/default.asp*

March
THE MOISTURE FESTIVAL brings modern-day, family-friendly burlesque to Seattle. *moisturefestival.com*

April
WHIRLIGIG. The Seattle Center's Center House transforms into a lively house of bounce for two weeks during spring; kids can play on supersized inflatable rides. *seattle center.com/events/festivals*

May
GIANT MAGNET (formerly Seattle International Children's Festival). Live musical and theatrical performances, activity centers, and giant bouncing balls. *seattleinter national.org*

NORTHWEST FOLKLIFE. A celebration of folk music from around the world; don't miss the children's stage and activities area. *nwfolklife.org*

June
FREMONT SOLSTICE PARADE is a big, naked, bike-riding party. No, really. You don't have to be naked or ride a bike to join, but it's part of the parade's draw. Most kids will giggle at the body-painted riders, but the Solstice Parade also offers floats designed by local schools, "art cars," live music, food, and a freewheeling atmosphere. Very old-school Seattle. *fremontfair.org*

July
SEAFAIR. Seafair is Seattle's annual celebration of summer, with community parades, weekend mini-festivals, and big parties along the waterfront. *seafair.com/events/community*

BITE OF SEATTLE. More than fifty of Seattle's finest restaurants host the Bite of Seattle, giving you a chance to sample local delicacies, watch cooking demos, and eat your way through Seattle. *biteofseattle.com*

September
BUMBERSHOOT. With more than twenty indoor and outdoor venues, a wide variety of festival cuisine, and a diverse collection of indie retail vendors, Bumbershoot embodies an eclectic mix of artists that has inspired summer festival-goers for nearly four decades. *bumbershoot.com*

November
TREE LIGHTING CELEBRATION AND HOLIDAY PARADE. Take in a holiday parade through downtown, the official lighting of Westlake Center's holiday tree and Macy's star, then fireworks.

December
WINTERFEST. Seattle Center transforms into a giant ice rink, to the delight of Seattle denizens. Includes music, caroling, and more. *seattle center.com/winterfest*

SEATTLE

Street; bathrooms, coffee, kids' area, open 9 a.m.–10 p.m. weekdays, 9 a.m.–11 p.m. weekends). Or you can stop in downtown Bellingham for inexpensive, great grub.

GETTING AROUND

Finding your way around Seattle: Seattle might make you a little crazy. Each neighborhood is laid out in tidy grid format — but it may be a grid format unique to that neighborhood alone. When seeking an address, get directions from your favorite mapping software, or ask for cross streets and look at a paper map.

Seattle is extremely hilly — more so than Portland or Vancouver, B.C. — particularly in the downtown area. Bring a stroller for kids younger than six.

A neat (yet possibly profane) trick to figure out your orientation downtown is to use the local mnemonic "Jesus Christ Made Seattle Under Protest" (JCMSUP). JCMSUP lists downtown's twelve main streets in pairs; from south to north, they are: Jefferson, James, Cherry, Columbia, Marion, Madison, Spring, Seneca, University, Union, Pike, Pine. Although we think Jesus would like Seattle just fine.

Car: Buy a road map at one of the local supermarkets or grocery stores; alternately, map out your drive using an online mapping program. Seattle newcomers often find the city's dead-end streets, lack of on- and off-ramps, and far-flung

---

ESSENTIALS

Area code: 206

Baby accessories: Forgot the stroller? Check with *happylittletraveler.com* (or call 206-935-0733) to see if they've got what you need.

Emergencies: Call 911. With urgent or emergency conditions, go to Seattle Children's Hospital at 4800 Sand Point Way N.E., or call 206-987-2000.

Mail a postcard: Head to the USPS at 301 Union Street, in downtown Seattle.

News: *The Seattle Times* is Seattle's newspaper of record; *Seattle Weekly* and *The Stranger* are two free alternative newspapers. For kid-friendly fun, pick up a free copy of *ParentMap* (or go to *parentmap.com*).

Parks: Find all of Seattle's parks at *seattle.gov/parks*.

Pharmacy: Bartell Drugs' Queen Anne store is open 24 hours at 600 First Avenue N., 206-284-1353; pharmacy, 206-284-1354.

Taxes: 12.5 percent hotel tax, 8.8 percent tax on goods, 10 percent tax on dining.

neighborhoods confusing. You may also be challenged by some of our 18-percent-grade streets, particularly if you drive a clutch. But it's really fun for the kids.

Metered on-street parking is available in most neighborhoods, but it can be next to impossible to find a spot in downtown Seattle. Save yourself the time (and spare your kids some choice swear words) — pay to park in one of the many paid-parking lots for the day, and then rely on your feet or public transit.

Public transportation: Fashionably late to the public-transportation party, Seattle opened its first large-scale light rail line (connecting the airport to downtown Seattle) in 2009. Other routes include the Seattle Streetcar (*seattlestreetcar.org*), connecting downtown to Seattle's South Lake Union neighborhood.

Almost every Seattle location listed here is easy to reach by public transport. As always, if traveling on public transportation, it makes sense to either stay downtown (from which public transportation radiates outward, like spokes of a wheel) or in the neighborhood in which you plan to spend most of your time.

All transportation is free within the "ride free area" (RFA), which includes much of Seattle's downtown. Read more about Seattle's public transportation and find the current fare schedule at *tripplanner.metrokc.gov*.

Ride the Duck: In Seattle, you can take a sightseeing trip via water and land on an amphibious World War II–era boat-van. "The Duck" takes riders through downtown Seattle, into Lake Union and then through Fremont before heading back downtown. Kids and adults blow "quackers," and the Duck Drivers work hard to entertain on the journey. *ridetheducksofseattle.com*

Bike: Find bike maps at *cityofseattle.net/transportation/bikemaps.htm*.

Traffic notes: Gridlock in Seattle is particularly notorious along I-5 during morning (7–9 a.m.) or evening (4–7 p.m.) rush hours. Try to avoid going into or out of the city when everyone else is doing the same thing, and take public transportation or surface streets during the day.

DOWNTOWN

This area covers a lot of ground — specifically, the miles between Seattle Center and the International District. But space-age transportation options (including the beloved yet irregular Monorail) keep all activities accessible.

The downtown core is Seattle's business, arts, and shopping center. Head to the downtown library's glass structure, wrapped in arresting, mesh-like metal. Visit the Pike Place Market (not "Pike's Place," as many assume) for lunch and shopping, and then the Seattle Art Museum for art, Safeco Field for an afternoon game, or the Seattle Aquarium and the Seattle waterfront for views of Elliott Bay. Most of Seattle's hotels are concentrated in the downtown area; the three listed here (page 50) are especially unique and family friendly.

Even better, with kids, consider staying in a kitchen-equipped hotel in the Lower Queen Anne neighborhood, next to Seattle Center. You're a few blocks from all the run-around fun Seattle Center provides, but you're also near grocery stores; inexpensive, informal dining; and a short bus ride away from downtown activities.

SLEEP
Hotel Monaco $$$-$$$$
1101 Fourth Avenue; 206-621-1770 or 800-715-6513; *monaco-seattle.com*
Fun, sun-splashed décor reminiscent of the Mediterranean is on display here,
along with well-maintained interiors. Children love the age-appropriate kid
packs and the option to keep a goldfish in your room. Friday's wine hour
features Guitar Hero games in the lobby, and twice-per-week visits from a
fortuneteller. There's no pool (few Seattle hotels offer a pool), but Hotel
Monaco's milk and cookies should help compensate.

Inn at the Market $$$$
86 Pine Street; 206-443-3600 or 800-446-4484; *innatthemarket.com*
This hotel is not cheap, but when else will you get to sleep right above a
working market? Inn at the Market offers families seventy rooms of varying
styles, flowerpot-lined outdoor hallways, a gracious courtyard, and front-door
people watching. Worth a splurge, if you can swing it, and particularly wonderful for older children.

Mayflower Park Hotel $$$-$$$$
405 Olive Way; 206-623-8700 or 800-426-5100; *mayflowerpark.com*
The Mayflower Park offers a peek into the Gilded Age, with original 1927
stained glass, a grand lobby, and 161 rooms trimmed with crown molding. But
don't think that kids aren't welcome. In fact, upon arrival, they're given a lunch-
box stuffed with crayons, a miniature orca, and more. Book early — this hotel
often fills with repeat visitors who like the location next to Westlake Center,
which makes hopping on the Monorail a breeze. Fridges available upon request.

DO
Gameworks
1511 Seventh Avenue; 206-521-0952; *gameworks.com*
It's an endless wall of noise and excitement, but you're used to it, right? Modern,
fast-paced arcade games invite kids to drive cars fast, blow up buildings, and shoot
space aliens. Well, better here than in real life, I suppose. Game cards start at $2
(receive $3.50 worth of credit). Open Monday–Thursday, 11 a.m.–midnight;
Friday, 11 a.m.–1 a.m.; Saturday, 10 a.m.–1 a.m.; Sunday, 10 a.m.–midnight.

Qwest Field
800 Occidental Avenue S.; 206-381-7555; *qwestfield.com*
Home of the pro Seattle Seahawks football (*seahawks.com*) and Sounders soccer (*soundersfc.com*) teams. Check the Qwest Web site for year-round tours of
the facility. Not as many facilities for younger kids as Safeco, so it's a better
option for older children, teens, and die-hard sports fans. Hours and admission
prices vary; check the Web site for details.

Safeco Field
1250 First Avenue S.; 206-346-4001; *mariners.mlb.com*
Watching a game of Mariners baseball is an abiding tradition for many
Seattle families; you'll be surrounded by tons of kids cheering the home

team, eating garlic fries (whew!), and getting autographs from favorite players. Kids should bring their Nintendo DS; they'll get free access to MLB scores, player statistics, and a digitized version of the live game. A children's play area (Seattle Children's Hospital playfield) will distract children while you keep tabs on the game. There's even a nursing mother's lounge. Ticket prices vary; seats in the no-alcohol family section run $27 per seat; bleacher seats start at $7.

Seattle Aquarium
1483 Alaskan Way; 206-386-4320; *seattleaquarium.org*
The Seattle Aquarium was just given a fresh fish lift in 2007, adding the 17-by-39-foot Window on Washington Waters, where kids can catch their first glimpse of salmon. At the Touch Pool, stroke hubcap-sized peach and pink starfish, as aptly named sea cucumbers inch along the bottom and crabs pop their heads out to say hello. Descending into the aquarium, find yourself a visitor in the otherworldly Underwater Dome. Reef sharks, flounder, and rays glide around silently. Don't skip the gift shop if you're interested in local waters; it has plenty of great books, stuffed animals, and DVDs on Puget Sound animal life. Adults/$16; children (ages 4–12)/$10.50; ages 3 and younger/free. Open 9:30 a.m.–5 p.m. daily.

Seattle Art Museum
1300 First Avenue; 206-654-3100; *seattleartmuseum.org*
SAM's curators obviously know what tickles the fancy of a 4-foot-tall kid. Dangling Ford Taurus cars hang from the ceiling. The ceramics display on the third floor features a toilet on a patchwork ceramic tile floor. A used toilet. The kids love it, no surprise. SAM's family room offers a bit more refinement: vintage-style dress-up, a drawer of tools, and Kapla blocks. In the North Contemporary Gallery, a 6-foot-tall polyester-resin mouse sits upon a man's chest. In the fourth floor's African Gallery, the African masks can transform an everyday man into an elephant, ram, or antelope. Don't miss the free brochure titled "Please Growl! Highlight Tour for Families." Adults/$13; youth (13–17)/$7; children 12 and younger/free. Open Tuesday–Sunday, 10 a.m.–5 p.m.; Thursday and Friday, 10 a.m.–9 p.m.; closed Monday.

Seattle Public Library
1000 Fourth Avenue; 206-386-4636; *spl.org*
For downtime, nothing beats the Seattle Public Library's completely different, birdcage-shaped building. The puzzles and dollhouse, library programs, and eye-popping art are free for all. As a giant blue bull looks on, browse the library's manga collection or play a computer game. Ride the lime-green escalators and elevators past the talking eggheads (between floors two and three) and up to the top floor. From the tenth floor, look out through the diamond-shaped glass windows at Seattle's skyscrapers and sky. Free. Open Monday–Thursday, 10 a.m.–8 p.m.; Friday and Saturday, 10 a.m.–6 p.m.; Sunday, noon–6 p.m.

Seattle Symphony
200 University Street; 206-215-4747; *seattlesymphony.org*
If you visit Seattle during the school year (September–May), look for weekend opportunities to attend a Tiny Tots show (ages newborn–five) or Discover Music! performance (ages five–twelve) at Benaroya Hall, Seattle Symphony's home. For one price, enjoy the pre-concert activities, plus a show geared exclusively to your child's age group (and attention span). These shows are a gentle, engaging way to introduce kids to classical music. Call the box office to find out whether tickets are available; the symphony Web site can be confusing. Prices and performance times vary, but generally occur on weekend mornings or late afternoons: check Web site for details or call the ticket office.

PLAY
Olympic Sculpture Park
2901 Western Avenue; 206-654-3100; *seattleartmuseum.org*
Play and art collide at this fabulous sculpture-focused park, which offers lots of open space for running around, two-story-tall traffic cones, grassy lawns, slabs of rock sculptures (perfect for hide-and-seek), and amazing views of ferry boats and barges on the water. Free. Open day after Labor Day–April 30, Tuesday–Sunday, 10 a.m.–4 p.m.; May 1–Labor Day, Tuesday–Sunday, 10 a.m.–5 p.m.

EAT
Bottega Italiana $
1425 First Avenue; 206-343-0200; *bottegaitaliana.com*
A very small but special gelateria with real-deal treats (no day-glo coloring!), right outside the Pike Place Market. My family always votes for the stracciatella (chocolate chip), if they haven't sold out of it yet. Hours change with seasons; open seven days a week.

Cherry Street Coffee House $
1212 First Avenue; 206-264-9372; *cherryst.com*
This homey, centrally located coffeehouse offers fun seating, great food (soups, salads, freshly made sandwiches), and an interesting back room with a few toys and books. On Saturdays, the "Kids Café" includes a cup of free hot chocolate. Open weekdays, 6:30 a.m.–5 p.m.; weekends, 8 a.m.–4 p.m.

Cinnamon Works $
1536 Pike Place; 206-583-0085
Mmmm . . . cookies! Lots and lots and lots of cookies, all displayed beautifully in glass cases. The perfect midafternoon stop. Open daily in winter, 8 a.m.–5 p.m.; in summer, 7:30 a.m.–6 p.m.

Crumpet Shop $
1503 First Avenue; 206-682-1598; *thecrumpetshop.com*
Light, delightful, oh-so-Brit "crumpets" are like an English muffin, only better. Try savory crumpets (tomato pesto) or sweet crumpets (maple butter). There's limited stool-style seating inside, so you might need to get your crumpet to go. Open Monday–Friday, 7 a.m.–5 p.m.; Saturday and Sunday, 7:30 a.m.–5 p.m. Closes early on hot summer days.

Daily Dozen Doughnut Co. $
93 Pike Street; 206-467-7769

Also known as "The Doughnut Robot," because of the Daily Dozen's small rotating doughnut machine. This is the place to pick up a half-dozen mini-treats, dusted with cinnamon and sugar. They'll be placed in a bag for you, because they're usually too hot to handle. Cash only.

El Puerco Lloron $
1501 Western Avenue; 206-624-0541; *elpuercolloron.com*

Tucked away inside the Pike Place Market, this authentic, home-style Mexican-food cafeteria offers picante pork and more. Long, long lines at lunchtimes don't deter the dedicated — just wait your turn and enjoy your taco inside, or take it down to the waterfront. Open Monday–Thursday, 11 a.m.–7 p.m.; Friday and Saturday, 11a.m.–8 p.m.; Sunday, 11 a.m.–7 p.m.

Green Leaf Vietnamese Restaurant $–$$
418 Eighth Avenue S.; 206-340-1388; *greenleaftaste.com*

If you're going to visit Uwajimaya (page 57), visit this chic hole-in-the-wall for pho (pronounced "fuh"), noodles, or salads. Kids get plastic plates to make eating a little easier, and the staff is genuinely welcoming toward families. Don't skip the dipping sauces and rolls; kids generally love the peanut sauces. Open Monday–Sunday, 11 a.m.–10 p.m.

Ivar's Acres of Clams $$–$$$
1001 Alaskan Way; 206-624-6852; *ivars.net*

You might first write off this restaurant as a tourist trap (because it's along the waterfront), but smart travelers know when to take chances. Ivar's provides Northwest produce and fish in a stunning setting, looking out across Elliott Bay. Ask for a seat near the fireboat pier, and get your scuba-shaped kids' menu and crayons. Open Monday–Thursday, 11 a.m.–10 p.m.; Friday and Saturday, 11 a.m.–11 p.m.; Sunday, 9 a.m.–2 p.m. and 3:30–10 p.m.

Pike Place Chowder $$
1530 Post Alley; 206-267-2537; *pikeplacechowder.com*

Eight types of chowder are served here, including Southwestern, scallop, vegan, and salmon. Kids like chowder served in sourdough bread bowls, and the pocket-size restaurant still offers plentiful indoor and outdoor seating, perfect in both rainy and sunny weather. Don't order too much though — this chowder is truly rich. Open Monday–Sunday, 11 a.m.–5 p.m.

Pink Door $$–$$$
1919 Post Alley; 206-443-3241; *thepinkdoor.net/menus.html*

Look carefully for the simple door in the middle of the Pike Place Market's Post Alley. Not only does this high-quality restaurant provide some of the best Italian food in Seattle, but it also has two high chairs, so even the youngest epicureans won't miss out. There's the squid-ink spaghetti for the adventurous family, "straw and hay" (white and green) fettuccine for the farm-friendly family, and straight-up spaghetti for the no-nonsense family. Truly amazing

SEATTLE DOWNTOWN

food sourced from local farms, whenever possible. Also a romantic restaurant, so take the kids at lunch time, or make a reservation for the early evening hours. Open Monday–Friday, 11:30 a.m.–11 p.m.; Saturday and Sunday, 11:30 a.m.–midnight.

Piroshky Piroshky $

1908 Pike Place; 206-441-6068 ; *piroshkybakery.com*

Triangles of dough wrapped around cheese, vegetables, and meat, these delectable Russian versions of pocket pizzas are easy to carry and eat as you walk through the Market. Traditional flavors include beef and onion, or potato, mushroom, and onion; updated options include smoked salmon pâté or smoked mozzarella, broccoli, and mushroom. Polish it off with a Moscow roll. Summer hours (May–September): Monday–Friday, 7:30 a.m.–6:30 p.m.; Saturday and Sunday, 7:30 a.m.–7:30 p.m. Winter hours (October–April): Monday–Sunday, 8 a.m.–6:30 p.m.

TASTE Restaurant $$-$$$

1300 First Avenue; 206-903-5291; *tastesam.com*

TASTE offers fresh Northwest vegetables in sleek, modern style. The chic restaurant is still welcoming to families, but perhaps lunchtime is best with kids in tow. Evening draws more of a romantic crowd. Open Wednesday–Saturday, 11 a.m.–10 p.m.; Sunday, 9 a.m.–8 p.m.

Three Girls Bakery $$

1514 Pike Place; 206-622-1045

Your kids will probably spot Three Girls' windows of goodies before you do; by then, it's too late to resist. At the walk-up window, order your full meal to go: a sandwich, soup, and cinnamon stick or cookie. Perfect to take back to your downtown hotel. Open daily, 7 a.m.–6 p.m.

Top Pot Doughnuts $

2124 Fifth Avenue; 206-728-1966; *toppotdoughnuts.com/locations.html*

Flamboyant, "hand-forged" doughnuts for doughnut connoisseurs. Kids love the coconut-crusted Feather Boa, but the chocolate old-fashioned inspires much love as well and may help your kids finish the walk to downtown or Seattle Center (Top Pot is about midway between the two). If you can't make it to the Fifth Avenue location, many of the Starbucks scattered throughout Seattle offer Top Pot doughnuts in their pastry cases. Open Monday–Friday, 6 a.m.–7 p.m.; Saturday and Sunday, 7 a.m.–7 p.m.

Tutta Bella $$

2200 Westlake, Suite 112; 206-624-4422; *tuttabellapizza.com*

Pick up a hand-thrown pie, and eat while watching pedestrians and Seattle's streetcar pass by. While you wait, the kids can play with pizza dough and funny, bendable wax sticks. Don't eat too much; you'll need to leave room for Tutta's delicious gelato. Open Sunday–Thursday, 11 a.m.–10 p.m.; Friday and Saturday, 11a.m.–11 p.m.

SEATTLE DOWNTOWN

Wild Ginger $$-$$$

1401 Third Avenue; 206-623-4450; *wildginger.net*

Seattle's Southeast Asian restaurant scene is legendary; some say we have just as many Thai restaurants as Starbucks coffee shops — one on nearly every corner. Wild Ginger is a reliable recommendation for those new to our Asian fusion scene, as the restaurant combines the best of the pan-Asian palate, served in an upscale, white-linen setting. The restaurant isn't snobby: Servers present a children's menu with simple items, such as meat skewers. Open Monday–Saturday, 11:30 a.m.–3 p.m., 5–11 p.m.

SHOP

Boston Street Baby

1902 Post Alley; 206-634-0580

A fabulous store offering primarily cotton tees, pants, dresses, and shirts for kids. You'll find political tees (leaning left), Seattle screen prints, and fluffy ballerina petticoats. Look for the locally made, reversible Imp Wear overalls, and Cotton Caboodle's plain cotton shirts and pants that also work well as pajamas — they're all specially dyed in a garden of colors. Monday–Sunday, 10 a.m.–6 p.m.

Dragon's Toybox

1525 First Avenue; 206-652-2333; *dragonstoybox.net*

Nothing but innovative toys here! If you're staying downtown, check out Dragon's Toybox's retro Smurf and Rubik's Cube collections, kids' hiking kits, European board games and play food, plus the obligatory stuffed animals and puppets. Open Monday–Sunday, 10 a.m.–6 p.m.

The Elliott Bay Book Company

101 S. Main Street; moving in Spring of 2010 to Tenth Avenue between Pike and Pine (in Seattle's Capitol Hill district); 206-624-6600; *elliottbaybook.com*

One of the most hallowed literary institutions in this book-loving city, Elliott Bay Book Company is a popular site for lazy-Sunday browsers and book authors on the chat circuit. Visit on a rainy day to fully appreciate the ambiance of a well-stocked new and used bookstore. Children's area features a small castle and extensive collections for all ages. Open Monday–Saturday, 9:30 a.m.–9 p.m.; Sunday, 11 a.m.–7 p.m.

The Great Wind-Up

93 Pike Street; 206-621-9370; *greatwindup.com*

Here's one of Seattle's most unusual stores, packed with hundreds of buzzing wind-up toys, most costing less than $5. Choose from animal, religious, or politically themed wind-up toys, including self-propelled unicorns, pigs, and cows. The store does not look kindly upon broken or damaged merchandise (particularly the larger tin nostalgia robots and other toys), so supervise your kids closely. Next to the Pike Place Market. Open Monday–Saturday, 10 a.m.–6 p.m.; Sunday, 11 a.m.–5 p.m.

SEATTLE DOWNTOWN

Market Magic Shop

1501 Pike Place, #427; 206-624-4271;
generalrubric.com/magicposters/marketmagic
A magic shop in just the right environment: the slightly creepy alleys of the Pike Place Market's arcade, seemingly the perfect place for a séance. Go for the goofy (whoopee cushion) or the mysterious (tarot card deck). The store offers plenty of entry-level parlor tricks and gags, but if the autographed walls could talk, they'd tell you that even pro magicians shop here. Open Monday–Saturday, 10 a.m.–6 p.m.; Sunday, 10 a.m.–5 p.m.

Metsker Maps

1511 First Avenue; 206-623-8747; *metskers.com*
Maps might not seem like the most fascinating subject at first, but wait until you get the kids in here. Pick up old maps, new maps, map games, and puzzles; maps of land and sea, maps of near and far. Open Monday–Friday, 9 a.m.–6 p.m.; Saturday and Sunday, 10 a.m.–6 p.m.

The Pike Place Market

1501 Pike Place; 206-682-7453; *pikeplacemarket.org*
Explore Seattle's permanent homage to traditional open-air markets. Stop to scratch Rachel the brass pig's ears, watch the men at Pike Place Fish sling silvery salmon through the air, or sample a few bites of fresh, farm-grown nectarines from a market vendor. Each store within the Market must stay within its defined specialty, so there are plenty of unique shops: a boulangerie, a cheesemonger, an Italian deli. On rainy days, the downstairs market's warren of DownUnder shops is moody and ghostly; thankfully, the Market's fifty different restaurants are mostly covered, but you'll probably jostle for a good dining spot. Visit the information booth at First Avenue and Pike to pick up a map . . . and don't miss the "gum wall" — a tribute to ABC (already been chewed) gum. Open Monday–Saturday, 10 a.m.–6 p.m.; Sunday, 11 a.m.–5 p.m.; DownUnder stores: Monday–Sunday, 11 a.m.–5 p.m.

Pike Place Market Creamery

1514 Pike Place, #3; 206-622-5029
Pop into proprietor Nancy's creamery for a sweet ice cream treat from her case, or ride the small cow toy out front. If you liked Mae's Phinney Ridge Café in Seattle's Phinney neighborhood, this is the perfect place to pick up a black-and-white Jersey cow Seattle souvenir. Open Monday–Saturday, 9 a.m.–6 p.m.; Sunday, 10 a.m.–5 p.m.

Pirates Plunder

1301 Alaskan Way, Pier 57; 206-624-5673; *piratesplunder.com*
All pirate, all the time. Pirate backpacks, costumes, clothing, rubber ducks, and baby onesies. Sure, it's a store full of shlock, but it's funny shlock — how can you resist? Just down the street from the Seattle Aquarium. Open Sunday–Thursday, 9:30 a.m.–8 p.m.; Friday and Saturday, 9:30 a.m.–8:30 p.m.

REI
222 Yale Avenue N.; 206-223-1944; *rei.com*
Visit the flagship REI store, which features a climbing wall, mountain bike test trail, and all the REI outdoor and sporting gear you can imagine. Seattle kids flock like birds to the second floor's giant tree, where they can crawl, slide, and scramble. The store is immense, so if you get lost on your way, stop another parent and ask for directions — or just listen for the rumpus. Open Monday–Saturday, 9 a.m.–9 p.m.; Sunday, 10 a.m.–7 p.m.

Tottini
259 Yale Avenue N.; 206-254-0400; *tottini.com*
Pick up übermodern kid gear here: sleekly designed beds, no-mess wall decals, and new-design feeding supplies. There's also a small, tidy collection of baby and toddler clothing. Most items are perfect for small-home living and taking home via plane or car. Open Monday–Saturday, 10 a.m.–6 p.m.; Sunday, 11 a.m.–5 p.m.

Uwajimaya
600 Fifth Avenue S.; 206-624-6248; *uwajimaya.com*
An emporium of Asian gifts, produce, baked goods, pantry items, and frozen goods, imported from Japan, China, Thailand, India, the Philippines, and other exotic locales. We love the Japanese candy aisle, the Hello Kitty section, and school-sized bento boxes. The store's clean, well-lit takeaway area offers cooked-to-order foods from Asia, plus tables to sit at and slurp your noodles. This supersized international grocery even hosts a Japanese bookstore (Kinokuniya). Open Monday–Saturday, 7 a.m.–10 p.m.; Sunday, 9 a.m.–9 p.m.

Ye Olde Curiosity Shop
1001 Alaskan Way; 206-682-5844; *yeoldecuriosityshop.com*
Vaudeville-style entertainment and cheap tourist stuff abound in this waterfront Seattle classic. My kids love the teeny-tiny origami creations at the store's front, folded from dollar bills; I have a thing for Sylvester and Sylvia, the mummies at the store's rear. Along the downtown's waterfront boardwalk, among the sightseeing crowds, just as it should be. Summer hours: Monday–Sunday, 9 a.m.–9:30 p.m. Winter hours: Sunday–Thursday, 10 a.m.–6 p.m.; Friday and Saturday, 9 a.m.–9 p.m.

SEATTLE CENTER/QUEEN ANNE
305 Harrison Street; 206-684-7200; *seattlecenter.com*
Seattle Center acts as Seattle's playground. The indoor-outdoor complex contains a children's museum, a children's playhouse, a science museum, a science fiction museum, a music museum — and all of the city's biggest and best seasonal festivals. When you're not busy with those fests, play in an enormous fountain resembling an upside-down salad bowl; it volleys water as high as 120 feet in the air from more than 200 nozzles. Shred it at the 8,900-square-foot skate bowl, or catch a family-friendly concert at the amphitheater in the evening. Check the center's Web site to find out what's going on while you're in town.

A word to the wise: Don't eat here. Head "off-campus," into lower Queen Anne instead, or catch the Monorail back to downtown for Pike Place fare.

SEATTLE CENTER/QUEEN ANNE

SEATTLE

SLEEP

Inn at Queen Anne $-$$

505 First Avenue N.; 206-282-7537 or 800-952-5043; *innatqueenanne.com*
A brick, budget-style hotel for those traveling with fewer dollars (and expectations), the Inn at Queen Anne may have cracked plaster-and-lathe walls, chipping bathrooms, and dreary hallways, but it's still appealingly vintage, with glass doorknobs and sweet wall alcoves. Offers all-day coffee and juice, plus a continental breakfast. Ask for the Deluxe Room (queen-twin combination) with kitchenette (two-stove burner, mini-fridge) or the Bedroom Suite (there's only one).

MarQueen Hotel $$-$$$

600 Queen Anne Avenue N.; 206-282-7407 or 888-445-3076; *marqueen.com*
Enter this 1918 brick building, pass through its dark wood lobby, and head up the grand staircase to hardwood-floored rooms, sitting areas with fold-out couches, and beds. Full-size fridges, stoves, and roomy kitchens are also available. Families should ask for the "quiet side" of the MarQueen, which is calmer than the side facing the sometimes hard-partying Queen Anne Avenue. Free shuttle service within the greater downtown area is provided, including Fremont and the University of Washington. If you can swing it, this is my pick for a hotel-style Seattle stay.

Mediterranean Inn $$-$$$

425 Queen Anne Avenue N.; 206-428-4700 or 866-525-4700;
mediterranean-inn.com
Ironically, this newer complex feels more corporate than many hotels in Seattle, but the beige walls and floors are impeccably clean. The rooftop patio deck offers spectacular views of Mount Rainier along with green lawn chairs, and the location is just a few blocks from Seattle Center's kid-friendly action. Also sweet: the kitchenettes (microwave and mini-fridge only).

DO

EMP | SFM

325 Fifth Avenue N.; 206-367-5483 or 206-770-2702; *emplive.com*
The Experience Music Project and Science Fiction Museum are housed under the same roof in an undulating, iridescent building that shines (rain or shine) like a dragon's scales. View Jimi Hendrix's threads or learn more about the Northwest's influential rock scene; study Nirvana's guitar licks and Tori Amos' vocal tricks with the help of EMP's hands-on tutorials. In the SFM, a spherical Death Star looms ominously as you enter, flickering images from space-age film hits. Check out the computer-generated Cities of Tomorrow, with scenes from the utopian *Jetsons* and the dystopian *Blade Runner*; the Space Dock area allows you to view spaceships from *Futurama*, *Star Trek*, and dozens of other sci-fi favorites. Adults (ages 18–64)/$15; youth (ages 5–17)/$12; children (ages 4 and younger)/free. Open 10 a.m.–5 p.m. daily (fall/winter/spring); 10 a.m.–7 p.m. daily (summer).

Pacific Science Center

200 Second Avenue N.; 206-443-2001; *pacsci.org*

This is a six-acre hands-on indoor/outdoor science discovery zone. Growl back at the animatronic *T. rex* and triceratops, interact with a robotic human-size praying mantis, and warm up in PSC's Butterfly House, where hundreds of butterflies float through the air. The Science Center's toddler zone offers water play, kid-size foam blocks, and marimbas. Adults/$11; children ages 6–12/$8, ages 3–5/$6, younger than 3/free; check to see if membership at your local science center gets you in free. Monday–Friday, 10 a.m.–5 p.m.; Saturday, Sunday, and holidays, 10 a.m.–6 p.m.

Seattle Children's Museum

305 Harrison Street; 206-441-1768; *thechildrensmuseum.org*

The Children's Museum is a great choice for kids younger than ten. My son takes orders in the pint-size Mexican-themed restaurant (complete with plastic tacos), while my daughter visits a multi-room reproduction of a Japanese home (shoes off, please). Kids can star in their own play or climb a mountain; babies can crawl through their very own underwater adventure. $7.50/general, ages 1 and younger/free. Open Monday–Friday, 10 a.m.–5 p.m.; Saturday and Sunday, 10 a.m.–6 p.m.

Seattle Children's Theatre

201 Thomas Street; 206-443-0807; *sct.org*

Seattle Children's Theatre, set in the heart of Seattle Center, offers book-themed plays throughout the year aimed at all age ranges, from toddler through adult. Check SCT's Web site to snag weekend matinee tickets far in advance. They go very, very quickly. Children's tickets range from $15 to $28; adults, $20–$34. Hours vary; matinees available.

Seattle Storm

KeyArena at 305 Harrison Street; 206-217-WNBA; *wnba.com/storm*

Enjoy pro women's basketball that's genuinely welcoming to families, right down to the Storm's tween and teen dance troupe. Look at the online schedule for family days, bring-your-daughter days, and other special events. Kids love Doppler, the Storm's meteorological mascot, and the energy of cheering for an exciting team. Single-game tickets range from $14 to $55. Season runs June–September; game times vary.

Space Needle

400 Broad Street; 206-905-2100; *spaceneedle.com*

Built for the 1962 World's Fair, the Space Needle represented the Northwest's forward-thinking attitude. It's still pretty cool today and worth at least one ride to the top during your visit. With the Needle reaching 520 feet high and featuring a panoramic, rotating view of mountains, city, and sea, the steep entry fee is worth it if you visit twice — once in daytime and once at dark. For a major splurge, eat at the Needle's rotating restaurant. Ride to the top: adults (ages 14–64)/$16; youth (ages 4–13)/$8; child (ages 3 and younger)/free. Open Sunday–Thursday, 10 a.m.–9 p.m.; Friday and Saturday, 9:30 a.m.–10 p.m.

EAT

Dick's Drive-In $

500 Queen Anne Avenue N.; 206-285-5155; *ddir.com*

An inexpensive experience and a favorite for many local families, Dick's has served Seattle residents since 1954, and not much has changed: Walk up to the '50s-style window and place your order of burgers, real ice cream shakes, and hand-cut french fries. Open daily, 10:30 a.m.–2 a.m.

McMenamins Queen Anne $$

200 Roy Street; 206-285-4722; *mcmenamins.com*

McMenamins provides solid bar fare: burgers, fries (with malt vinegar on your table), pastas, and salads. In the relative absence of family-friendly options on Queen Anne, the brewpub is a welcomed friend, particularly for families of picky kids, with kids' entrées averaging $3.50. Open Monday, 11 a.m.–midnight; Tuesday–Saturday, 11 a.m.–1 a.m.; Sunday, noon–midnight.

Phuket $

517 Queen Anne Avenue N.; 206-284-3700

Queen Anne has many Thai dining options, but Phuket's seating arrangement and intimate dining spaces make it more fun for families. Ask to sit in the bench seats, next to the Thai puppets on the walls. Or sit on the barstools facing the cooks and watch all the stir-fry action. Most kids love pad Thai and the big jar of lollipops at the end of the cooking station. Hours vary: generally open Monday–Thursday 11:30 a.m.–9:30 p.m.; Friday, 11:30 a.m.–10:30 p.m.; Saturday, 12:30–10:30 p.m.; Sunday, 12:30–9:30 p.m.

Uptown Metropolitan Market $

100 Mercer Street; 206-213-0778; *metropolitan-market.com*

If you're staying in a kitchen-equipped hotel on Queen Anne, Metropolitan Market offers all the general and gourmet groceries you're looking for, plus a nice deli selection. Open daily, 5 a.m.–midnight.

GREENWOOD/PHINNEY

Greenwood/Phinney may sometimes be overlooked by out-of-town visitors. After all, it has to compete with its flashier downtown neighbors. But just a quick bus ride away, this area offers one of the Northwest's best animal experiences at the Woodland Park Zoo, plus fabulous coffee shops, restaurants, and little stores (don't miss Greenwood Space Travel Supply Co.). Bring a stroller — the entire expanse is more than thirty (short) blocks long — or plan to hit the zoo, then drive up to the corner of Greenwood Avenue and Eighty-fifth Street, where you'll find toy stores, restaurants, and more.

SLEEP

Sea to Sky Rentals $$$–$$$$

206-632-4210; *seatoskyrentals.com*

This rental agency offers two coveted, bungalow-style homes for rent in the Phinney neighborhood, both of them on bus lines that efficiently deliver you to downtown attractions. Contact agency for specific addresses, but both are located just a block or two off Greenwood's main drag — convenient to video rental shops, restaurants, and just a short hike to the Woodland Park Zoo.

DO

Woodland Park Zoo

750 N. Fiftieth Street; 206-548-2500; *zoo.org*

The Northwest's top zoo, this wild place displays more than 1,100 animals in lush landscapes of more than 57,000 plants, trees, and shrubs, set on ninety-two acres. On cool days, park by the zoo's west entrance and visit the kid-designed Zoomazium; climb a giant fig strangler tree, spelunk in a rock cave, and zip down a slide. Out in the zoo's wilds, head for a favorite continent (Africa, Asia, North America, South America, or Australia) and visit lions, tigers, bears, or really cute little monkeys, oh my. Spend a happy half-hour (and $2 extra) riding the zoo's vintage carousel, or pay a buck to feed parrots at Willawong Station. The zoo's south entrance (at Fiftieth and Fremont) offers a large pay parking lot; the west entrance (at Phinney and Fifty-fifth) is closer to the indoor Zoomazium, limited free on-street parking nearby. October through April: adults/$11; children (3–12)/$8; 2 and younger/free. May through September: adults/$16.50; children/$11; 2 and younger/free. Open October through April: 9:30 a.m.–4 p.m. daily; May 1–September 30: 9:30 a.m.–6 p.m. daily.

PLAY

Green Lake

7351 E. Green Lake Drive N.

This popular lake is a serious hike from the Phinney/Greenwood neighborhood, but doable, if you'd like to see where locals flock on sunny days. Visit Green Lake's nearly three-mile loop around a sparkling lake, by foot, bike, or inline skates. You may be rewarded with eagle and turtle sightings; you'll enjoy fantastic views of the surrounding neighborhoods; and last but no where near least, there's a feature-filled playground (located at Latona and Green Lake, near the very full parking-lot entrance), perfect for toddlers and preschoolers. On summer days, kids play in the lifeguard-monitored lake and buy ice cream cones from kiosks. Rent a paddleboat from Green Lake Boat Rental (7351 E. Green Lake Drive N., 206-527-0171) for around $7/per person. Parking can be very difficult, but look for spaces on the southwest side of the lake.

Woodland Park

Aurora Avenue N. and N. Fifty-ninth Street; 206-684-4075;
cityofseattle.net/parks/parkspaces/woodland.htm

Run up and around a snail shell, hide under stone arches, and swing high on old-fashioned swings (the kind with long chains). The snail shell seems to herd the children into happily cooperative groups in some bizarre way — see for yourself! Woodland Park is located right outside the Woodland Park Zoo; on sunny days, get pizza from Zeeks and eat at the picnic tables or on the grassy fields. Big caveat: no bathroom here.

SEATTLE GREENWOOD/PHINNEY

EAT

Fresh Flours $-$$

6015 Phinney Avenue N.; 206-297-3300; *freshfloursseattle.com*

One of Seattle's most interesting cafés is just down the street from the Woodland Park Zoo. Pick up a midzoo snack here. Fresh Flours serves the typical coffee found throughout the Northwest, along with fresh-baked Japanese pastries, incorporating exotic yet accessible tastes like kabocha (Japanese pumpkin), sweet red bean, and green tea. Even the pickiest kids won't be able to turn down a kabocha, pecan and white chocolate muffin, or an azuki cream brioche. Open weekdays, 6 a.m.–5 p.m.; weekends, 7 a.m.–5 p.m.

Gordito's $-$$

213 N. Eighty-fifth Street; 206-706-9352; *gorditoshealthymexicanfood.com*

No one goes here expecting a quiet, romantic meal — which makes it perfect for families. Brick-size burritos are filled with sturdy ingredients: beans, meat, cheese, rice, lettuce, tomatoes, and toppings. They're huge enough to share, but kids twelve and younger can also order a plate of beans and rice or a mini-quesadilla for around $2. Eat your affordable food inside or on the back patio in a boisterous atmosphere. Open Sunday–Thursday, 10:30 a.m.–9 p.m.; Friday and Saturday, 10:30 a.m.–9:30 p.m.

Mae's Phinney Ridge Cafe $$

6412 Phinney Avenue N.; 206-782-1222; *maescafe.com*

Mae's famous breakfast nook provides plenty to feast your eyes on while you wait. Ask to be seated in the back room, where you can eat your green eggs and ham, heaps of chocolate-kiss-kissed pancakes, or Mae's cinnamon rolls while you look at a room full of cow paraphernalia on the move. The extremely lucky (or early) get to sit inside the bat-cave-style booth or the booth set inside a giant, open mouth. Must be seen to be believed. Open Monday–Friday, 8 a.m.–2 p.m.; Saturday and Sunday, 8 a.m.–3 p.m.

Red Mill Burgers $

312 N. Sixty-seventh Street; 206-783-6362; *redmillburgers.com*

More than just a burger joint, this place is a cult! Seattle's Red Mill acolytes love the hefty meat (or veggie) patties, smorgasbord of dressings, and delicious shakes and malts. Red Mill is consistently voted one of Seattle's best burger joints. The '50s-style interior is always hopping with friends, couples, and families; bring your patience for the long order line and wait for tables, and you'll be richly rewarded. Note: Cash only, so stop at the ATM before coming in. Open Tuesday–Saturday, 11 a.m.–9 p.m.; Sunday, noon–8 p.m.

Zeeks Pizza $

6000 Phinney Avenue N.; 206-285-8646; *zeekspizza.com*

Easier (and cheaper) than zoo food, Zeeks Pizza is just a few blocks up from the zoo and provides hearty pizza for around $2. They also serve beer for grownups and dough for kids to play with while you wait. In summer, ask to sit outside on the small patio and listen quietly; from your perch, you may be able to hear trumpeting elephants and screeching monkeys. Open daily, 11a.m.–10 p.m.

SEATTLE GREENWOOD/PHINNEY

SHOP

Beach Comber Kids Cuts

6417 Phinney Avenue N.; 206-783-1554; *beachcomberkidscuts.com*

If you're in town for a few days, make an appointment here, where kids get to sit on a wood-carved sea animal, watch a movie, and get sparkles in their hair. A large waiting area in back provides a ball pit, a tricycle, and tons of toys. Not just a haircut — it's an experience! One of the most comprehensive kids' haircut spots I've ever seen. Open Tuesday 11 a.m.–7 p.m.; Wednesday–Friday, 10 a.m.–7 p.m.; Saturday, 10 a.m.–5 p.m.; Sunday, 11 a.m.–5 p.m.

Berserk Games

7217 Greenwood Avenue N.; 206-523-9605; *berserkgames.com*

A sweet selection of role-playing, card, and board games for the older child in your house, at competitive prices. Open daily, 11 a.m.–7 p.m.

Dolly's Dollhouse

5821 Phinney Avenue N.; 206-783-1033

Just up the street from the zoo, Dolly's is a long-lasting legacy of miniature wonders. Even if the kids don't yet possess a dollhouse, they may still plead to bring home a strange and tiny toaster. Open Monday–Saturday, 11 a.m.–5 p.m.

Greenwood Space Travel Supply Co.

8414 Greenwood Avenue N.; 206-725-2625; *greenwoodspacetravelsupply.com*

You must take your space monsters and mini-scientists to this store full of quirky, tongue-in-cheek toys. Pick up portable oxygen pockets, black hole starter kits, and near-death rays (a more peaceful alternative). The store is one of Dave Eggers' national writing centers, which support the literary arts through sales of unusual themed merchandise (the NYC store has a superhero theme, and San Francisco's location has a pirate theme). Proceeds from sales of space food, planets, and other novelties go to fund 826 Seattle, a nonprofit group providing after-school tutoring, writing classes, and school field trips. Open Monday–Friday, noon–6 p.m.; Saturday, 10 a.m.–6 p.m.

Mimi Rose

6001 Phinney Avenue N.; 206-361-1834

Follow the dancing babies above the door, and discover flowery, funky clothing for babies and toddlers inside. All clothing is designed and sewn in Seattle before being hung on the racks in this extremely tiny shop, which also offers hand-selected stuffed animals and books. Open Tuesday–Sunday, 10 a.m.–6 p.m.

Rising Stars

7321 Greenwood Avenue N.; 206-781-0138; *rising-stars.biz*

This cheery shop is a hodgepodge of shopping options, including consignment and new, clothing and toys, organic and conventional. A nice selection of sale items is usually on hand, as are wooden and natural-themed toys. Open Monday–Saturday, 10 a.m.–6 p.m.; Sunday, 10 a.m.–5 p.m.

Santoro's Books
7405 Greenwood Avenue N.; 206-784-2113; *santorosbooks.com*
Cozy up on the bitty couch in Santoro's shop, or ponder in the rocking chair. Not a wide selection of children's books, but what's here is golden. Open Monday–Wednesday, 10 a.m.–7 p.m.; Thursday and Friday, 10 a.m.–8 p.m.; Saturday, 10 a.m.–6 p.m.; Sunday, noon–5 p.m.

Top Ten Toys
104 N. Eighty-fifth Street; 206-782-0098; *toptentoys.com*
As a matter of principle, Top Ten Toys doesn't carry toy guns, Barbies, or Leap Pads (or other electronic toys). But even if your kids looove those toys, they'll still find something in this cornucopia of playthings. Hundreds of classic toys, art supplies, stickers, science kits, building sets, puppets, kids' kitchen gear, costumes, and music are all laid out on the store's well-organized shelves. Open Monday–Friday, 9 a.m.–9 p.m.; Saturday and Sunday, 9 a.m.–7 p.m.

BALLARD
Ballard was once a sleepy enclave of fishermen, Scandinavian immigrants, and bar hoppers. Today, it's a bustling neighborhood of families, shops, and . . . bar hoppers. Some things just don't change.

However, families enjoy Ballard for the same reason your family might: The area's walkable core offers the free public Ballard locks, movie theaters, cupcakes, a skate bowl, small water park, and a variety of ethnic eateries, from Thai to Greek. Keep your eyes peeled for the neon signs of "old Ballard," try some lutefisk, or wander up to the Nordic Heritage Museum to find out more about Ballard's history. Unfortunately, there are no hotels in Ballard at this time.

DO

Ballard Library
5614 Twenty-second Avenue N.W.; 206-684-4089; *spl.org*, click on "locations"
While not every Seattle library is worth a stop, this one is unique, because of a grassy roof, light-drenched reading areas, and an open bank of kids' computers, preloaded with games.

Ballard Sunday Farmers' Market
Ballard Avenue between Twentieth Avenue N.W. and Twenty-second Avenue N.W.; 206-851-5100; *fremontmarket.com/ballard*
Get the full Ballard experience by visiting on a Sunday, when you can also check out the neighborhood's farmers' market. You'll probably see some distinctly Northwest foods at this market, including fiddlehead ferns, nettles, and wild mushrooms. Kids love the free samples and fiddling buskers; be sure to bring a few quarters to throw into the hard-working musicians' cases. And save a few dollars for a freshly baked pie, cookie, or pastry. Open 10 a.m.–3 p.m., year-round.

Golden Gardens

8498 Seaview Place N.W.; 206-684-4075;
seattle.gov/parks/park_detail.asp?ID=243
Located at the end of the Burke-Gilman Trail, this sandy beach is often packed with sunscreened-toe-to-sunhat crowds in summer; less so during other times of the year. A playground, covered picnic facility, wetlands area, and kite-flying field are all available, along with a small, lazy stream that kids love to play in. On hot days, it's one of Seattle's best places to cool off, due to strong winds coming in off the water. Bring sand toys, a picnic, and plenty of time. Open 6 a.m.–11:30 p.m.

Hiram M. Chittenden Locks

3015 N.W. Fifty-fourth Street; 206-783-7059;
www.nws.usace.army.mil: click on "locks and dams"
Kids love Seattle's low-key locks, which connect the Puget Sound with the Lake Washington Ship Canal. They enjoy running through the colorful gardens, rolling down the grass-covered steppes, and making their way through a maze of locks, as boats wait for waters to rise and fall. Continue on a gangplank across roaring waterfalls (and look for gulls, leaping salmon, and other creatures to the west). Then descend into the viewing area, where you'll see salmon struggling to move upstream. On summer Sundays, families play Frisbee and enjoy afternoon concerts. Fish ladder is open 7 a.m.–8:45 p.m. year-round. Visitor center: summer hours (May 1–September 30) daily, 10 a.m.–6 p.m. Winter hours (October 1–April 30) 10 a.m.–4 p.m.; closed Tuesday and Wednesday.

Majestic Bay Theatres

2044 N.W. Market Street; 206-781-2229; *majesticbay.com*
First-run flicks in a three-screen neighborhood theater, and most current kid hits will be playing on at least one screen. But don't fill up on the real-butter-drizzled popcorn — this theater is right next door to Cupcake Royale, which sells the perfect post-movie treat. Open daily, noon–midnight.

Nordic Heritage Museum

3014 N.W. Sixty-seventh Street; 206-789-5707; *nordicmuseum.org*
Roughly a thirty-block walk from Old Ballard, this museum is a must if you're interested in the area's Nordic roots. Re-created slums and storefronts depict the Scandinavian immigrant's long journey to Ballard. Upstairs, view real reindeer clothing, a replica of a logging camp, Viking ships made from Legos, and even a troll or two. Outside, there's a playground that features a cool tubular climbing structure, swings, and more. Open Tuesday–Thursday, 10 a.m.–4 p.m.; Friday and Saturday, 10a.m.–4 p.m.; Sunday, noon–4 p.m.

PLAY

Ballard Commons Park

5701 Twenty-second Avenue N.W.; 206-684-4075; *seattle.gov/parks*
On a hot summer day, stop by to let the kids run through shell-shaped fountains, stomp across a green lawn, or watch teens roll around Ballard's own skatebowl.

Caveat: not much shade and lots of glare from new concrete. Bring sunglasses, or buy some at a neighborhood store. Open year-round, water feature open from late May until early September, 11 a.m.–8 p.m.

EAT

Café Besalu $
5909 Twenty-fourth Avenue N.W.; 206-789-1463
No need to go to France for killer pastries; my French friend says these are as good as the ones she gets in Paris. Grab your flaky, chocolate-filled croissants and sit outside under a shady tree, or walk a few blocks over to the park at the Ballard Community Center, located at the corner of Sixtieth and Twenty-eighth. Open Wednesday–Sunday, 7 a.m.–3 p.m.

Cupcake Royale $
2052 N.W. Market Street; 206-782-9557; *cupcakeroyale.com*
Cupcake Royale's pint-size babycakes might seem like a good idea at first, but then the kids will ask you to share your grownup-sized peppermint-frosted chocolate cupcake. Resign yourself to sharing plenty of bites. Lines are out the door year-round, but it's worth every minute of the wait. Look for the winter treats, which are cupcakey twists on old classics: figgy pudding, eggnog, and candy cane. While Cupcake Royale locations dot Seattle like sprinkles, the Market Street shop features an enormous, glittering cupcake (look above the door) and lots of seating. Monday–Thursday, 6:30 a.m.–10 p.m.; Friday and Saturday, 6:30 a.m.–11 p.m.; Sunday, 7:30 a.m.–10 p.m.

Firehouse Coffee $
2622 N.W. Market Street; 206-784-2911
Get your coffee, get the kids' hot chocolate, then head to the right of the front entry. There's a small playroom stocked with toys and tables, perfect for a late-morning snack; the door shuts, so the kids can't get away. Bwa-ha-ha. Open Monday–Friday, 6 a.m.–7p.m.; Saturday–Sunday, 7 a.m.–7 p.m.

Hi-Life $$-$$$
5425 Russell Avenue N.W.; 206-784-7272; *chowfoods.com/hilife*
This retired firehouse, built in 1911, now houses a favorite Ballard restaurant. Families flood into the dark-paneled room at 8:30 (opening time) every morning for the Mickey Mouse Cake, Kids' Grand Slam, or to share the adult-and-a-half-sized hazelnut and mascarpone French toast. There are plenty of lunch and dinner items available later in the day, but I recommend breakfast. The cuisine theme changes every three months. "Blunch," 8:30 a.m.–3 p.m. daily; dinner, Sunday–Thursday, 5–10 p.m.; Friday and Saturday, 5–11 p.m.

Old Town Ale House $$
5233 Ballard Avenue N.W.; 206-782-8323; *oldtownalehouse.com*
Kids are welcome at this quintessential brewpub, deep in the heart of Old Ballard. Children can choose from items on the kids' menu ($5 for fish 'n' chips, chicken fingers or tortellini, plus carrots and choice of beverage). You'll enjoy Old Town's craft-brewed ales alongside a wedge (sandwich), salad, or

pasta dish, inside the pub's dark wood interior. Open Sunday and Monday, 11:30 a.m.–10 p.m.; Tuesday–Thursday, 11:30 a.m.–11 p.m.; Friday and Saturday, 11:30 a.m.–midnight.

Pho Than Brothers $

2021 N.W. Market Street, #A; 206-782-5715; *thanbrothers.com*
Kids love Than Brothers mostly for the vanilla-filled cream puffs, which inexplicably arrive before the meal. Food is served within minutes of ordering, and the fish tank will entertain fidgety kids. Service is often terse, but the low prices (a family can easily eat for less than $20, because soup portions are large enough for kids to share) compensate. Open daily, 11 a.m.–9 p.m.

Scooter's Burgers $

5802 Twenty-fourth Avenue N.W.; 206-782-2966
While many rave about Red Mill Burgers, Scooter's is a neighborhood favorite. Extremely limited seating inside, so take your burgers to the Ballard Commons for a pickle-packed picnic. Try the juicy meat burgers and Gardenburgers, no-salt fries (add your own), and thick shakes in dozens of flavors. Open Monday–Saturday, 11 a.m.–9 p.m.; Sunday, noon–9 p.m.

Snoose Junction Pizzeria $–$$

2305 N.W. Market Street; 206-789-2305; *snoosejunctionpizzeria.com*
For train-crazy toddlers, there's nothing better than Snoose's miniature train table. But you can also check out the books or small selection of toys while you wait for your pizza. Most of Snoose's interior is from reclaimed, demolished buildings; older kids may enjoy hearing about the surprising origins of the walls, seats, and décor. Caveat: Pizzas here are high quality, but a bit on the small side. Order appetizers or a salad to satisfy larger appetites. Open Sunday–Thursday, 11 a.m.–11 p.m.; Friday and Saturday, 11 a.m.– 3 a.m.

SHOP

20Twenty

5208 Ballard Avenue N.W.; 206-706.0969; *myspace.com/twenty_twenty*
This store's staff members are superstars, but the new and used threads rock, too. Come here with your indie-tee-loving teen for a locally made screen-printed shirt, or just find some way-back clothes from your youth for your own child. Polyester blend mix with butterfly collars? Check. Supersweet '80s stripes? Definitely. Open Monday–Saturday, 11 a.m.–7 p.m.; Sunday, 11 a.m.–5 p.m.

Clover

5335 Ballard Ave. N.W.; 206-782-0715; *clovertoys.com*
This store celebrates the traditional toy, and it's hard not to stroke all the wooden, felt, and metal playthings, much less tell the kids to keep their hands off. Little rooms of art supplies, puzzles, stuffed animals, dress-up clothes, and room décor are hand-selected by the store's proprietor. The kids' clothes ride that fine line between hip and affordable, including Zutano, Tea, and imported labels. Open Monday–Saturday, 10 a.m.–6 p.m.; Sunday, 10 a.m.–5 p.m.

Cookies

2211 N.W. Market Street; 206-297-1015; *cookiesinseattle.com*

A store devoted to a kid's favorite activity — making cookies! A wall of cookie cutters offers holiday, animal, and symbol shapes; the sprinkle aisle is a confetti-like festival of sugary goodness. The jam-packed store is so small that you can't really fit a large stroller in here, so park it outside and hold younger children's hands tight; there's plenty to accidentally knock over here. Open Tuesday–Saturday, 10 a.m.–6 p.m.; Sunday, 11 a.m.–5 p.m.

Me 'n Moms

2821 N.W. Market Street, #B; 206-781-9449; *menmoms.com*

Need it? Me 'n Moms has it, and at the right price. It's the largest consignment shop I've ever seen, jam-packed with used and new items. You'll find consigned clothes, receiving blankets, Halloween costumes, and baby furniture. They also carry brand-new baby carriers, Melissa and Doug Toys, shoes, train sets, creams and lotions for baby, and more. A great place to go if you've forgotten something at home; a great place to go just because you want to stock next year's wardrobe at this year's prices. Open Monday–Friday, 9:30 a.m.–6 p.m.; Saturday and Sunday, 10:30 a.m.–5 p.m.

Secret Garden Bookshop

2214 N.W. Market Street; 206-789-5006; *secretgardenbooks.com*

A tiny rocking chair, a children's table, and shelves and shelves stocked with kids' books make this independent bookstore a must-visit place in Ballard. Don't miss the clinking bricks lining the picture-book section at the store's front. Check store's Web site for author readings and other events. Monday–Friday, 10 a.m.–8 p.m.; Saturday, 10 a.m.–6 p.m.; Sunday, noon–5 p.m.

Sonic Boom Records

2209 N.W. Market Street; 206-297-2666; *sonicboomrecords.com*

Ballard's music shop sells new and used CDs and vinyl records, music magazines, and supercute Sonic Boom tees. Kids like the headphones in back, where they can listen to new indie bands. Local and national acts sometimes stop by the store to put on a show; check the Web site for details on who's playing next. Open Monday–Saturday 10 a.m.–10 p.m.; Sunday, 10 a.m.–7 p.m.

Venue

5408 Twenty-second Avenue N.W.; 206-789-3335; *venueballard.com*

You'll find jewelry, T-shirts, purses, paintings, and other arts and crafts made by locals — sometimes created while you watch. Stop in to view an artist at work (if you're lucky) in one of the small ateliers, or just browse for the perfect gift for a preteen or teen you know. My kids love to take their chances on the automatic art dispensers, located just inside the door: Pay a dollar, get some art. Tuesday–Friday, 11 a.m.–6 p.m.; Saturday, 10 a.m.–5 p.m.; Sunday, 10 a.m.–4 p.m.

FREMONT

Fremont's odd art defines one of Seattle's favorite areas. Where else can you see dinosaurs, trolls, and Vladimir Lenin all in one neighborhood? The self-described "Center of the Universe," Fremont has long been recognized for its arty culture and funky feel. If you can, try to visit during the Fremont Solstice Parade in June; it's the neighborhood's annual celebration of the bohemian lifestyle, featuring food stalls, kids' areas, car art (cars made into art), live music, costumed locals, and naked bike riders.

DO

Fremont art stroll

On a sunny Seattle day, nothing's better than a (free) walking tour of Fremont's sculptures. Pick up an self-guided art walk map at a local business and meet giant dinos, a Lenin statue (often decorated by locals), and a group of life-size stone statues, decorated with scarves, hats, and bags. But you must pay homage to the most famous resident, the Fremont Troll — an enormous beast with glittering eyes, holding a VW bug in one hand and waiting under the Fremont Bridge. The kids will never forget him.

Fremont Outdoor Cinema

Parking lot at N. Thirty-fifth Street and Phinney Avenue; *fremontoutdoormovies.com*

Geeky good times for movie nerds (and everyone else) at Fremont's Outdoor Cinema, where cinephiles huddle under blankets and watch '50s-era B movies, crack jokes, play games, watch improv, and more. Check the Web site to make sure the movie is family friendly, and be aware that the movies start quite late (dusk in Seattle means 8 or 9 p.m., or perhaps even later). The lot opens at 7:30 p.m.; summers only. Suggested donation: $5.

Sunday Market

N. Thirty-fourth Street between Evanston Avenue N. and Phinney Avenue N.; 206-781-6776; *fremontmarket.com/fremont*

The eccentric bachelorette cousin to Ballard's farmers' market, Fremont focuses more on the flea-market feel of used clothing and furniture, plus new art and household décor created by local artisans. Best for tweens and teens who want to find something that nobody else has. Winter hours: Sunday, 10 a.m.–4 p.m. Summer hours: Sunday, 10 a.m.–5 p.m.

PLAY

Gas Works Park

2101 N. Northlake Way; 206-684-4075; *http://seattle.gov/parks*

Gas Works forgoes the usual playground and instead offers a kite-flying hill, views of downtown Seattle, and an exhauster-compressor building converted into a colorful children's play barn. Open 4 a.m.–11:30 p.m. daily.

EAT

SEATTLE
FREMONT

Blue C Sushi $

3411 Fremont Avenue N.; 206-633-3411; *bluecsushi.com*
An urban, fast-paced solution to hunger: Small dishes of sushi whisk around on a conveyor belt, ready to be plucked off and enjoyed. Blue C is a favorite for children, with a one-story-tall screen playing Japanese children's cartoons, vivid Tokyo subway décor, and a frenetic vibe. When you're done, hit the blue button and a server comes to total your plates ($1.50–$5 per plate of sushi). Check Web site for other Seattle locations. Open Monday–Thursday, 11:30 a.m.–9 p.m.; Friday, 11:30 a.m.–10 p.m.; Saturday, noon–10 p.m.; Sunday, noon–9 p.m.

Dad Watson $–$$

3601 Fremont Avenue N.; 206-632-6505; *mcmenamins.com*
This McMenamins restaurant in Fremont provides beer, pub grub, and a kids' menu. Slide into a dark booth and sip a cold one (lemonade or raspberry-flavored beer). Monday–Thursday, 11:30 a.m.–1 a.m.; Friday and Saturday, 11:30 a.m.–2 a.m.; Sunday, 11:30 a.m.–midnight. Kids allowed until 10 p.m.

Kaosamai $

404 N. Thirty-sixth Street; 206-925-9979; *kaosamai.com*
Somehow, Thailand got sucked into the Center of the Universe, and around five Thai options sit in Fremont's core. They're all just fine; most kids love peanut buttery dips and pad Thai. But Kaosamai's outside eating patio and superfast service make it a standout. Open Monday–Thursday, 11 a.m.–9:30 p.m.; Friday, 11 a.m.–10:30 p.m.; Saturday, noon–10:30 p.m.; Sunday, noon–9:30 p.m.

PCC Natural Markets $

600 N. Thirty-fourth Street; 206-632-6811; *pccnaturalmarkets.com*
Seattle's cooperative natural food store doesn't smell like goji berries and hemp, thank goodness. Head in here for slices of pizza, a premade sandwich, hard-boiled eggs, wraps, and a large variety of deli foods. PCC also encourages kids to pick out a free piece of fruit with every purchase — just tell the cashier when checking out. You can eat your deli items outside on a covered patio, or across the street in the park. Open daily 6 a.m.–midnight.

SHOP

Fremont Place Bookstore

621 N. Thirty-fifth Street; 206-547-5970; *fremontplacebooks.com*
Pull up the rocking chair in the kids' area and browse Fremont Place Bookstore's excellent selection of board books. This compact store's size means it's easy to look for your own book right next to the kids' section. Open Monday–Saturday, 10 a.m.–8 p.m.; Sunday, noon–6 p.m.

Ophelia's Books

3504 Fremont Avenue N.; 206-632-3759; *opheliasbooks.com*
Two resident cats will greet your kids at the door (and may want to play, depending on the day). After saying hello, head up to Ophelia's charming, attic-like nook, which welcomes elementary-school-age kids and preteens. Open Monday–Saturday, 11 a.m.–6 p.m.; Sunday, 11 a.m.–5 p.m.

Portage Bay Goods

706 N. Thirty-fourth Street; 206-547-5221; *portagebaygoods.com*
This store has something for every age, including snarky tees for babies, Uglydolls for preschoolers, and savvy jacket pins for teens. It's a clever place to pick up a completely unique birthday gift and a card. It's also located right next to the headquarters for the popular eco-card game Xeko (*xeko.com*), and Portage Bay carries the complete line of Xeko decks. Open 10 a.m.–7 p.m. daily.

Theo Chocolate

3400 Phinney Avenue; 206-632-5100; *theochocolate.com*
Walk into Theo for a unique Seattle souvenir — organic chocolate truffles and bars, made on site from raw cacao. Older kids may enjoy Theo's tours, which demonstrate how chocolate is crafted, from bean to bar. Call for scheduled tours and to reserve a spot. Open daily, 10 a.m.–6 p.m.

WEST SEATTLE

West Seattle's multicultural population, sweeping views of the water, and bustling shopping and dining opportunities fill the neighborhood with sights and sounds. Connected like the thumb of a glove to Seattle, West Seattle maintains its own identity and well-established, self-sustaining neighborhoods. A day trip — from downtown via the Elliott Bay Water Taxi — is a classic, low-key Seattle experience.

SLEEP

Sea to Sky Rentals $$–$$$

206-632-4210; *seatoskyrentals.com*
This rental agency offers two rental options in West Seattle: a small condo (good for a family of three — two adults and one baby) and a larger house (OK for kids six and older), both very affordably priced. Ask the agency for specific addresses and locations, but either is a nice option if you hope to stay out of the downtown core and in a neighborhood.

DO

Elliott Bay Water Taxi

Downtown: Pier 55, 1101 Alaskan Way
West Seattle: Seattle and Seacrest Park, 1660 Harbor Avenue S.W.;
206-205-3866; *kingcounty.gov/transportation/kcdot/Marine/WaterTaxi.aspx*
Half the charm of going to West Seattle is the journey there; in summer, hop aboard the passenger-only Elliott Bay Water Taxi and ride from downtown Seattle to West Seattle on a twelve-minute, $3 trip. Take the taxi's bus shuttle to the West Seattle Junction for shopping and eating, or to Alki Point to stroll along Alki Beach Park's boardwalk (page 72).

Farmers' Market

California Avenue and S.W. Alaska Street; 206-935-0904; *wsjunction.org*
Pick up nuts, veggies, fruits, and flowers from small, local family farms; listen to live old-time music; enjoy activities for kids; and sample just-picked produce. Smaller than Pike Place or Ballard, so West Seattle's market packs vendors

densely into a crowded core, and encourages an elbow-to-elbow, neighborhood vibe. Open Sundays year-round, 10 a.m.–2 p.m.

West Seattle Bowl
4505 Thirty-ninth Avenue S.W.; 206-932-3731; *wsbowl.com*
Check Web site for excellent coupons. Saturday night features glow bowling under black lights — a great option for tweens and teens. One of Seattle's last bastions of retro fun, this bowling alley will spin your pins. $19 per lane per hour (day), $26 per lane per hour (evening after 6 p.m.), shoe rental extra. Open Monday, 11 a.m.–1 a.m.; Tuesday, noon–1 a.m.; Wednesday–Saturday, 11 a.m.–1 a.m.; Sunday, 10 a.m.–midnight.

PLAY
Alki Beach Park
1702 Alki Avenue S.W.; 206-684-4075; *seattle.gov/parks*
On warm, sunny days, make your way out to the windy Alki Beach Park, a two-and-a-half-mile paved strip bordering a sandy beach and Elliott Bay. Picnic spots are located at the south end (Alki Point), where white settlers first arrived in 1851. There are plenty of beach-style coffee and ice cream stops along the way, or bring picnic goodies with you. Pick up breakfast or lunch in either the full-service Alki Cafe (2726 Alki Avenue S.W.) or deli-style Alki Bakery & Cafe (2738 Alki Avenue S.W., #1); both popular spots offer children's menus, crayons, and lovely views. Or pick up your order of halibut at **Spud Fish & Chips** (2666 Alki Avenue S.W.). Hours: April 15–Oct. 1, daily 6 a.m.–11 p.m.; Oct. 2–April 14, daily 4 a.m.–11:30 p.m.

EAT
Coffee to a Tea $
4541 California Avenue S.W.; 206-937-1495; *sugarrushbakingcompany.com*
While tweens and teens might prefer the cool atmosphere at Cupcake Royale, most tots would rather head for Coffee to a Tea, the only coffee shop I've ever seen that offers wooden riding toys. Of course, there's the ubiquitous train set and kitchen, but the rocking horse and airplanes really take the cupcake (they serve those, too). Young elementary-school-age kids love the board-game library. Adults enjoy the coffee, pastries, and ample window light. Open Monday–Thursday, 8 a.m.–8 p.m.; Friday, 8 a.m.–10 p.m.; Saturday, 8 a.m.–8 p.m.; Sunday, 9 a.m.–6 p.m.

Easy Street Records $–$$
4559 California Avenue S.W.; 206-938-3279; *easystreetonline.com/cafe*
Glowing neon signs direct you inside this supercool West Seattle eatery and record shop. Western-style breakfasts are Easy Street's specialty, and they don't disappoint. Dig into the Los Lobos (chorizo sautéed with black bean salsa, eggs, and cheese) or the Dolly Parton Stack (two pancakes, two eggs, two strips of bacon). And expect to share with the kids, because the portion sizes hit you like a two-ton truck. Lunch offerings include sandwiches and quesadillas. Café open daily, 7 a.m.–3 p.m.; record shop open Monday–Saturday, 9 a.m.–9 p.m.; Sunday, 9 a.m.–7 p.m.

Elliott Bay Brewery & Pub $-$$

4720 California Avenue S.W.; 206-932-8695; *elliottbaybrewing.com*
Kids get plastic cups with lids, children's menus, and a coloring sheet filled with activities; you get a cup filled with beer. It's a deal! Try some Whidbey Island mussels, a grilled salmon sandwich, or pesto Brie. The parsley-flecked fries may even convince your kids to eat green food (if only once). Open Monday–Saturday, 11 a.m.–midnight; Sunday, 11 a.m.–11 p.m.

Husky Deli $

4721 California Avenue S.W.; 206-937-2810; *huskydeli.com*
Widely known for its thick and creamy homemade ice cream, Husky Deli is a West Seattle favorite. Pick up a cone of luscious strawberry and go for a walk, or sit on the barstools and watch the people along California Avenue. Monday–Saturday, 9 a.m.–9 p.m.; Sunday, 9 a.m.–7 p.m.

SHOP

Curious Kidstuff

4740 California Avenue S.W.; 206-937-8788; *curiouskidstuff.com*
At first, this shop might look small, but once inside you keep going . . . and going . . . and going. A loop takes you through Curious Kidstuff's great stuff for kids — everything from Calico Critters to kites. Building toys, chemistry sets, puzzles, dolls, and trains are available here, and many toys are out of the box for sample play. And Curious Kidstuff certainly wins the award for one of the best bathrooms I've seen, with a tiny toilet and light-up faucet. Open Monday–Friday, 9:30 a.m.–7 p.m.; Saturday, 10 a.m.–6 p.m.; Sunday, 11 a.m.–5 p.m.

Electric Train Shop

4511 California Avenue S.W.; 206-938-2400; *electrictrainshop.com*
Stop by this small shop to watch a miniature train shoot down the tracks, or pick up a train cap or die-cast train to play with at home. Open Tuesday–Saturday, 11 a.m.–6 p.m.; closed Sunday and Monday.

AROUND SEATTLE

DO

Burke Museum

On University of Washington campus at Seventeenth Avenue N.E. and N.E. Forty-fifth Street; 206-543-5590; *washington.edu/burkemuseum*
The Burke Museum may be the closest we'll ever get to a dino's living room. Towering skeletons (real and replica) fill the Burke's upstairs level, and kids love playing in the small children's area filled with toys and puzzles. Downstairs, older kids may be interested in the "Pacific Voices" permanent display; be sure to open the drawers throughout the exhibit to find surprise hands-on activities. The museum doesn't take long to go through, but it's an attraction that kids love. Parking is expensive here on school days; go on a

weekend, or in the evening or summer. Adults/$9.50; seniors/$7.50; students and youth/$6; younger than 4/free. Open daily, 10 a.m.–5 p.m.

Museum of Flight

9404 E. Marginal Way S.; 206-764-5720; *museumofflight.org*

This six-story building is one of the largest flight museums in the world and offers lots for families, including a children's area where kids can run around (and fuss as much as they want), miniature riding planes, and an air traffic control tower replica, so kids can pretend to direct traffic. You won't be able to miss the fighter planes hanging from the ceiling in the Great Hall, but also wander down below, so you can see the odd little plane-car, born of some flight of fancy. The museum's historic wing gives details on Boeing's beginnings, which may interest older children. A well-stocked gift shop offers model kits, lots of flight-related toys, and an excellent selection of books for kids who are fascinated by all things aero. Adults/$14, youth (5–17)/$7.50, children (4 and younger)/free. Open daily 10 a.m.–5 p.m.; until 9 p.m. the first Thursday of the month.

Recycled Cycles

1007 N.E. Boat Street; 206-547-4491; *recycledcycles.com*

Rent road bikes, trail-a-bikes, and Burleys at this full-service cycle shop, then cruise down the paved and even Burke-Gilman Trail (*ci.seattle.wa.us /Parks/BurkeGilman/bgtrail.htm*) to either Fremont (head west) or North Seattle (head east). I would suggest Fremont, where you can incorporate a snack, lunch, or dessert break into your day. Open Monday–Friday, 10 a.m.–7 p.m.; Saturday and Sunday, 10 a.m.–6 p.m.

Seattle Asian Art Museum

1400 E. Prospect Street; 206-654-3100; *seattleartmuseum.org*

Check the museum's Web site to see if there's an exhibit that piques your interest; this is a small museum with limited offerings. However, many visiting exhibits are accompanied by a small children's area with coloring, crafts, books, and videos. Adults/$7; students with ID, seniors (62 and older), and youth (13–17)/$5; children younger than 12/free. Open Wednesday–Sunday, 10 a.m.–5 p.m.; Thursday, 10 a.m.–9 p.m.; closed Monday and Tuesday.

Volunteer Park Conservatory

1402 E. Galer Street; 206-322-4112; *volunteerparkconservatory.org*

This donation-based hot spot is one way to beat winter's rainy doldrums. Wander through window-shrouded rooms full of towering cacti, fragrant blooms, and caged orchids. Check out the air plants, which get their nutrients from sky (not soil), and the antler-shaped rainforest plants. The Seattle Asian Art Museum and Volunteer Conservatory aren't far from Vios (page 76); make a day of it. Winter hours: Tuesday–Sunday, 10 a.m.–4 p.m. Summer hours: Tuesday–Sunday, 10 a.m.–6 p.m.

PLAY

Carkeek Park
950 N.W. Carkeek Park Road; 206-684-0877;
cityofseattle.net/parks/environment/Carkeek.htm
Six miles of easy hiking trails crisscross through 216 acres of maples, Douglas fir, and pine. End your hike at the grassy picnic area and funky playground (look for the salmon slide). Cross the bridge (wave to trains passing below your feet) and head to Carkeek's beach. During summer low tides, a beach naturalist is on hand to explain what the tide left behind, such as starfish and seashells, anemones, sea cucumbers, and hermit crabs. Open daily, 6 a.m.–10 p.m.

EAT

Agua Verde $-$$
1303 N.E. Boat Street; 206-545-8570; *aguaverde.com*
If you're lucky enough to come here during a lull, you may be able to sit out on the year-round outdoor patio with views of the water. Even if you have to sit inside, the kids will love the funky folk-pop art décor. Here, you'll find a salsa bar, enormous quesadillas, a casual atmosphere, and some of the best Mexican food in Seattle, made from authentic ingredients like Cotija cheese, guajillo chiles, and jicama. Not your brother's Taco Bell. Walk-up window open Monday–Friday, 7:30 a.m.–2:30 p.m.; restaurant open Monday–Saturday, 11 a.m.–3:30 p.m., 4–9 p.m.; Sunday, noon–6 p.m.

Chinook's at Salmon Bay, Little Chinook's $$-$$$
1900 W. Nickerson Street; 206-283-4665; *anthonys.com*
Located between Ballard and downtown Seattle, Chinook's at Salmon Bay is a midrange restaurant with dependable seafood platters, fresh off the boats. (You'll see the Seattle Fishermen's Terminal right outside the enormous windows — more than 700 commercial fishing vessels come home here in winter.) In summer, the outdoor patio is divine. A popular family spot (kids' menus available), but still a sit-down affair. Little Chinook's is the grab-and-go option, and found right outside Chinook's. Take rowdier toddlers here for fish 'n' chips in a basket. Just watch out for greedy seagulls and don't get too close to the boats (that water is cold!). Open Monday–Thursday, 11 a.m.–10 p.m; Friday, 11 a.m.–11 p.m.; Saturday, 7:30 a.m.–11 p.m.; Sunday, 7:30 a.m.–10 p.m.

Mosaic: A Community Coffee House $
4401 Second Avenue N.E.; no phone; *mosaiccoffeehouse.org*
Mosaic's unique approach to coffee shops makes it my favorite in Seattle. Located in a residential area's church basement, you pay as much as you can afford for your mocha, quiche, or cookie; then head to the Demitasse playroom for toys and fun. I try to always pay a little more than street value for my coffee, because I feel like Mosaic's innovative approach should be encouraged and rewarded. A percentage of all profits goes toward a rotating charity of the month. Accessible by car or by foot, located in the Wallingford neighborhood. Monday–Thursday, 9 a.m.–9 p.m.; Friday, 9 a.m.–5 p.m.; Saturday, 9 a.m.–2 p.m.

SEATTLE AROUND SEATTLE

Molly Moon Ice Cream $

1622½ N. Forty-fifth Street; 206-547-5105; *mollymoonicecream.com*
When you get here, there will be a line out the door, day or night. Wait your ten minutes; Molly Moon's ice cream is worth it, in thick, rich flavors like salted caramel, lavender, and birthday cake. By evening, they may have run out of a few ingredients or flavors, so go earlier if you can. Open daily, noon–11 p.m.

Vios Café $–$$$

903 Nineteenth Avenue E.; 206-329-3236; *vioscafe.com*
Vios is very much out of the way on Seattle's Capitol Hill (with a second location in North Seattle), and requires either a taxi or a car to reach. However, it's probably Seattle's best family-friendly restaurant. Enjoy counter-style Greek fare at lunch (hummus and pita), including kid plates with kebabs. Take your food and sit near the fenced children's play area (we like to grab seats at the counter) or at a table nearby. The kids' area has a small kitchen, Legos, and toys. In the evening, the scene's the same, but with more upscale dining options and table service. The biggest problem at Vios? Taking the children away from the play pit and convincing them to eat their dinner. Families are always treated to wonderful service here — it's a knockout! Open Tuesday–Saturday, 11 a.m.–4:30 p.m. for lunch, 5–9 p.m. for dinner.

SHOP

Archie McPhee

1300 N. Forty-fifth Street; 206-297-0240; *archiemcpheeseattle.com*
Wacky low-brow fun: Archie McPhee presents an avalanche of inexpensive, strange, and culturally perfect items. Kids love this place, and parents do, too. Few other stores offer the opportunity to juggle a toddler-size plastic tarantula, a "Crazy Cat Lady" board game, and 1950s-style, cowboy-decorated metal lunch pails. While many Northwest stores have trafficked in the gag-gift arena for years, Archie did it first and still does it best. Open Monday–Saturday, 9 a.m.–9 p.m.; Sunday, 9 a.m.–7 p.m.

Blue Highway Games

2203 Queen Anne Avenue N.; 206-282-0540; *bluehighwaygames.com*
This game store — one of the largest in the Northwest — boasts more than 500 puzzles, board and card games. Games are categorized by type and audience; check out the travel, geography, and mind-boosting games. In the back corner, families sit and play games from Blue Highway's "game library" of already-opened games. Open Monday–Wednesday, 10 a.m.–7 p.m.; Thursday 10 a.m.–9 p.m.; Friday and Saturday, 10 a.m.–11 p.m.; Sunday, 11 a.m.–5 p.m.

Izilla Toys

1429 Twelfth Avenue; 206-322-8697; *izillatoys.com*
This store features fantastic free events, along with the dedicated attention the owners — parents themselves — bring to selecting toys of all types. Enter in a quandary (perhaps an eight-year-old boy who hates everything) and walk out with the perfect item. Check out the cool "Reading Rocket Ship" in the store's book area. Open Monday–Friday, 10 a.m.–7 p.m., Saturday, 9 a.m.–7

p.m., Sunday, 10 a.m.–6 p.m. If in the Wallingford neighborhood (by Archie McPhee), see the store's second location at Wallingford Center (1815 N. Forty-fifth St., 206-547-5204. Open Monday–Saturday, 10 a.m.–8 p.m.; Sunday, 10 a.m.–6 p.m.).

Wide World Books and Maps
4411 Wallingford Avenue N.; 206-634-3453; *wideworldtravelstore.com/shop/index.php*
This is one of my favorite travel stores in the Pacific Northwest; it's loaded with works for both armchair travelers and gonna-leave-tomorrow types. A small toy basket keeps toddlers happy, and the well-chosen selection of children's travel books provides plenty for older children to browse. Open Monday–Saturday, 10 a.m.–7 p.m.; Sunday, 10 a.m.–6 p.m.

getaway
BAINBRIDGE ISLAND

If you'd like to go on an island getaway, but aren't really ready for a hours-long sojourn to Victoria or the San Juan Islands, try Winslow. On Bainbridge Island, this small city offers the same mix of high-quality food, laid-back, kid-friendly activities, gorgeous views aboard the ferry, and walkable pleasures — but it's only a half-hour ferry ride from Seattle. Better still, all the stores and attractions are packed within about a one-mile radius. Leave the car at home, board the walk-on ferry, and discover small-town Washington for a half-day.

GETTING THERE

Going in summer is rewarding and beautiful, and provides an excuse to go to Mora Iced Creamery (page 80); spring's and summer's early sunsets mean you can eat dinner, then watch the sunset on the ferry ride home ; winter is chilly but still great for indoor activities like the museum, movie theater, and bookstore.

Catch the Washington State Ferry at Seattle's Pier 52. Play "Name that Mountain" if it's a sunny day — the Olympics are to the west (where you're headed, toward Winslow), Mount Rainier is toward the south, and the Cascades are directly east (behind Seattle). Drinks and food are available on board. Passenger-only round-trip cost: adult/$6.70; child (6–19)/$5.40; younger than 6/free. Ferries generally leave once an hour. See the full schedule at the Washington State Ferries' Web site (*wsdot.wa.gov/ferries*).

SLEEP

Eagle Harbor Inn $$–$$$$
291 Madison Avenue S.; 206-842-1446; *theeagleharborinn.com*
If you want to stay within walking distance of downtown Winslow, the ferry docks, and easy transport to Seattle, Eagle Harbor Inn might be your best bet. There are four hotel-style rooms (including one with a queen bed and a fold-out couch) and three town homes.

SEATTLE GETAWAY

About a mile out of the downtown core, two hotels offer affordably priced kitchen-equipped suites: Best Western Bainbridge Island Suites (350 N.E. High School Road; 206-855-9666 or 866-396-9666; *bestwesternwashington.com*) and Island Country Inn (920 Hildebrand Lane; 206-842-6861 or 800-842-8429; *islandcountryinn.com*); both are about a half-mile from the Aquatic Center.

DO
Bainbridge Aquatic Center
8521 Madison Avenue N.; 206-842-2302;
biparks.org/parksandfacilities/ifaquaticscenter.html
Just because Bainbridge Island has a laid-back charm doesn't mean it skimps on state-of-the-art swims. This center offers a 180-foot water slide, a lazy river, tot play area, and diving boards. At times, a large inflatable toy floats in the pool's center — perfect for working off excess winter energy. Adults/$5, ages 3–17/$4, ages 2 and younger/free. Check Web site for open hours.

Bainbridge Cinemas at the Pavilion
403 Madison Avenue N.; 206-855-8173; *bainbridgepavilion.com*
First-run movies on five screens, up the street from the Kids Discovery Museum. Typically, at least one or two kid-, tween- or teen-friendly movies play here. Try one of the ten powdered popcorn toppings. Tickets: adult/$9, child/$7; matinee $7.

Bainbridge Island Historical Museum
215 Ericksen Avenue N.E.; 206-842-2773; *bainbridgehistory.org*
A sleepy museum, housed in a renovated 1908 schoolhouse, with probably about fifteen to thirty minutes (max) of appeal. Old-fashioned toys in pull-out drawers will probably engage kids long enough for you to read about Bainbridge's history, including the sad internment of citizens of Japanese ancestry. Adults/$2.50; students and seniors/$1.50; family pass/$5; younger than 5/free. Open Wednesday–Monday, 1–4 p.m.; Saturday (summer), 10 a.m.–4 p.m.; Saturday (winter), 1 p.m.– 4 p.m.; closed Tuesday.

Farmers' Market
Town Square at City Hall Park (spring, summer, fall), Eagle Harbor Church on Madison Avenue at Winslow Way (winter market);
bainbridgefarmersmarket.com
Wander among white-awning-covered stalls where vendors sell fresh fruits and vegetables, handcrafted cheeses and breads, artisan jewelry, and clothing. The rules stipulate that items sold must be handmade, homemade, or homegrown on Bainbridge Island or in North Kitsap County, so you can count on local, fresh, and unique items. Open mid-April to mid-October, 9 a.m.–1 p.m.; late November to the Saturday before Christmas, 10 a.m.–3 p.m.

Kids Discovery Museum (KiDiMu)
150 Madrone Lane N.; 206-855-4650; *kidimu.org*
Open in a temporary location until about mid-2010 while a museum building is being constructed; it will re-open in the new building at the intersection of Winslow Way and Highway 305.

KiDiMu is Bainbridge Island's enthusiastic embrace of children's play and learning. It's currently morphing from a small temporary space to bigger digs. The new space will include rotating attractions, a toddler-only playroom, a science hall with a rainforest exhibit, and an "our town" area where kids can act out daily life in Washington (grocery store, medical center, and ferry ride). The two-story facility will keep kids busy and cool on hot days, but an outside play area will offer summer fun. Check *nwkidtrips.com* for updated details and a review of the new location. Adults and children (12 months and older)/$5; younger than 12 months/free. Open Tuesday–Saturday, 10 a.m.–4 p.m.; Sunday, noon–4 p.m.; closed Monday.

PLAY

Waterfront Park
Eagle Harbor off Brien Drive (across from the Bainbridge Commons)
Delight in vast expanses of lawn, bird-watching opportunities, and a playground in this five-and-a-half-acre park ringed by trees and water. During summer, you might catch a family-friendly concert here, or just grab some food from a grocery store or deli and have a picnic. Older children, teens, and their adults can rent a kayak.

EAT

Blackbird Bakery $
210 Winslow Way E.; 206-780-1322
Pastries include wheat-free and vegan options, along with rich pies and quiches. No toys, and only a few books, but the window-front seating perched over Winslow Way gives kids a bird's-eye view of passersby. Open Monday–Saturday, 6 a.m.–6 p.m.; Sunday, 7 a.m.–6 p.m.

Café Nola $$-$$$
488 Winslow Way E.; 206-842-3822; *cafenola.com*
Looking for one of the best breakfasts in the Pacific Northwest? Line up at this bistro and discover a dining treasure. Sleepy-eyed moms and dads drink ever-refilled coffee while kids decorate paper-covered tables with crayons. Soon, your enormous plate of pecan-orange challah bread, Dungeness crab melt, or sweet-potato hash arrives. The menu follows the seasons, so hopefully you'll be lucky enough to score some island greens. Kids' menu ($5–$7) includes pasta, quesadillas, ravioli, Gardenburgers, or just a PB&J; for each item ordered, Café Nola donates $1 to the nonprofit Spoons Across America. Big lines; get here early or late, but avoid the rush or be prepared to wait. Open Monday–Friday, 11 a.m.–2:30 p.m. and Monday, Thursday and Friday, 5–9 p.m.; Saturday and Sunday, 9:30 a.m.–2:30 p.m. and 5–9 p.m.

Doc's Marina Grill $-$$
488 Winslow Way E.; 206-842-8339; *docsgrill.com*
Here's waterfront dining at its best, with a view of boats on Eagle Harbor from both indoor and outdoor tables, and a noisy, gregarious scene. Kids will enjoy the selection of burgers, sandwiches, hand-cut Northwest fish and chips, and

SEATTLE GETAWAY

other familiar options. Doc's gets crazy-busy during sunny summer weekends and evenings (half-hour- to hour-long waits), but if you call ahead, you can get on the waitlist. Open daily, 8 a.m.–10 p.m.

Mora Iced Creamery $

139 Madrone Lane; 206-855-1112; *moraicecream.com*

Mora's clinical-feeling white interior seems almost jarring after the browns and honeys of Bainbridge's surroundings, but it's hard not to warm up to the dozens of flavors available. Made locally on Bainbridge, Mora's creations include seasonal favorites like eggnog, lavender, rose petal, and Mexican chocolate. Ask to sample one of these unusual tastes, or select a standard, like chocolate mousse, pistachio, blueberry, or banana split. A bit expensive (around $3.59 for a single scoop; $5–$8 for sundaes), but the exotic flavors are unbelievably good.

Pegasus Coffee $

131 Parfitt Way S.W.; 206-842-6725; *pegasuscoffeehouse.com*

The 27-year-old coffeehouse welcomes all ages to build their own breakfast panino, or order a lunchtime salad, soup, and bruschetta; and there's evening open-mike and music hours (weekends only, year-round). It also serves as a springboard for island musicians, so you might just hear the next alt-folk star here. The kids' menu options include fontina panino, milk, and a fresh veggie pack. Go with island-roasted Pegasus coffee, and get the kids a cup of drinking chocolate (just remember, there's caffeine in them thar cacao beans). Open Sunday–Tuesday, 7 a.m.–6 p.m.; Wednesday–Saturday, 7 a.m.–10 p.m.

That's a Some Pizza $–$$

488 Winslow Way E.; 206-842-2292; *thatsasome.com/tasp.htm*

A quick stop on the way to the ferry dock; buy thick-crust slices of pizza to go, or call ahead for the crust and toppings of your choice. No family seating inside. Open Sunday–Thursday, 11 a.m.–9 p.m.; Friday and Saturday, 11 a.m.–10 p.m.

SHOP

Bon Bon Confections

123 Bjune Drive, Suite 103; 206-780-0199; *bonboncandies.com*

Get a taste of the sweet island life: Bainbridge Island Fudge, saltwater taffy, and enough chocolate to keep you awake all night long. You'll also find dozens of varieties of licorice, including some that will make even licorice haters take a second look. Open Monday–Saturday, 10 a.m.–6 p.m.; Sunday, noon–5 p.m.

Calico Cat Toys

104 Winslow Way W.; 206-842-7720; *calicocattoys.com*

In the Winslow Green shopping center off Madison, Calico Cat Toys offers a train table, helmet-wearing monkeys flying from the ceiling, and other whimsical décor, along with Playmobil toys, puzzles, craft kits, and little playthings for the ferry ride home. Open Monday–Saturday, 9:30 a.m.–6 p.m.; Sunday, 10 a.m.–5 p.m.

Eagle Harbor Book Company

157 Winslow Way E.; 206-842-5332; *eagleharborbooks.com*

Sit in a large, squishy armchair big enough for two and delve into a picture, board, or chapter book. Or sit on the floor. Or sit in a corner — no worries! There are plenty of places to kick back with a good book. This is a great afternoon pit-stop, and you may find that it's difficult to drag the kids back out of this serene, hardwood-floored store with its quintessential Northwest vibe. Open Monday–Friday, 9 a.m.–7 p.m.; Saturday, 9 a.m.–6 p.m.; Sunday 10 a.m.–5 p.m.

Lollipops Children's Boutique

278 Winslow Way E.; 206-780-9012

Kids can play with a wooden ferry or consider a fanciful television-shaped aquarium while you peruse Lollipops' selection of Le Top, Deux Par Deux, and Roxy clothing. Best for parents of girls and babies, although the store stocks garments for kids as old as sixteen. Look for the Bainbridge-made sweatshirts on the racks and boat headbands at the register — a perfect souvenir.

Oil & Water Art Supply

278 Winslow Way E.; 206-842-0477; *oilandwaterarts.com*

Check out the kids' corner in this small art store, particularly the bare wooden animals practically growling for a coat of paint. You can pick up both the paint-your-own beasts and paint supplies here, or an old-fashioned turn-your-kid's-art-into-a-plate kit. Open Monday–Saturday, 10 a.m.–6 p.m.; Sunday, 11 a.m.–5 p.m.

Possum's Boutique

146 Winslow Way W., Bldg. 2; 206-780-0611; *possumsboutique.com*

Possum's sells a variety of European-, Canadian-, and American-made clothes and toys in both organic and conventional, up to size 6. Look for the adorable mom (or dad!) 'n' me aprons, made by a Bainbridge mom. Possum's play kitchen room is in the store's rear. Open Monday–Saturday, 10 a.m.–6 p.m.; Sunday, 10 a.m.–5 p.m.

vancouver

vancouver

Vancouver's diverse history, people, and big-city flair are an instant match for families. The outdoor activities can't be beat; there's skiing, snowboarding, snowshoeing, boating, and biking — all within the city limits or just outside. The entire city is one big playground for children and adults alike. Dozens of gardens dot the city, from the blooms surrounding swing sets in Stanley Park to the exploding flower-shaped fireworks at VanDusen Garden. Here's a city that takes kids seriously: There's even a shopping center just for them, the Granville Island Kids Market.

There's so much to do here that one short stay just won't be enough. Vancouver is best tasted in multiple small bites — a weekend here, a half-week there — so you can sample the huge variety Vancouver has to offer.

SUGGESTED ITINERARIES

If you're staying for two days: Arrive at Granville Island early and stay for two hours or so. Drive or take the Aquabus to Science World. The next day, go to the Vancouver Aquarium before the crowds arrive, then spend a lazy afternoon at Stanley Park.

If you're staying for three days: Do all of the above, plus take a side trip to Capilano, Lynn Canyon, or Burnaby. Plan to go swimming in an outdoor pool in summer, biking in spring or fall, or ice-skating in winter.

If you're staying for five days: Take in all of the activities above, plus visit two neighborhoods and a museum (Vancouver or Maritime), and take a trip to either Grouse Mountain or Cypress Mountain.

If you're staying for a week: Include all the the attractions above, plus take a side trip to Victoria or Whistler.

MATCH YOUR TRAVEL ITINERARY TO YOUR FAMILY STYLE:

Active families: Hike or ski on Grouse Mountain or Cypress Mountain, bike through Stanley Park to the Variety Kids Water Park, catch a ballgame at Nat Bailey Stadium. Stay at Rosellen Suites, which offers plenty of room and is a hop, skip, and bike path away from Stanley Park.

Artsy families: See modern art at the Vancouver Art Gallery and eat in the upstairs cafe. Gaze at Granville's indie galleries, which feature paintings, glasswork, and sculptures.

Foodie families: Shop at the public market on Granville Island, try a new food dish at a dim sum, izakaya, or Indian restaurant. Stay at the Granville Island Hotel.

Retro families: Travel back in time at the Vancouver Maritime Museum, the Vancouver Museum, and the Burnaby Village Museum. Sleep at the Sylvia Hotel, a gracefully aging doyenne.

VANCOUVER

SIX THINGS YOU MUST DO IN VANCOUVER

1. Explore life above ground at **Science World at Telus World of Science** (page 93) and under the sea at **Vancouver Aquarium** (page 95). Both are world-class experiences, and Science World has the benefit of being free for Oregon Museum of Science & Industry and Pacific Science Center members.

2. Visit Vancouver's Chinatown, the third largest in North America. It's chock-a-block with fantastic and affordable little shops, restaurants, and bakeries (page 111).

3. Explore Stanley Park's playgrounds, water features, bike paths, hiking trails, and public art (page 94).

4. Go to Granville Island Kids Market, a two-story shopping, eating, and adventure emporium (page 99).

5. Eat a hot dog from one of downtown Vancouver's little takeaway hot dog carts. Bonus points for trying a "Japadog"! (page 98)

6. Eat at an izakaya or dim sum restaurant; two different takes on small-plate Asian food. Izakaya is Japanese pub food that's just the right size for kid tummies; dim sum's family-style service and hectic pace mean kids are welcome.

Shopping families: Shop your heart out on Robson Street, with its indoor malls and pedestrian thoroughfares. Stay at the swank Carmana or a thriftier Priceline-booked hotel, right in the thick of downtown shopping.

WHAT KIDS LIKE BEST, AGE BY AGE

Babies: Take advantage of babe's portability and hit up the Vancouver Art Museum, and then go shopping and eating on The Drive (Commercial Avenue).

Toddlers and preschoolers: Head for the Vancouver Aquarium, Science World's toddler- and preschool-aged play zones, and Stanley Park's train. Don't miss the Variety Kids Water Park in summer, and the Granville Island Kids Market year-round.

Elementary-school-age kids: Vancouver Aquarium and Science World are still big hits, but now you can also add in the imagination-fueled Vancouver Museum and Maritime Museum, plus pools such as the one at Stanley Park's Second Beach. Ride bikes or 'blades (inline skates) to cruise around Stanley Park's seawall.

Middle-school-age kids: At this age, kids are ready for sports that accommodate more independence, like swimming, biking, skiing, snowboarding, and snowtubing. Vancouver has plenty of these options to explore.

VANCOUVER

Teens: Often fascinated by moves on the slopes and people in the streets, teens can hit the slopes and then take in Vancouver's bustling street life. Visit Commercial Avenue's (The Drive's) neighborhood for used threads and Robson Street for Keds.

TRAVEL INFORMATION

Tourism Vancouver provides travel deals and promotional materials. For more information, visit *tourismvancouver.com/visitors* or call 604-682-2222. Make hotel reservations through Tourism Vancouver at 877-826-1717.

VANCOUVER IN THE MEDIA

Hundreds of films and TV shows have been shot in Vancouver, because the city produces films less expensively than cities south of the border. A few titles your kids might recognize: *Sisterhood of the Traveling Pants*, *X-Men*, *Scooby Doo* (sequels two and three), *Scary Movie* (and sequels two through four), and *Air Bud*. Encourage the kids to keep an eye out for roving bands of actors, directors, and camera jockeys.

Several celebrities were born in and around Vancouver, including Meg Tilly, Michael J. Fox, and Hayden Christensen ("Anakin Skywalker" in episodes two and three of the *Star Wars* movies).

Author Phyllis Grant Lavelle writes chapter-book mysteries centered on Vancouver, best for elementary-school-age kids. For younger children, check out *Who Hides in the Park*, by Warabe Aska (about Stanley Park's residents), along with books by Per-Henrik Gurth: *Oh, Canada!*, *Canada in Colours*, and *Snowy Sports: Ready, Set, Play!*

Kids of all ages will enjoy finding Vancouver's highlights using *My Vancouver Sketchbook* by Robert Perry, who also wrote the BC Ferry–centric *The Ferryboat Ride*. There's a companion coloring book, "The Ferryboat Ride Coloring Book."

VANCOUVER

FUN FACTS

- There are more than 200 parks in Vancouver.

- In 1791, Captain José María Narváez of Spain became the first European to explore the area.

- Vancouver is the second-driest Canadian city during the winter months.

- Vancouver is the setting for 10 percent of Hollywood movies.

- The port of Vancouver is the most diverse and largest port in Canada.

- In 1922, motor vehicles in B.C. switched from driving on the left side of the street to driving on the right.

- Not-so-fun fact: In 1886, almost all of Vancouver's buildings caught fire and burned down.

- BOOM! Hear that sound? Every night, the Nine O'clock Gun is fired (really, a cannon in Stanley Park) – as it has been for more than 100 years.

VANCOUVER NICKNAMES

Van
Terminal City
The Big Smoke
Vanhattan
Vansterdam
Hollywood North

SAFETY

Vancouver is safe to walk day or night — with one very important exception: Families should avoid walking on Hastings Street past Carrall (East Hastings). You may have to drive through this stretch to get to Commercial or Pacific National Exhibition (PNE); if you do, you'll probably have to explain some unusual or shocking behavior (most denizens appear to be experiencing a combination of mental illnesses, drug abuse, and drunkenness) to curious older children. While most people here probably won't hurt you, the afflictions on very public display can be disturbing and sad. On the other hand, witnessing this pain is probably a better anti-drug and anti-drink PSA than any schoolteacher's lecture.

Keep valuables out of your car, and don't walk through dark, lonely places at night. It's common sense in the Pacific Northwest, or anywhere in the world.

GETTING THERE

Plane: If arriving by plane, you'll land at Vancouver International Airport (YVR), about a half-hour drive from downtown Vancouver. Rent a car, take a taxi, take a shuttle bus directly into downtown Vancouver, or ride the new SkyTrain Canada Line (*translink.ca*). Find all your options at the Vancouver Web site: *yvr.ca*.

Ferry: You can reach Vancouver from Victoria by BC Ferries (*bcferries.com*), which makes the crossing between Swartz Bay and Tsawwassen multiple times per day. Check real-time lineups, schedules, and prices at *ferrylineups.com*.

Amtrak: Amtrak Cascades trains (*amtrakcascades.com*) leave Seattle for Vancouver twice a day, with one-way trips starting from about $28 and lasting three hours or more. Arriving at the gorgeous brick Pacific Central Station (1150 Station Street), you'll jump aboard the SkyTrain to reach downtown. Carefully plan your trip — Amtrak's departures at some times are often actually buses, which aren't as relaxing with kids.

Car: You'll drive toward Vancouver along I-5 from points either north or south. Coming from Seattle, it's roughly a two- to two-and-a-half-hour drive to Vancouver through rolling countryside; about five hours from Portland (depending on wait times at border crossings).

One trouble spot: the Peace Arch border crossing. When coming from Seattle, try leaving very early in the morning (5 or 6 a.m.), missing late-rising border traffic, and arriving at Granville Island by 9 a.m., just in time to score a great parking spot. Leaving midday or late afternoon can be an exercise in

VANCOUVER

frustration at the border. You can also try an alternate crossing point if traffic is terrible. Check *borderlineups.com* to find out current wait times.

A nice place to stop en route is off Bellingham's exit 256 (take a left on Meridian Street), at the Barnes & Noble bookstore (4099 Meridian Street); bathrooms, coffee, kids' area; open weekdays, 9 a.m.–10 p.m.; weekends, 9 a.m.–11 p.m. Or you can stop in historic, downtown Bellingham for good grub.

GETTING AROUND

Finding your way around Vancouver: Outside the downtown core, Vancouver's streets are in an orderly grid shape — for the most part. Avenues run east-west, and streets run north-south. A neat trick: Locate addresses on north-south streets by subtracting sixteen from the first two digits of the numbered address to find the correct block (for example, 2110 Burrard Street — 21 minus 16 — is between Fifth and Sixth avenues). Ontario Street divides the city into east and west.

Buy a map to locate cross streets. Downtown's peninsula shape means it's fairly difficult to get truly lost — just memorize where Robson Street is located

CALENDAR

January
POLAR BEAR SWIM. Brrr! Don a costume, then jump into English Bay's frigid waters and swim off winter's excesses. *vancouver.ca/parks/events /polarbear/2009/index.htm*

CHINESE NEW YEAR PARADE (January or February). A fantastic parade, storytelling, lucky red packets, and more on the first Sunday of the Chinese (lunar) new year. *vancouverchinatown.ca*

February
CHUTZPAH FESTIVAL. Jewish performers from around the world sing, play klezmer, and dance. *chutzpahfestival.com/programs.html*

VANCOUVER INTERNATIONAL STORYTELLING FESTIVAL. Stories geared toward older kids, teens, and adults, but a kids' stage keeps little ones entertained. *vancouverstorytelling.org*

March
CHERRY BLOSSOM FESTIVAL. This Japanese-themed festival features taiko drumming performances, koto performances, and more in honor of the city's more than 36,000 ornamental cherry trees. *vcbf.ca*

May
VANCOUVER INTERNATIONAL CHILDREN'S FESTIVAL. Theater, acrobats, puppetry, and song to entertain all ages. *childrens festival.ca*

CHINATOWN NIGHT MARKET. Vendors set up displays of clothing, music, toys, and household items, from May through early September. Family performances. *vcma.shawbiz.ca/home_e.htm*

June
WEST POINT GREY PARK offers a small-town carnival, parade, and

other fun events, including a bike-decorating contest, live music, and carnival rides. *pointgreyfiesta.org*

July
HSBC CELEBRATION OF LIGHT. Barges fire explosions of light and sound over English Bay, a display representing the talent of fireworks designers from around the world. *celebration-of-light.com*

RIOTINTO ALCAN DRAGON BOAT FESTIVAL. Watch teams race down False Creek, eat fish 'n' chips, and enjoy dancing and music performed on the World Beat Stage. *dragonboatbc.ca*

KIDS MINI GRAND PRIX RACES. Kids between the ages of three and five race little electric sports cars while dressed in official F1 gear. July through September. *thedrive.ca/event_kids_grand _prix.shtm*

VANCOUVER FOLK FESTIVAL. Families can play with bubbles, create art, enjoy workshops, and listen to music at Kitsilano's Jericho Beach. *thefestival.bc.ca/little-folks -village*

August
ANNUAL CHINATOWN FESTIVAL. Features children's performances, food tasting, BMX stunts, and a kids' corner. *vcbia.brinkster.net /CF/Festival.htm*

BARD ON THE BEACH. An annual presentation of Shakespearean plays, best suited for older children. Grab an Aquabus from downtown and watch the Bard's plays in the midst of Vanier Park. *bardonthebeach.org*

MUSICFEST. More than fifty events over the span of two weeks, featuring international musicians at indoor and outdoor venues. *musicfest vancouver.ca/home/venueList.php*

THE FAIR AT PNE. This fair brings more rides — and waaay more people — to the Pacific National Exhibition (PNE). Expect long lines, frantic parking situations, and lots of sticky cotton-floss fun. *pne.ca/thefair/*

October
HARVEST FESTIVAL. At Capilano Bridge, kids can visit a jack-o'-lantern display, have their fortunes told, listen to ghost stories, or go trick-or-treating. *capbridge.com*

December
ROGERS SANTA CLAUS PARADE. Santa's parade route takes him right through downtown Vancouver; afterwards, enjoy family festivities in front of the Vancouver Art Gallery, including the world's largest mailbox to Santa. *rogerssantaclausparade.com /christmas-square*

WINTER SOLSTICE LANTERN FESTIVAL. Drum jams, lantern processions, dance instruction, and music light up winter's darkest nights. Lantern festivals are popular throughout the Northwest; this is a great one to experience. *secretlantern.org*

BRIGHT NIGHTS AT STANLEY PARK. Get through winter's bleakest months with millions of tiny lights, train rides, roasted chestnuts, and hot chocolate. *vancouver.ca /PARKS/events/brightnights*

VANCOUVER

ESSENTIALS

Area code: 604

Baby accessories: Wee Travel, Inc. (604-222-4722; *weetravel.ca*) rents strollers, car seats, and more.

Emergencies: Call 911. Vancouver General Hospital's emergency services are on call 24 hours a day at 855 Twelfth Avenue W. (604-875-4111). Vancouver police: 604-717-3321. The B.C. Children's Hospital: 4480 Oak Street and also offers an emergency department. Call 604-875-2345 for more information.

Mail a postcard: You can mail your postcard at many pharmacies with full mail services inside. Red mailboxes dot Vancouver's streets.

Money: U.S. citizens should have no problems taking money out of the ATMs found throughout downtown Vancouver. You can also use your Visa card, just as you do at home. Call the bank before leaving; international spending can sometimes trigger holds, and you'll also want to ask if using your Visa internationally incurs special fees.

News: Pick up an issue of the *Vancouver Sun* to find out what's going on in local news. Families will enjoy *Urban Baby & Toddler* (*urbanbaby.ca*), *BC Parent* (*bcparent.ca*), and *WestCoast Families* (*westcoastfamilies.com*).

Parks: See *vancouver.ca/parks* for a complete listing of all parks, including a searchable database.

Pharmacy: London Drugs at 1187 Robson Street is open from 9 a.m. to 11 p.m., even on holidays. Call the pharmacy at 604-669-7374.

Taxes: As of mid-2010, purchases are subject to the new 12 percent Harmonized Sales Tax. Some additional hotel taxes may apply.

vis-à-vis your hotel. But if you get turned around, remember that the big mountains (e.g., Grouse Mountain) are to the north of downtown.

Car: Buy a road map at one of the local supermarkets or grocery stores; alternately, map out your drive online. Vancouver's sprawl makes it more challenging to navigate, but it's still primarily grid-based, so it's not too tricky.

Street parking is virtually nonexistent downtown; you'll park in lots (and pay for the privilege). Parking in neighborhoods is usually ample, with the exception of Granville Island. Bring coins in case you need to pay to park (not always necessary).

Note to U.S. visitors: Gas is priced per liter. (No, gas is not on super-sale in Canada. Quite the opposite!) Fill up in the U.S. before crossing the border.

Public transportation: Vancouver's smorgasbord of sea and bus connections includes ferry boats, catamarans, above- and below-ground urban rail lines, and buses. You can even reach ski destinations — like Grouse Mountain and Cypress Mountain — by bus. Plan your family's routes, figure out the pricing system (hint: it's often cheaper to buy passes), and memorize schedules here: *translink.ca/en/Schedules-and-Maps.aspx.*

Private transportation: The Aquabus (*theaquabus.com*; 604-689-5858) criss-crosses stations at Hornby Street, Granville Island, Yaletown, Science World, and Stamp's Landing. Ferries run from 7 a.m. to 10:30 p.m. (to 8:30 p.m. in winter), run at least twice an hour during the peak hours between 10 a.m. and 5 p.m. Adults/$3–$4; kids/$1.50–$2. Check Web site for prices and details.

The False Creek Ferries (*granvilleislandferries.bc.ca/map.html*) connect Granville Island, Yaletown, Stamp's Landing, the Aquatic Centre, and the Maritime Museum. Some routes operate weekdays from 7 a.m. until 9 p.m.; others only run on weekends and holidays. Adults/$3–$6; kids/$1.50–$3. Check the schedule and prices online.

Taxis are also available, although not plentiful. Call one up from Blacktop (604-731-1111) or Yellow Cab (604-681-1111).

Bike: Vancouver is still developing safe bike paths for commuting purposes, but many recreational trails exist. View bike path routes and find suggestions from B.C.'s Translink (*translink.ca/en/Cycling/Cycling-Routes.aspx*) or connect with advocacy group Vancouver Area Cycling Coalition: *vacc.bc.ca/home.php*.

Traffic notes: Avoid going into or out of the city when everyone else is doing the same thing. That means staying away from the downtown core between 7 and 9 a.m. on weekdays from either North Vancouver or South Vancouver: and again between 4 and 7 p.m. on weekdays. Weekend midmornings can be equally bad during winter, as Vancouverites head north toward the ski slopes.

DOWNTOWN/WEST END (STANLEY PARK)

If you're visiting Vancouver with younger kids, you'll probably want to stay in a West End apartment-style hotel, close to Stanley Park and, thankfully, grocery stores and very inexpensive restaurants. The whole downtown and West End don't have much in the way of shops or services catering directly to kids, so that's why families often head for Stanley Park, as soon as possible.

With teens, you might try bidding on Priceline or selecting a downtown hotel (like the Carmana), so your shopaholic (or peoplewatcher) can get his or her fix. Downtown is also excellent for families that want to be in the thick of Vancouver's international-tourist core, have arrived by train, or wish to make lots of trips on the SkyTrain. Pricey parking is the norm (around $18–$24/day), but if you're on foot, it won't matter.

SLEEP
Carmana Plaza $$$–$$$$
1128 Alberni Street; 604-683-1399 or 877-686-9988; *carmanaplaza.com*
It's a nondescript building, but Carmana doesn't need to advertise with flash. Indoors, you'll find one of the most amazing values in Vancouver: luxe, upscale suites with separate bedrooms, dark wood furniture, wood-laminate flooring, full kitchens, DVD players and televisions, and plenty of room for strollers. Most of the clientele are business travelers, but don't let this deter you. No on-site restaurant or room service, but this hotel's swank more than makes up for the lack of service-based amenities.

VANCOUVER DOWNTOWN/WEST END

Robson Suites $$$–$$$$
777 Bidwell Street; 604-685-9777 or 800-404-1398;
robsonsuitesvancouver.com
Despite the name, Robson Suites is actually located on a street off Robson.
Fourth-floor suites feel bigger due to high ceilings, but these quarters are a bit
tighter than other Vancouver options, right down to the two-person dining
table. The rooms feel a bit drab, but there's a spare, empty room with a desk
for working parents. It may be a good fit for small families.

Rosellen Suites $$–$$$$
2030 Barclay Street; 604-689-4807 or 888-317-6648; *rosellensuites.com*
In a quiet, leafy section of Vancouver's West End and just two blocks from
Stanley Park, Rosellen Suites is a great value: large rooms for families of three
to eight people, with studio, one- and two-bedroom rooms. Room layouts
vary, but all have a kitchen, dining area, and living room with DVD player.
As a renovated apartment building, some rooms have seen better days,
although the owners try to replace furnishings as they wear out. Front-desk
staff hours are limited, but the staff is chatty and helpful.

Sylvia Hotel $$–$$$
1154 Gilford Street; 604-681-9321; *sylviahotel.com*
Vancouver visitors flock here for sweet vintage sleeps at affordable prices.
Built as apartments in 1912, the Sylvia's pale green walls, marble staircases,
oak accents, and vine-covered exterior speak to a bygone age. Several rooms
offer kitchenettes and sofas. And even if you don't stay here, stop by the
Sylvia Restaurant, which fronts windy English Bay, for a meal or a warm
drink.

Times Square Suites $$$–$$$$
1821 Robson Street; 604-684-2223 or 877-684-2223; *timessquaresuites.com*
Families will particularly appreciate the one-bedroom options, which include
a kitchen stocked with everything you need, cable TV and DVD player, and
stackable washer/dryer. Ask for a quieter room, and the staff will try to do
what it can — but be warned, this is on a popular part of Robson, and in sum-
mer, can be a little noisy. Kitty-corner from a new Safeway, one block from
bike-rental shops, and just a few blocks from Stanley Park, this is definitely
one of my family's favorite stays in Vancouver.

YWCA $
733 Beatty Street; 604-895-5830 or 800-663-1424; *ywcahotel.com*
Sure, the Y in your hometown might cater to the down and out, but this Y's
income depends upon travelers — male and female, poor and wealthy, young
and old alike. At check-in, children receive a "magic suitcase" with games.
Larger families will appreciate the configurations (as many as six single beds).
Amenities include a coin-operated laundry, Wi-Fi , and a community kitchen.
But don't expect the Ritz at these prices; front-desk staff can be brusque, and
you'll want to lock up your valuables.

VANCOUVER
DOWNTOWN/WEST END

DO

CN Imax and Canada Place

201-999 Canada Place; 604-682-2384; *imax.com/vancouver*
Set in the impressive Canada Place (the structure with five billowing white sails above), this is a great place for a movie on an immense screen. Short (forty-five-minute) movies geared for general audiences and longer feature films play here, and either are nice options during rainy days or cooler months. Canada Place was originally built as a pavilion for the 1986 World's Fair; the sails are spectacular around Christmas, when they are lit up in bright red and green. Adults/$12–$14; children/$11–$13. Show times change daily; check Web site.

Commodore Lanes & Billiards

838 Granville Street; 604-681-1531;
where.ca/vancouver/guide_listing~listing_id~914.htm
With bowling alleys rapidly disappearing from urban cores, Commodore keeps the all-ages fun rolling along. Pool tables are also available. No alcohol is allowed in the lanes, but it is served in the bar (and in all the bars around this area), so families feel most comfortable on weekdays and on weekends before 6 p.m. Per game: weekdays/$4.50; weekends/$7; shoe rental/$2. Open Sunday–Thursday, 11 a.m.–midnight; Friday and Saturday, 11 a.m.–1 a.m.

General Motors Place

800 Griffiths Way; *generalmotorsplace.com*
Watch a National Hockey League game and cheer on the Vancouver Canucks for an only-in-Vancouver experience. The 18,000-plus-seat General Motors Place offers family washrooms and booster chairs, so even little hockey fans won't be left out. $55–$131 for single-game tickets. Check Web site for game times.

Robson Square Ice Rink

Corner of Robson and Howe; *yougottabehere.com/robson-square*
For skating right downtown, check out Robson Square's refurbished outdoor ice rink. Skate rentals/$3, helmet rentals/$2 (free and mandatory for kids 12 and younger). Open daily, noon–9 p.m.

Science World at Telus World of Science

1455 Quebec Street; 604-443-7443; *scienceworld.ca*
Science World is not in downtown Vancouver, but easily accessible by SkyTrain (or your car) from downtown. My kids clamor to revisit the same areas again and again, including the Eureka! Gallery with waterfalls, a giant kid-cranked windmill, and other ways to explore sound, light, and movement, plus the eco-themed "Our World" garbage slide. Toddlers have their own area to ramble and roam, behind a chest-high staffed (and shut) gate, where there are also bathrooms and a private nursing room. The staff keeps exhibits clean and in good working order; the frequently changing traveling exhibits mean that there's always a new section to explore. If you're a member of OMSI, the Pacific Science Center, or another member of ASTC (*astc.com*), bring your ID card, because you'll get in for free. Adults/$19.75; teens (13–18)/$16.25; children (4–12)/$13.75; families, up to six people/$71.50; OMNIMAX film/$10. Open Monday–Friday, 10 a.m.–5 p.m.; Saturday and Sunday, 10 a.m.–6 p.m.

VANCOUVER
DOWNTOWN/WEST END

Stanley Park

Vancouver's 1,000-acre playground offers so much for families, from tree-shaded playgrounds to sun-dappled water parks. There's also an aquarium, a miniature train, a bird-populated lagoon, a petting zoo, a lighthouse, an artist's corner, a family-friendly music venue (*malkinbowl.com*), and seaplanes taking off and landing in Coal Harbour. Once you think you've seen it all, you turn a corner and . . . totem poles sprout from the ground. Families with young children may plan to spend a lot of time here, so it's best to find a hotel or apartment close to Stanley. A free shuttle goes around the park's perimeter from mid-June through late September, although much of what kids will want to see is concentrated at the park's southeast corner.

Stop at the park's information booth (inside the Georgia Street entrance to Stanley Park) to find out what's going on and to pick up a map. Parking is available at Stanley, but in anything less than a downpour, the walk to the park from downtown is worth the work. Warning: There isn't much to eat beyond hot dogs and overpriced food inside Stanley, so eat big beforehand, bring snacks, or pack a lunch.

STANLEY PARK

Bike the seawall

vancouver.ca/engsvcs/transport/cycling/index.htm

Bike out to Prospect Point Lookout, and you'll never forget the tremendous views of downtown Vancouver, sweeping sky, and encircling mountains. More adventurous and/or athletic families can take bikes out to Granville Island, Kitsilano's Vanier Park, or all the way around Stanley Park's perimeter. Check out Spokes Bicycle Rentals' fleet of family cycles: cruisers, tandems, child's bikes, trail-a-bikes, and pull-along trailers (1798 W. Georgia Street; 604-688-5141; *vancouverbikerental.com*), or one of the other bike shops along the same street. Open 9 a.m.–4:30 p.m. daily. Hourly rates range from around $5 to $15; from $19 to $65 for the full day.

Lost Lagoon Nature House

604-257-8544; *stanleyparkecology.ca/programs/natureHouse*

Nature House offers Sunday hikes and naturalist-guided tours of Stanley Park, often focusing on animals and plants. Adults/$10; children/$5. Hours vary; check the Web site for upcoming programs.

Miniature Train

604-257-8531; *vancouver.ca/parks/parks/stanley/fun.htm*

The quick ten-minute ride around a track is over too soon, but the waterfall and tunnel features often make young kids want to go again (and again and again). Luckily, the replica of Canada's first transcontinental train is right next to a playground, which might help convince the kids to leave. Adults/$6; teens (13–18)/$4.25; children (2–12)/$3. Hours vary (check Web site), usually open on weekends, weather permitting.

STANLEY PARK *continued*

Second Beach and Pool

Stanley Park Drive; 604-257-8731; *vancouver.ca/parks/rec/pools*
Twenty-seven-degree C (80-degree F) water right on English Bay, in a
fairly shallow (5 feet deep at maximum), infinity-style pool. Hop into
the pool one of four ways: three slides or beach-style entry (no diving).
Next to a well-loved playground with all the toddler favorites (swings,
slides, etc.) and wide, grassy spaces perfect for Frisbee, soccer, or your
portable lunch. Adults/$5.15; teens (13–18)/$3.60; children (5–12)/$2.60.
Open mid-May through early September, noon–8:45 p.m.

Stanley Bright Nights

Around Christmas, the park puts up thousands of little lights and
Christmas-themed décor, and families line up for Stanley Bright Nights.
Grab some freshly roasted chestnuts from a vendor to keep your hands
warm while you wait, but make sure you've already reserved your tickets.
Read more here: *vancouver.ca/parks/events/brightnights/index.htm*.

Vancouver Aquarium

845 Avison Way; 604-659-3474; *vanaqua.org*
A must-see, despite the steep entry price. Even if you can only do
it once every few years, you should do it. Visit child-size arapaima
fish and sleek sharks in the Tropic Zone. Watch your kids get lost in
quiet wonder indoors, or catch a splashy beluga show outdoors.
Awesome eight-and-younger "Clownfish Cove" contains a stuffed-
seal hospital, Venus flytraps, and miniature tunnels. The food in the
outdoor-seating Upstream Cafe isn't terrible and is probably the only
quasi-decent food in Stanley Park. Of course, the irony of eating
a salmon burger or fish 'n' chips won't be lost on some kids, so pizza,
cheese sandwiches, and pretzels are also available. Adults/$22; youth
(13–18)/$17; children (4–12)/$14; younger than 3/free. Open 9:30
a.m.–5 p.m.

Variety Kids Water Park

Stanley Park, near the junction of Avison Way and Park Drive;
604-257-8400; *city.vancouver.bc.ca/parks/parks/stanley/fun.htm*
A riot of color, water, and shrieks resounds through this outdoor water
park. Bring towels and a change of clothes if you're even considering walking past, because the freezing cold water doesn't deter any child from
jumping into a trickling stream, dodging overhead sprinklers, or running
under the waterfall. Watch out for the water cannon (older kids particularly love dousing adults). There's an outdoor dryer, but it often seems to
be broken — perhaps due to overuse. Grassy spaces and benches provide
sitting spots for adults and shivering kids. Free. Open from the end of May
through Labour Day; check Web site for hours.

VANCOUVER
DOWNTOWN/WEST END

Vancouver Art Gallery

750 Hornby Street; 604-662-4719; *vanartgallery.bc.ca*

If the gallery is showing an exhibit that interests you, this attraction is a great stop with older children. And even if you're not, visit the gallery's gift shop, which offers a wide variety of crafts, art books, finger puppets, and drawing guides for kids. Check the Web site for weekend offerings; child-oriented tours are often presented on Saturdays; on the second and fourth Sundays, "The Making Place" provides art workshops. Adults/$20.50 (September–May, $19.50); teens (with student ID)/$15 (September–May, $14); children (5–12)/$7; 4 and younger/free; family (maximum two adults and two children)/$50. Open daily, 10 a.m.–5:30 p.m.; Tuesday until 9 p.m. year-round.

Vancouver Public Library

350 W. Georgia Street; 604-331-3603; *vpl.vancouver.bc.ca*

The library's Coliseum-style architecture is an instant classic, as is the indoor, glassed-in atrium, where families can enjoy a coffee or hot chocolate and look up at the sky, no matter the weather. Indoors, there's a small — and a bit tattered — children's area with computers, a fenced-in toddler area, plus lots and lots of books to ramble through. Open Monday–Thursday, 10 a.m.–9 p.m.; Friday and Saturday, 10 a.m.–6 p.m.; Sunday, noon–5 p.m.

Vancouver Symphony Orchestra

Performance venues vary; 604-876-3434; *vancouversymphony.ca*

At the Vancouver Playhouse Theatre, the Vancouver Symphony presents orchestral arrangements for toddlers (Tiny Tots) through tweens (Kids' Koncerts). Tickets can be purchased singly or as a set; visitors can order single tickets online: $7–$15.

West End Community Centre

870 Denman Street; 604-257-8333; *westendcc.ca*

This nondescript building holds some treasures for families seeking inexpensive fun: drop-in playtime on cars and other riding vehicles, parent-tot ice skating (October–April) and family skating, and one-time classes and workshops. Check the online schedule to find an event, and meet local families on your vacation. Membership may be required for some events. Hours vary; check Web site.

PLAY

Coal Harbour Community Center

480 Broughton Street at W. Hastings Street; 604-718-8222; *coalharbourcc.ca*

If you're staying downtown but don't want to walk all the way to Stanley Park for a playground, head here. The small playground looks over Coal Harbour and presents toddler swings, a climbing structure, and slides atop soft, rubberized blacktop. Best for younger children. Open dawn to dusk.

EAT

Café Crepe $

1032 Robson Street; 604-488-0045

Crêpes with savory fillings (blends of egg, Emmenthal cheese, ham, or spinach) or sweet (Nutella, jam, sugar) make for a quick, satisfying, and inexpensive lunch. Order from the outside window and take it to the park, to your hotel, or as you walk; service indoors can take a long time. Open Sunday–Thursday, 8 a.m.–midnight; Friday and Saturday, 8 a.m.–2 a.m.

Caffè Artigiano $

763 Hornby Street (604-694-7737) and 1101 W. Pender Street (604-685-5333); *caffeartigiano.com*

The café's espresso drinks are served with intricate patterns swirled in the foam, guaranteed to wake up mom and dad. Once you make it through the long line (and there's always a long line), you can order breakfast items, pastries, or lunch sandwiches from a deli case. Hornby hours: Monday–Friday, 6:30 a.m.–9 p.m.; Saturday, 7 a.m.–9 p.m.; Sunday, 7 a.m.–7 p.m. Pender hours: Monday–Friday, 6 a.m.–6 p.m.; Saturday and Sunday, 6:30 a.m.–5 p.m.

Canada Safeway $

1766 Robson Street; 604-683-6155; *safeway.com*

No-nonsense foodstuffs like you get at home, wherever that home might be. Open daily, 7 a.m.–midnight.

Capers Whole Foods Market $

1675 Robson Street; 604-687-5288; *wholefoodsmarket.com/stores/robson*

Capers stocks primarily health food, but it's a good place to pick up sandwiches, deli takeaway, soups, salads, and muffins that won't make you feel guilty (they have whole wheat and chocolate chips). The bulk section makes sense if you want to pick up a pound of oatmeal for breakfast in your kitchen, or handfuls of trail mix or sweet stuff (such as chocolate and candy) to reward the kids after the Grouse Grind. Open daily, 8 a.m.–10 p.m.

Guu with Garlic $

1698 Robson Street; 604-685-8678; *guu-izakaya.com/robson.html*

My favorite kid-friendly izakaya in Vancouver, Guu's noisy, vibrant atmosphere makes it a great fit for toddlers. Shed your shoes and snag a pillow seat; wipe your hands with the hot washcloth, then dig into edamame, noodles, Japanese-style pancakes, or an unusual and delicious boiled egg wrapped in fried pumpkin. Open Tuesday–Sunday, noon–2:30 p.m. and 5:30 p.m.–midnight.

Hon's Wun-Tun House $$

1339 Robson Street; 604-685-0871

Hon's dim sum isn't the most spectacular, but the extensive menu, fast service, large seating capacity, and child-friendly service makes it an option to consider when staying downtown or visiting Chinatown. Vegetarian options are available, and they proudly use trans-fat-free oil when frying. Go for the classic (noodles, won-tons, or chicken) or more unusual; my kids liked the taro-root dumplings. Open Sunday–Thursday, 11 a.m.–10:45 p.m.; Friday and Saturday, 11 a.m.–11:45 p.m.

VANCOUVER DOWNTOWN/WEST END

Japadog $

899 Burrard St.; *japadog.com/en*

East meets West in a bun. Order a hot dog with a side of soy sauce, wasabi mayo, or seaweed sprinkles. Combining two of my kids' favorite food groups (hot dogs and sushi), I can't go wrong. You can add items as you wish, or just a straight-up dog is also fine. Open Monday–Thursday, noon–7:30 p.m.; Friday and Saturday, noon–8 p.m.; Sunday, 12:30–7 p.m.

Vancouver Art Gallery $–$$

750 Hornby Street; 604-688-2233;

vanartgallery.bc.ca/visit_the_gallery/gallery_cafe.html

If the kids are a little too wild for the gallery's exhibition, you'll probably find something to tame them here. Most art gallery restaurants aren't known for value, but this one provides some nice options in a casual setting: Try soup for around $4, panini for $8, and deluxe nourishment — like baked salmon — for $10. And even if you don't want to make a meal of it, the gallery's dessert window is drool-worthy; you can pick up everything from a cookie to a slice of cake. Open Monday, Wednesday, Friday, 9 a.m.–7 p.m.; Tuesday and Thursday, 9 a.m.–9 p.m.; Saturday, 9:30 a.m.–6 p.m.; Sunday, 10 a.m.–6 p.m.

White Spot $$

1616 W. Georgia Street; 604-681-8034; *whitespot.com/locations.htm*

Ah, the White Spot. It's not a small restaurant, but any book on B.C. would be remiss without a mention of it. While most B.C. residents will tell you it's like a "Canadian Denny's," the truth is that it's far more worldly (imagine Denny's serving Thai-style prawns over rice). And kids really do love those Pirate Packs: a few bucks for a kids' meal that sails in on a ship. For adults, there's everything from naan bread with dips to B.C. salmon Caesar salad, to risottos and stir-fries. Open daily, 6:30 a.m.–11 p.m.; Friday and Saturday, open until midnight during the summer.

SHOP

Konbiniya Japan Centre

1238 Robson Street; 604-682-3634; *konbiniya.com*

Catering to homesick Japanese students, curious travelers, and little kids, Kobiniya stocks Japanese groceries, little boxed toys (Pokemon and Thomas fans will find a few unique items here), and Pocky, that addictive dipped treat. You won't miss it — just look for the huge, window-sized Pocky signs. Open daily, 11 a.m.–2 a.m.

Robson Street

Robson between Granville and Denman; 604-669 8132; *robsonstreet.ca*

Like British high streets, Robson Street lays out store after store along a wide pedestrian strip. Appealing most to tweens and teens, Robson's stores are mostly chain brands like Banana Republic, MEXX, Lululemon Athletica, and Roots. Nice for people watching and a coffee. However, you won't see a lot of young families here. One long, steep hill on the way to Stanley Park can be challenging, so bring a stroller for little kids if you're going to try to walk the whole thing. If you're located at a downtown hotel and want to walk to Stanley Park, choose a parallel street, because the pedestrian traffic can slow you down.

GRANVILLE ISLAND

SLEEP

Granville Island Hotel $$$
1253 Johnson Street; 604-683-7373 or 800-663-1840; *granvilleislandhotel.com*
This offers one of the best locations in Vancouver, if you'd like to make a summer weekend of Granville. Rooms are tight, but who needs to spend much time in the room, with dining, splashing, playing, and entertainment options right outside your hotel, within easy walking distance? If you'd like to splurge during winter, the top-floor penthouse offers a whirlpool, full kitchen, a luxe living room, and balcony; some suites provide soaking tubs with a view of False Creek Harbour.

DO

Adventure Zone
Inside Kids Market; 604-689-8447; *theadventurezone.ca/index.html*
This four-level mazelike foam structure contains everything from balls to pointy spikes, rollers to slides. The only downside is that younger children (younger than three or less than 3 feet tall) need to be accompanied by an adult; the maze's tiny spaces can be physically challenging for even the most fit (don't eat a big lunch before going inside). Perfect for kids ages four to seven. There's also a noisy game room with skee ball and video games right next door, where you can win tickets, then exchange them for the cheap toy du jour. $6.25. Open daily, 10 a.m.–6 p.m.

Carousel Theatre
1411 Cartwright Street; 604-685-6217; *carouseltheatre.ca*
Here's a fun way to meet the locals: Head for their theaters! The small, intimate Carousel Theatre, on Granville Island next to the Kids Market, provides winning stagecraft to keep all ages entertained. A cash-only intermissions café offers drinks for grown-ups and kids, plus candy. We were impressed by the comedic timing of the actors, and the theater's staff takes kids seriously; no skimping on sets or costumes. Check Web site for show times.

Granville Island Kids Market
1496 Cartwright Street; 604-689-8447; *kidsmarket.ca*
At this Granville Island building, two floors stuffed with more than twenty stores geared directly for kids are the main attraction. Gaze upward to spot the Giant and Jack crawling their way up the beanstalk, and kites flying overhead. Little coin-operated cars and Ferris wheels dot the market, giving toddlers something to look forward to around every corner. Go to the "Shop" section (page 101) for best shopping picks in the market. Open daily, 10 a.m.–6 p.m.

Granville Island Public Market
1689 Johnston Street; *granvilleisland.com*
An enormous indoor marketplace of locally grown foods and exquisite imports. Dozens of vendors line narrow corridors, but the glass roof above

provides a feeling of spaciousness. Try to arrive at Granville around 9:30 a.m., when great parking spots are still plentiful. Stay all morning, then pick up an early lunch at one of the dining options available. Wait for a family-sized table in the atrium, or head outside. If you're lucky, a busker will entertain you while you eat your perfectly sized (portion- and price-wise) meal. Open daily, 9 a.m.–7 p.m.

PLAY
Granville Island Water Park and Adventure Playground
Granville Island; *vancouver.ca/parks/cc/falsecreek/website/waterpark.cfm*
Just follow the happy shrieks to the largest free public water park in North America, which features fountains, sprinklers, a toddler area, and a big, loopy yellow slide that doesn't go too fast. Not a lot of shade available in the watery areas, so bring the sunscreen. Open mid-May to Labour Day, daily, 10 a.m.–6 p.m.

Sutcliffe Park
Behind Kids Market
During cooler months — or if you need to dry off after the water park — wander over to Sutcliffe Park's greenery-lined trails. You'll see lots of joggers and dog walkers, wildflowers, small ponds (oops, watch the kids), and tennis players getting their game on.

EAT
Blue Parrot Organic Coffee $
1689 Johnston Street; 604-688-5127; *blueparrotcoffee.com*
A favorite warm- and cold-weather spot inside Granville Public Market, because of the coffee shop's two-story glass peninsula with plentiful seating. Order a coffee for yourself and a hot chocolate (served with whipped cream) for the kids, or get a kids' grilled cheese and your own bagel sandwich. Open daily, 7 a.m.–8 p.m.

Go Fish Ocean Emporium $–$$
1505 First Avenue W.; 604-730-5040
Go Fish serves up a menu of mouthwatering, sustainably caught seafood. Try beer-batter-dipped fish and chips or salmon tacones (taco cones). The conundrum: It's outdoors with limited seating, so best visited during warmer months — yet the lines during summer mean you'll probably wait fifteen to twenty-five minutes for your lunch. It's also a little tricky to find (not among the Granville Island shops). Get directions beforehand or ask a local how to get there. Open Tuesday–Friday, 11:30 a.m.–6:30 p.m.; weekends, noon–6 p.m.

La Baguette & L'Echalote $
1680 Johnston Street; 604-684-1351; *labaguettebakery.com*
You'll stumble upon smatterings of travelers munching on sandwiches while listening to buskers and wonder where they picked up those sandwiches. Then you'll follow your nose and find this petite bakery by scent. La Baguette has been creating warm, fresh loaves of French-style bread, sweet macaroons (pastel-colored cookies), and picnic lunches since 1986. Open daily, 7:30 a.m.–7:30 p.m.

Laurelle's Fine Foods $

1689 Johnston Street; 604-685-8482

On a rainy day, Laurelle's is one of my very favorite stops. This glorified deli case displays dozens of Old World flaky-crusted pastries, including meat and pot pies, sausage rolls, pasties, and turnovers. Affordable and filling, it's an efficient way to get the calories you (and your kids) will need to power through the Kids Market. For a regional twist, try a wild B.C. salmon roll. Open daily, 9 a.m.–7 p.m.

Pedro's Organic Coffee $

1550 Anderson Street; 604-899-0741

Take a break from Granville's buzz and pick up a cup of espresso at Pedro's sweet little coffee shop. A small play corner welcomes kids indoors, or you can take your coffee outside on the patio and watch the kids play on a mini-boat. The grilled cheese sandwich and Goldfish crackers are an easy hit, while you can try a red rooibos (caffeine-free) tea or a white chocolate pecan cookie. Open Monday–Saturday, 8 a.m.–6 p.m.; Sunday, 8:30 a.m.–6 p.m.

Stock Market $

1689 Johnston Street; 604-687-2433

If you're renting or staying someplace with a kitchen, the Stock Market is a must. Let the kids pick from dozens of soups, sauces, and other quick-to-heat consumables. Go right next door to Laurelle's to pick up bread or pie — and voilà! Instant dinner. Open daily, 8 a.m.–6 p.m.

Terra Breads $

1689 Johnston Street; 604-685-3102; *terrabreads.com*

A simple stop for kids who want nothing more than a PB&J or focaccia sandwich; parents should try the sweet-tart fig and anise bread, homemade soup, or a roasted leg of free-range lamb sandwich, served with roasted red onion, fresh pear, organic mixed baby greens, and fresh mint. Open daily, 9 a.m.–7 p.m.

SHOP

These are our family's favorite stores at the Kids Market, but there are so many to choose from, you can't go wrong. The address for all is 1496 Cartwright Street. Open 10 a.m.–6 p.m.

Camelot Kids

604-688-9766; *camelotkids.com*

Stuff to keep your infants and toddlers quiet, safe, and happy while traveling — a tiny play table, booster seats, portable placemats.

The Granville Island Toy Company

604-684-0076; *toycompany.ca*

Basic toys at decent prices: Lego, Playmobil, Schleich figurines, play food, and a make-your-own-doll kit.

Hairloft

604-684-6177; *princessspa.ca*

There's nothing more interesting to some kids (and some parents) than getting a haircut in a new location. Hairloft will cut your kid's curls in one of four chairs, while a television plays overhead and you wait on the couch.

VANCOUVER GRANVILLE ISLAND

Half Time Sports
604-689-8637
Vancouver 2010 mascots, Mountie-dressed bears, plus coins, tees, and caps featuring favorite Canadian teams (like the Oilers).

Humpty Dumpty Books and Music
604-683-7009
Chapter, educational, picture, and work books. Want a book to teach your kids the Canadian ABCs, from "eh" to "zed"? You'll find that book here.

I'm Impressed
604-684-4657; *imimpressed.ca*
A quick place to pick up a postcard for grandma and mail it, too (there's a post office inside).

Kaboodles Toy Store
604-684-0066; *kaboodlestoystore.com*
Check out the miniature B.C. ferries and old-school Sandylion stickers, art kits, and 8-foot-tall wall of toys.

Kites and Puppets
604-685-9877; *kitesandpuppets.ca*
Seriously, Einstein puppets! Also, da Vinci, Freud, Chekhov, and Emma Goldman. With stringed marionettes and kites dangling from every corner, this isn't the place for a puppetphobe.

Knotty Toys
604-683-7854; *knottytoys.com*
An all-wood-toy store with imported European, Canadian, and American wooden toys. We like the wooden name puzzles; you can either buy your child's name in stock or request a special order.

Scallywags
604-682-3364
Funky, cute clothes and shoes (particularly for girls), stuffed into a room the size of a walk-in closet. Great off-season sale racks right outside the store's main entrance.

Stay Tooned
604-689-8695
Cartoons of every color in here, from Pokemon yellow, to Thomas the Train blue, to Bob the Builder plaid — on plates, sippy cups, key chains, backpacks, and wallets. And stickers. And notebooks.

IN GRANVILLE MARKET

Beadworks
Net Loft 5-1666 Johnston Street; 604-682-2323
Inside Beadworks, you'll find a rainbow of glass waiting to be arranged into necklaces, bracelets, key chains, and hairclips. Beadworks smartly offers a small work table where you can sit, chat, and create — and the staff is nearby if you have a technical question (like "How do I get this thingy onto that thingy?"). Open daily, 10 a.m.–7 p.m.

VANCOUVER GRANVILLE ISLAND

Edie Hats
Net Loft 4-1666 Johnston Street; 604-683-4280; *ediehats.com*

Encourage your girl to channel her great-great-great-grandmother — or at least her hat — in this decadent cap shop. Vintage lamps glow over and around Victorian-inspired confections, floppy sunhats (easier than SPF 90), and antique-era boaters. The store's enthusiastic, dapper staff encourages photographs, so stop by to adore a fedora, don it, and play Bugsy for a day. Open weekdays, 10 a.m.–7 p.m.; weekends, 9:30 a.m.–7 p.m.

Original Paper-Ya
Net Loft 9-1666 Johnston Street; 604-684-2531; *paper-ya.com*

It's easy to imagine the just-logged trees happy in their new paper incarnations, as long they end up here. Paper-Ya offers sheets of paper as spectacular as fine cloth, card-making kits, paper puppets, and more. Teens can possess the coolest backpacks with Vancouver-made pins straight from Etsy, notebooks, leather wallets, and magnetic bookmarks. Open daily, 10 a.m.–7 p.m.

KITSILANO

If you're looking for an alternative to Granville, Kitsilano's West Broadway provides lots of nice little shops, pedestrian-friendly sidewalks (fewer tourists), and good dining deals for young families (with kids about ten and younger). The beach area by "Kits'" museums is pleasant for a walk; the museums themselves keep kids busy on rainy afternoons. Kitsilano would be the perfect home base for a Vancouver family vacation, if only there were more places to spend the night . . . if you check listings on VRBO (*vrbo.com*), you may be able to rent a home or condo during summer.

SLEEP
Kitsilano Cottage By the Sea $$$
1350 Walnut Street; 604-261-4951; *kitsilanocottagebythesea.com*

Heading to Vancouver with grandma and grandpa, or have a large family? You might want to look into this sweet basement rental, set in the perfect location. Within walking distance to the beach, the Maritime Museum, Vancouver Museum, and many restaurants and shops, the cottage offers three bedrooms, can sleep eight to ten people, and includes all necessities (full kitchen, washer/dryer). The owner can pull out tubs of kids' videos, toys, puzzles, and games, as well as high chairs and booster seats.

DO
Museum of Vancouver
1100 Chestnut Street; 604-736-4431; *museumofvancouver.ca*

Play with your history at the Vancouver Museum, where you can travel back in time to Vancouver's past in a series of hands-on displays and galleries. Favorites include the turn-of-the-century toys, a dress-up trunk stuffed with top hats and Victorian-era wear; a 1950s-era diner, car, and neon signs; and a 1970s hippie crash pad with a groovy couch and even groovier clothes (whether you explain how that fancy pipe was used is up to you!). Pick up the fliers featuring Vancouver landmarks through the eras; for example, the "Seek Out the 1960s and '70s in Vancouver" points out important landmarks of those decades, like the founding of Naam Restaurant and Granville Island. The Vancouver Museum is housed in the same building as the H.R. MacMillan Space Museum, which may be OK for kids who happen to be insane over outer space, and it does offer educational star shows — but I prefer to spend my money at the Vancouver Museum. Adults/$11; youth (5–17) $7; children (younger than 5)/free; family/$32. Open daily, 10 a.m.–5 p.m. (Thursdays until 8 p.m.); closed Mondays in winter.

Vancouver Maritime Museum
1905 Ogden Avenue; 604-257-8300; *vancouvermaritimemuseum.com*
My favorite maritime museum in all of the Northwest, the Vancouver Maritime Museum makes boats interesting to people who don't typically love boats (like me). Walk onto the RCMP Arctic schooner *St. Roch* and climb a scary ladder to visit the captain's quarters, try on Inuit sunglasses, find out about unsavory pirates, or drive a helicopter. Phew. And that's before you even reach the well-stocked children's playroom, which provides a telescope, educational drawers for exploration and play, plus dress-up gear. Afterwards, head outside to Vanier Park. You'll see wonderful views of downtown Vancouver, along with perfect air currents for flying kites. A great spot for photos. Adults/$10; youth (6–19) and seniors/$7.50; children/free; family/$25. Open daily, 10 a.m.–5 p.m. Winter hours: Tuesday–Saturday, 10 a.m.–5 p.m.; Sunday, noon–5 p.m.

PLAY
Kitsilano Beach and Pool
2305 Cornwall Avenue; 604-731-0011;
vancouver.ca/parks/rec/beaches/kitsb.htm
Only a thin strip of concrete (and a fence) separates the gray English Bay from the bright-blue Kitsilano Pool, Canada's longest pool. The 137-meter saltwater pool features three slides, 25-degree C (77-degree F) water, and a gentle, shallow end for little ones. This pool has little shade, so bring an umbrella.

The sandy beach is perfect for sandcastles or picnics, and a playground occupies kids on cooler days. It's wonderful to look out at the bay and count the sailboats, which look like tiny cut-paper triangles. Pool admission: adults/$5.15; teens (13–18)/$3.60; children (5–12)/$2.60. Beach is open year-round; pool is open mid-May through mid-September; check Web site for details.

EAT
East Is East $$–$$$
3243 W. Broadway; 604-734-5881; *eastiseast.ca*
Sit at heavy wooden tables and dig into exotic Indian-style wraps on stainless steel plates. Kids like sitting against pillow-packed benches and downing smoothies, shakes, and yogurt lassis. For dessert, try the pistachio, cardamom, rosewater, and ice cream shake. Open daily, 11 a.m.–10 p.m.

The Noodle Box $-$$

1867 W. Fourth Avenue; 604-734-1310; *thenoodlebox.net*
This is one of my favorite spots to catch a quick meal. The restaurant's high ceilings and kitchen clatter absorb most kid sounds, but you can also wait on a bench for your to-go order and salivate over other diners' noodles. Sit on stools facing Fourth or along long wall benches. Sauces are spot on; you select from seven different spice levels (the no-heat level is just right for little ones), or you can just order a kids' meal. If you choose heat level seven, call me when your mouth heals. Open daily, 11:30 a.m.–9 p.m., Friday until 10 p.m.

Rocky Mountain Flatbread Company $$

1876 W. First Avenue; 604-730-0321; *rockymountainflatbread.ca*
Inside the warm red walls of this Kits eatery, you'll find flatbread-style pizzas, pastas, and salads made with local and organic ingredients. While you wait (not long) for your pizza, kids can play in the wooden toy kitchen, cooking up a storm with felt veggies and pots and pans. And on Sundays, kids can truly go pro: The staff takes kids into the back to top their own pizzas. Open daily, 11:30 a.m.–9:30 p.m., Friday and Saturday until 10 p.m.

Serano Greek Pastry $

3185 W. Broadway; 604-739-3181
Vivid pink, purple, and green meringue cookies, plus polysyllabic pastries featuring layers of phyllo, cream, and sugar. Excellent grab 'n' go spanakopita (a pie of spinach, feta, and phyllo). Get here by noon for the best selection, particularly on weekends. Open Monday–Saturday, 9:30 a.m.–6 p.m.; Sunday, noon–6 p.m.

Solly's Bagelry $

2873 W. Broadway; 604-738-2121; *sollysbagels.com*
Amazing N.Y.C.-style bagels, boiled, then topped with a shmear. Need more reasons to go? How about fill-you-to-the-brim matzoh ball soup, cinnamon buns, or a sandwich? Beware of the long lines that can form outside the door, and be ready to eat on the run if there's no place left to sit inside. But don't worry — it's that good and absolutely worth it. Open Monday–Saturday, 7:30 a.m.–6 p.m.; Sunday, 7 a.m.–5 p.m.

Sophie's Cosmic Café $

2095 W. Fourth Avenue; 604-732-6810; *sophiescosmiccafe.com*
Get your pancakes with a helping of irony on top. The giant spoon and fork at Sophie's front door should tell you everything you need to know. Inside, it's a crazy kitschy world, with nearly every surface of the interior covered with figurines and ephemera from the '50s through the '80s. For kids, it's fun to look around or read one of Sophie's collections of kids' books while waiting for your helping of thick-cut toast, buttermilk pancakes, or yogurt-topped Belgian waffles. A warning: This is one of *the* places to go in Vancouver for breakfast, so there may be a line. Go early or be prepared to wait a very, very long time. Open daily, 8 a.m.–8 p.m.

VANCOUVER KITSILANO

Zakkushi $$

1833 W. Fourth Avenue; 604-730-9844; *zakkushi.com*
Head into this tiny izakaya, or Japanese small-plates pub. Kids love removing their shoes and sitting on benches by the tabletop fountain, where adventurous eaters (deep-fried squid with plum mayo) and picky ones (sauced-up meat skewers) get their fill. (Two other locations: 823 Denman Street and 4075 Main Street). Open 5:30–11:30 p.m. daily.

SHOP

3H Craftworks Society

2208 W. Fourth Avenue; 604-736-2113; *3hcraftworks.com*
Shop here and feel good about your purchases; they're designed and made locally by physically or mentally challenged adults. Don't miss the sock-monkey wall, finger puppets, felt picture books, kids' clothing, and delightful felt stories (depicting classic picture books and nursery rhymes, for use on felt boards). You'll definitely recognize your child's favorite tale here, such as *If You Give a Mouse a Cookie* or *Goldilocks*. It's authentic and earnest here, refreshingly free of irony and snobbishness. Beyond cool. Open Monday–Friday, 10 a.m.–6 p.m.; Saturday and Sunday, 10 a.m.–5 p.m.

Babes on Fourth

2354 W. Fourth Avenue; 604-739-9870
Contemporary and comfortable are key at this clothing shop serving ages newborn–twelve. There are excellent sales here; don't miss the back room, where you'll find items as much as (and sometimes more than) 50 percent off the original prices on French and Canadian brands. The play corner with toys keeps very little ones entertained, while older kids will appreciate the big-top-tent-style dressing room. Open Monday–Saturday, 10 a.m.–6 p.m.; Sunday, noon–5 p.m.

Candy Aisle

2083 W. Fourth Avenue; 604-739-3330; *candyaisle.com*
Right inside the door, this sweets shop boasts 1,000 reasons why locals voted it "best candy store." And it certainly feels like there are more than 1,000 varieties of candy inside. Whirl the candy powder machine to make your own powder tube, create a grab bag from the mix 'n' match wall or Jelly Belly bins, and seek out a favorite Brit bar. For your hard-to-please teens, see if a box full of Crick-ettes won't spark an "Ew, gross" reaction. Open Sunday–Wednesday, 10 a.m.–9 p.m.; Thursday–Saturday, 10 a.m.–10 p.m.

The Comicshop

2089 W. Fourth Avenue; 604-738-8122; *thecomicshop.ca*
Pick up a quick-read comic (e.g., "Archie") to entertain the kids while you wait for your food at Sophie's, up the street. Right inside the door, you'll find a rack of all-ages choices, plus a red rocket holding *Tintin* books. The Comicshop also stocks vintage *Mad* magazines and newspaper favorites. Open Monday–Tuesday, Thursday, 11 a.m.–6 p.m.; Wednesday, 11 a.m.–7 p.m.; Friday, 11 a.m.–8 p.m.; Saturday, 10 a.m.–6 p.m.; Sunday, noon–6 p.m.

Crocodile

2156 W. Fourth Avenue; 604-730-0232; *crocodilebaby.com*
If you've forgotten a key item at home for your baby or toddler, check out Crocodile's extensive collection of organic, sustainable, and conventional kids' gear. From furniture to feeding utensils, this store offers a good variety of items (albeit toward the posh end). Open Monday–Saturday, 10 a.m.–6 p.m.; Sunday, 11 a.m.–5 p.m.

Does Your Mother Know?

2139 W. Fourth Avenue; 604-730-1110
Does Your Mother Know . . . that you have a zillion magazines stashed inside this store? U.S., Canadian, British . . . worldwide! . . . glossy reading material piled into long aisles. This place is great for fashion-obsessed (or foreign-language-learning) tweens and teens. Open Monday–Saturday, 10 a.m.–9 p.m.; Sunday, 11 a.m.–7 p.m.

Duthie Books

2239 W. Fourth Avenue; 604-732-5344; *duthiebooks.com*
Every Northwest city in the U.S. and Canada has its shining knight of indie bookstores, and this is Vancouver's. Books for adults, books for kids, books for readers, and books for non-readers — Duthie has it all. The knowledgeable, friendly staff wants to make you happy — ask a question! Open Monday–Friday, 9 a.m.–9 p.m.; Saturday, 9 a.m.–6 p.m.; Sunday, 10 a.m.–6 p.m.; holidays, 11 a.m.–5 p.m.

Grand Prix Hobbies

3038 W. Broadway; 604-733-7114; *grandprixhobbies.ca*
Classic craft kits, paints, balsawood planes, and other busy stuff; this store is fine for a walk-by browse, if your kids enjoy hobbyist pastimes. Open Monday–Saturday, 9 a.m.–6 p.m.; Sunday, 10 a.m.–5 p.m.

Gum Drops

2029 W. Fourth Avenue; 604-733-1037; *gumdrops.ca*
A rainy-day store, as colorful as its name suggests, this shop provides a wide assortment of rain gear. A candy-colored, diverse selection of umbrellas, coats, rain hats, and puddle-worthy boots for kids and adults — including animal-themed and sprightly attire — may make you actually *wish* for rainy days. Open Monday–Saturday, 10 a.m.–6 p.m.; Sunday, noon–5 p.m.

Hip Baby

2110 W. Fourth Avenue; 604-736-8020; *hipbaby.com*
Here, you'll find hundreds of everyday and unique items focusing on that first year of life, but with an organic and sustainable twist. Hip Baby has long been a Kits institution, but new owners Jen Maccormac and Michael Ziff have searched the world for cool new stuff, such as homemade dolls from Montreal and top-quality, easy-to-use cloth diapers. Check out the store's line of Fig Organic clothing. Open Monday–Wednesday, 10 a.m.–6 p.m.; Thursday–Saturday, 10 a.m.–7 p.m.; Sunday, 11 a.m.–6 p.m.

VANCOUVER
KITSILANO

Just Imagine Fun Clothing

3060 W. Broadway; 604-222-3523; *dressups.com*

Who needs Halloween or Purim as a reason to dress up? Wear your party clothes year-round with Just Imagine's fun costumes, which include minimal scary stuff (good for younger ones). The staff is incredibly helpful and fun loving. Visit the "Treasure Box" for costume hats costing less than $10. Open Monday–Saturday, 10 a.m.–6 p.m.; Sunday, noon–5 p.m.

Kidsbooks

3083 W. Broadway; 604-738-5335; *kidsbooks.ca*

This store is one of the very best children's bookstores I've ever seen, and worth a trip to W. Broadway. The incredibly helpful, friendly staff assists you (or your child) in locating the perfect novel, picture book, comic, or nonfiction masterpiece. Don't miss the store's complete Djecco sticker and paint-by-number collections — incredibly cute and sure to become pop masterpieces. Check out the excellent section focused on Canadian and First Nation titles, or just sit in one of the bookstore's cozy red chairs. Children's book authors often come through town, so check the Web site to see if one of your family's favorites is scheduled. Open Monday–Thursday and Saturday, 9:30 a.m.–6 p.m.; Friday, 9:30 a.m.–9 p.m.; Sunday, 11 a.m.–6 p.m.

Stepback

3026 W. Broadway; 604-731-7525; *stepback.ca*

If you've been looking for a distinctive, unique piece to add to your child's room, this is one of the best places to find it. The store stocks incredible furnishings with 1940s to '60s sensibility, in a mix of vintage and new. Find cool old-fashioned blocks, milk-glass cups, school readers, plus wall décor, such as mirrors and quaint old alphabet cards. The owners will even craft custom furniture on request. Head to the back to check out the sale room if you're on a budget, although most pieces are reasonably priced. Open Tuesday–Saturday, 10 a.m.–6 p.m.; Sunday, noon–5 p.m.

Toy Jungle

3002 W. Broadway; 604-738-4322; *toyjungle.ca*

This tropical treasure trove of puzzles, art supplies, building toys, dolls, and games will please children of all ages. The left rear corner of the store contains an impressive train table, a castle, numerous toddlers, and weary parents sitting on benches. Open Monday–Thursday, Saturday, 9:30 a.m.–6 p.m.; Friday, 9:30 a.m.–9 p.m.; Sunday, 11 a.m.–5 p.m.

VANCOUVER KITSILANO

RILEY PARK

This up-and-coming neighborhood offers plenty for families that think they've seen everything in Vancouver. Hey, rents are less expensive over here, so you'll find lots of small, locally owned businesses with art, books, coffee, toys, and completely different merchandise (don't miss my favorite, Regional Assembly of Text, page 110).

DO
Nat Bailey Stadium
4601 Ontario Street; 604-872-5232; *canadiansbaseball.com*
Vancouver families flock to this stadium to watch Vancouver's own Canadians baseball team. Don't expect a big, fancy experience. This is simple, no-frills fun, with hot dogs and pop, but there is a children's play area for antsy kids. Check Web site for game times and prices.

PLAY
Queen Elizabeth Park
Play in this park's seventy-jet fountain, run down floral-accented paths, or catch a breathtaking view of the mountains that ring Vancouver. Queen Elizabeth Park's peak is the highest point above sea level in Vancouver. The rehabilitated Quarry Gardens remind me of a scaled-down version of Victoria's Butchart Gardens.

EAT
Quejo's Cheesebuns $
4129 Main Street; 604-420-0832; *quejos.com*
The words "gluten free" don't really get my salivary glands going, but Quejo's uses a traditional Brazilian recipe to make manioc-flour buns with add-ins like jalapeños, cheese, and sun-dried tomatoes to make excellent, chewy, and unusual snacks. Those with gluten, wheat, and dairy sensitivities are all catered to equally, along with the rest of us. Open Monday–Saturday, 10 a.m.–6 p.m.; Sunday and holidays, 11 a.m.–5 p.m.

Splitz Grill $
4242 Main Street; 604-875-9711; *splitzgrill.com*
With burgers this great, it's no wonder that Splitz decided to build a second location (the first is a tiny 700-square-foot burger shack at Whistler). Children can get a Splitz Kids, which comes with burger, fries, and drink. You'll be able to choose from more than twenty free condiments to add to your burger, including sauerkraut, pickled banana peppers, hummus, tzaziki — or just plain ol' relish. The interior is a rehash of the '50s burger-style motif, but the big-screen television may keep hungry kids distracted while waiting. Open Sunday–Thursday, 11:30 a.m.–9 p.m.; Friday and Saturday, 11:30 a.m.–10 p.m.

Sun Sui Wah $–$$
3888 Main Street; 604-872-8822; *sunsuiwah.com*
Generations of Vancouverites flock to dim sum every Sunday at this Main Street institution. Upstairs in the wide, mirrored room, you can order from menus or choose from the bamboo dishes on rolling carts. Focus is on Cantonese seafood cuisine, with seafood so fresh it's still swimming in tanks before it arrives at your table. Open daily for lunch, 10 a.m.–3 p.m.; dinner, 5–10:30 p.m.

VANCOUVER
RILEY PARK

Zipang Sushi $

3710 Main Street; 604-708-1667

In a city of cheap sushi of dubious quality, this joint shines. Authentic offerings such as pan-grilled octopus, along with West Coast–style B.C. wild sockeye, are on offer here. There are few seats in the mostly mod restaurant, so you may want to gather your rolls and roll down to Edward Park (one block east of Main Street at Sophia Street and E. Twenty-first Avenue) for a picnic. Open Tuesday–Sunday for lunch, 11:30 a.m.–3 p.m.; dinner, 5 p.m.–10 p.m. Closed Monday.

SHOP

Beansprouts

4305 Main Street; 604-871-9782; *beansprouts.ca*

Smart parents shop here for preloved, upscale children's clothing and shoes sizes 0–6, or B.C.-made dolls and apparel for birthday gifts. Beansprouts also sells new clothes, mostly in smaller sizes. The play corner keeps smaller kids busy for a short while with vintage toys and wood puzzles. Open daily, 11 a.m.–6 p.m.

Lucky's Comics

3972 Main Street; 604-875-9858; *luckys.ca*

A veritable hobbit hole of comics, 'zines, graphic novels, and quirky books. The staff keeps some Pokemon cards behind the shoebox-size desk. Open Monday–Saturday, noon–6 p.m.; Sunday, noon–5 p.m.

Once Upon a Huckleberry Bush

4387 Main Street; 604-876-4010; *huckleberrychildrensbooks.com*

This small bookstore's owner welcomes curious browsers with a smile and open arms — and if you're lucky, a bilingual story time. Call and ask about weekly story times, author signings, and other fun events. Open Monday–Saturday, 10 a.m.–6 p.m.; Sunday, 11 a.m.–5 p.m.

The Regional Assembly of Text

3934 Main Street; 604-877-2247; *assemblyoftext.com*

This is one of my favorite stores in our region. Regional Assembly is devoted to that vanishing classic: old-fashioned type. Kids can make their own mini-buttons with the typewriter (!) and pens, or browse the children's toys (heavily emphasizing the alphabet), which include B.C.-made puzzles, chalkboards, and fabric letters. Open Monday–Saturday, 11 a.m.–6 p.m.; Sunday, noon–5 p.m.

Urban Source

3126 Main Street; 604-875-1611; *urbansource.bc.ca*

My daughter's school refers to it as "scrounge art" — Urban Source collects items from dozens of industries, then organizes them into bins and baskets. Bring the kids in and see how the staff turns eye-popping papers, tiles, and test tubes into fanciful mobiles, dragonflies, and octopi. A great way to stimulate creativity. Open Monday–Saturday, 10 a.m.–5:30 p.m.; Sunday, 11 a.m.–5 p.m.

VANCOUVER RILEY PARK

Voltage
4346 Main Street; 604-709-8214; *voltageland.com/shop*
Character-based vinyl and "magic box" Japanese toys, including Kid Robot and Tokidoki. Teens jam this store, trying on character-themed tees and buying cool purses and school bags. Open Tuesday, Wednesday, Saturday, and Sunday, noon–6 p.m.; Thursday and Friday, noon–8 p.m.

CHINATOWN

Vancouver's Chinatown is the third largest in North America. Storefronts selling fresh spices, dried fish, exotic fruits, and medicinal herbs pack the narrow, busy sidewalks, and the musky aroma of mushrooms mingles with the scent of dried fish and fresh fruit. You'll also see plenty for kids here, including stores selling licensed merchandise (in other words, this is a very inexpensive place to buy Hello Kitty erasers). We like to check out new stickers and toys, walk to a bakery to get well-priced buns, cookies, and tarts, then pick up deals in the flea markets (housed inside old buildings; look for the signs). Pick out jade jewelry, silken slippers, and . . . dried eel.

Bring cash to Chinatown, as many mom 'n' pop merchants don't want to deal with credit or debit cards. And be aware that you are only a few blocks from "Sketchville" (the intersection of Hastings and Main), so you may see some gritty urban dwellers here; just give them a wide berth and don't worry too much. In summer, you'll probably have more to fear from the tourist hordes trampling you. However, if you've brought a car, it's worth staking out a parking spot, so you don't have to make the haul from downtown on foot or by bus.

DO

Chinatown Night Market
Keefer and Main streets (between Main and Columbia streets); *vcma.shawbiz.ca/home_e.htm*
Night markets are common throughout the world, particularly in locales where the evening offers cool respite to daytime's high temperatures. While Vancouver isn't tropical, it does play host to the Chinatown Night Market, where kids can have their fill of sweet, salty, and sticky street food, and watch musical, martial arts, and dance acts. Open May–September: Friday–Sunday, 6:30–11 p.m.

Dr. Sun Yat-sen Classical Garden
578 Carrall Street; 604-662-3207; *vancouverchinesegarden.com*
This garden is especially nice for calmer children, who can restrain themselves from running through the quiet, peaceful courtyard, over the intricately carved bridges, and through the palatial-style interiors. Look for the small turtles and flitting dragonflies in the pond during summer; after a fresh snowfall, the garden feels magical. If the kids seem a little too wound up for the garden, you can visit the landscaped park — with a pagoda — right next door for

free. Adults/$10; children younger than 5/free; students/$8; family (two adults, two children younger than 18)/$24. Hours vary by season; check the Web site for details.

San Lee Enterprises
267 Keefer Street; 604-688-1383

While the scent outside might startle you, don't be too concerned; it's just the durians, the notoriously nasty-smelling fruit of Southeast Asia. San Lee offers a smorgasbord of exotic fruit, including fiery rambutan and boulder-sized jackfruit. A daring store for adventurous fruit-loving kids. Open daily, 9 a.m.–6 p.m.

EAT

The Boss Bakery and Restaurant $–$$
532 Main Street; 604-683-3860

You probably won't see Bruce Springsteen here, but visit the steamy and sweet dessert cases anyway! Try a red bean cake, winter melon cake, egg tart, a century egg puff, coconut tart, or melon bun. You just can't lose. Open daily, 7 a.m.–7 p.m.

Floata Seafood $–$$
180 Keefer Street; 604-602-0368; *floata.com*

With seats for more than 1,000, this is no small-scale dim sum operation. Take your pick from rolling trolleys stacked with bamboo steamers of Cantonese specialties (which may or may not include intestines) or order from the menu, but bring your sense of adventure. Less-than-adventurous kids (or adults) can stick to rice or pastries. Open daily, 8:30 a.m.–10 p.m.

Maxim's Bakery $
257 Keefer Street; 604-688-6281

You'll find even more delicious choices of custard buns, tropical-fruit-filled cakes, and crumbly cookies at Maxim's. Just follow the long line of grandmas out the door and stake your place in line. Open daily, 8 a.m.–7 p.m.

SHOP

Novelty Gifts Express Limited
114 E. Pender Street; 604-632-3893

My favorite Chinatown trinket shop, Novelty Gifts stocks tons of Snoopy, Miyazake, Pokemon, Hello Kitty, and other anime-style pop-icon goodies. Check out the impressive lite-rock-playing robot (in a cage, of course — one can never be too safe) at the store's rear. You can pick up teeny-tiny stickers or toddler-size stuffed animals, depending on how much room you've got left in your suitcase. The definitive Northwest stop for your next binge buy of tiny birthday souvenirs or a supersized Totoro. Open Monday–Saturday, 10:30 a.m.–6 p.m.; Sunday, 10:30 a.m.–5:30 p.m.

VANCOUVER CHINATOWN

THE DRIVE

Commercial Avenue, or "The Drive," has gone through multiple transformations over the past fifty years. Starting out as an Italian enclave, the neighborhood morphed into hippieville in the late '60s and early '70s. Many of the Italian coffee shops, vegan restaurants, and patchouli-scented shops still flourish. But families have been moving in, so you'll also see toy stores, playgrounds, and restaurants geared especially toward families. The Drive is good for exploration at every age: Tots will love the gelato, restaurants with play areas, and playgrounds; older kids will enjoy the trinket shops; and teens may break your budget in the secondhand clothing stores. Find more information at *thedrive.ca.*

PLAY

Victoria Park

1415 Victoria Drive; 604-257-8400; *vancouver.ca*

While you may first head for Grandview Park, right at Commercial Drive and Charles Street, this park is better — newly redeveloped with a fresh playground, a sandbox, and lots of local families. Grassy spaces and picnic tables provide amazing vantage points for watching a bocce ball game.

EAT

Café Deux Soleils $–$$

2096 Commercial Avenue; 604-254-1195; *cafedeuxsoleils.com*

In this bright, light-filled room with wooden tables and chairs, you'll find hung-over bohemians, fussy kids, hungry teens, and huge plates of vegetarian food. Go at breakfast and get a plate of incredibly filling omelet or tofu scramble for less than $7; you probably won't need to eat again until midafternoon. Kids tend to go a little nuts in here with all the noise, but on the other hand, all the noise means they can go a little nuts. Open daily, 8 a.m.–midnight.

Gelateria Dolce Amore $

1590 Commercial Avenue; 604-258-0006; *gelateriadolceamore.com*

Homemade gelato in a teeny Little Italy gelateria. Best bet: Pick up your vanilla, chocolate, or pistachio gelato and walk to Victoria Park. Open daily, noon–9 p.m.

The Little Nest $–$$

1716 Charles Street; 604-251-9994; *littlenest.ca*

Why didn't I think of this? Soothing '60s retro touches, such as vintage high chairs and mint-green walls. High-quality organic sandwiches and fruit "fries" with jam "ketchup" for the kids. No nasty, wilted lettuce here or subpar adult meals. The boisterous play area keeps kids busy while parents chat. The only downside? This place is never quiet, and you'll have to wait for one of the old-school couches or tables. But if you have young children, this is a must-do. Open Tuesday–Sunday, 9 a.m.–4 p.m. (kitchen closes at 3 p.m.).

Pane Vero $

952 Commercial Avenue; 604-216-3338; *panevero.com*
The store's name means "true bread" in Italian; this is truly a great stop for families. Pull up a high chair and bite into one of Pane's sandwiches (bread made on site) or soups (also made on site). And of course, here you'll find that kid mainstay, mac 'n' cheese. Very casual and informal, this restaurant works well, particularly if The Little Nest (page 113) is too crazy or your kids are older. Open Monday–Friday, 7 a.m.–5:30 p.m.; Saturday and Sunday, 8 a.m.–5:30 p.m.

Roundel Café $–$$

2465 E. Hastings Street; 604-253-2522
This child-friendly diner is not on Commercial Avenue, but up the street on the fun multicultural jumble of East Hastings. What makes it child friendly? A few crayons, a coloring book or two — and the genuinely welcoming attitudes of the café's owners. It doesn't hurt that Roundel's food is truly top quality. Freshness is infused in the omelets, pancakes, and Mexican-style breakfast goods. Open Saturday–Wednesday, 9 a.m.–4 p.m.; Thursday and Friday, 9 a.m.–9 p.m.

SHOP

Dandelion Kids

1206 Commercial Avenue; 604-676-1862; *dandelionkids.ca*
It's obvious that owners Maria and Stefanie carefully select everything inside this contemporary urban-baby store. Inside, you'll find boho luxe blankets, knit cupcakes, and fanciful furniture (the beanbag chairs are my favorite). The edgy, casual kids' clothes and shoes include brands such as GLUG, Katvig, and Vans; Dandelion also puts out private-label organic blankets and tees. Open Monday–Saturday, 10 a.m.–6 p.m.; Sunday, 11 a.m.–6 p.m.

It's All Fun & Games

1308 Commercial Avenue; 604-253-6727
Just around the corner from The Little Nest, this toy store provides plenty of opportunities to put your eye out (just kidding!). In reality, items from the shop's collection of basics (balls, figurines, trucks) are great to buy for play in Victoria Park, which is just down the street. Open Monday–Saturday, 10 a.m.–6 p.m.; Sunday, 11 a.m.–5 p.m.

Room For 2

1409 Commercial Avenue; 604-255-0508; *roomfor2.ca*
Room For 2's refreshingly no-nonsense attitude draws busy moms-to-be looking for nursing bras, cloth diapers, infant clothing, toys, and baby carriers. But owner Lorena Battistel also stocks unique items, such as belly-casting kits, tummy-support bands, and baby hair clips. If you're a breastfeeding mom, Room For 2's staff will help you find a quiet place to nurse your baby. Open Monday–Saturday, 10 a.m.–5:30 p.m.; Sunday, noon–5 p.m.

Urban Empire

1108 Commercial Avenue; 604-254-4700; *urbanempire.ca*
This store was named "Vancouver's best kitsch emporium" by *The Georgia Straight* newspaper, and it's hard to disagree. Full of novel, goofy gifts and cards; best for older kids or teens with an offbeat sense of humor. Open Monday–Saturday, 11 a.m.–5:30 p.m.; Sunday, noon–5 p.m.

VANCOUVER THE DRIVE

AROUND VANCOUVER

While many of these activities and restaurants don't fit neatly into any one neighborhood, they're all fabulous. VanDusen is great in spring, summer, and fall; Burnaby Village is essential for kids enamored by vintage playthings; and Lonsdale Quay's boat ride and shopping offer a lovely escape on rainy days. But Vancouver's true difference lies in those North Vancouver mountains; a quick zip out of the city, and you're playing in snow or hiking through wildflowers.

If you're heading north by car, avoid crossing the Lion's Gate Bridge during rush hours (weekdays, 7–9 a.m. and 4–8 p.m.) or be prepared for waits of as long as an hour. Lion's Gate bottlenecks traffic through Stanley Park into the downtown core and North Van.

DO

If you've forgotten some outdoor equipment at home and want to take advantage of Vancouver's nearby winter or summer attractions, head over to E. Broadway between Cambie and Main, where you'll find Mountain Equipment Co-op (*mec.ca*) and a host of used and new skiing, biking, snowboard, and hiking stores.

Burnaby Village Museum

6501 Deer Lake Avenue; 604-293-6500; *burnabyvillagemuseum.ca*

If you have a boy or girl who's fascinated by history (think American Girls), take them to this historical re-creation of early-twentieth-century West Coast life. Walk into an old schoolhouse and get a lesson, listen as a self-playing piano cranks out a plunky tune, watch a movie in the theater, churn butter, play with old-fashioned toys, or watch a blacksmith fashion a horseshoe. Top it all off with an ice cream cone (real and modern-day) at the Home Bakery. Winter brings a Christmas theme, and families love Halloween for mildly scary thrills. Caveat: Burnaby appears close to Vancouver on a map, but the drive, depending upon red lights and traffic, can take anywhere from a half-hour to an hour. Bring snacks. Nevertheless, the town is unparalleled in the Northwest for making history real, hands on, and fun. Bring a few extra loonies (the Canadian $1 coin) for the 1912 C.W. Parker Carousel. Adults/$12; teens (13–18)/$9; children (6–12)/$6; younger than 5/free; carousel ride/$2. Open May 2–September 7: Tuesday–Sunday, 11 a.m.–4:30 p.m. (later in October for the "Haunted Village"). December hours vary.

Capilano Suspension Bridge

3735 Capilano Road; 604-985-7474; *capbridge.com*

Forget the stories. The plank-and-steel-cable bridge, 230 feet above the Capilano Canyon, isn't too much to handle, even for a scaredy-cat mom like me. Once you cross the canyon, you delve into children's activities, First Nations history and totem poles, and the "Treetops Adventure," my favorite area. The Treetops Adventure allows you to walk 650 feet on cable bridges, suspended midway up old-growth rainforest trunks. Looking up or down is a thrill, and gives you a bird's-eye view of the forest floor. Overall, not great for strollers or tots just learning to walk, but very good for older kids and babes in carriers. We like going shortly before dusk, when most of the big tour buses have returned home for dinner. It's not cheap, so you might try Lynn Canyon as a less expensive alternative until you know whether your kids like it. Adults/$27.95; teens (13–16)/$18.75; children (6–12)/$10; younger than 6/free. Generally open 9 a.m.–dusk year-round (check Web site); open 5–9 p.m. during winter holiday season in late December for evening lights.

Cypress Mountain

6000 Cypress Bowl Road; 604-926-5612 (main switchboard); 604-419-SNOW (7669) (conditions and info); *cypressmountain.com*
Here you'll find snowtubing, snowshoeing, alpine, and cross-country skiing for families. Don snowshoes or Nordic skis and head through forested trails to Hollyburn Lodge, a 1926 fairy-tale-like place where you'll find soups, breads, and drinks. As with Grouse Mountain, get here very, very early (check the Web site and arrive shortly before opening) to pick up your rentals, before the crowds pack the parking lot. Night skiing available on 52 runs with nine lifts. In summer, enjoy breezy hiking through wildflower-carpeted meadows. In winter, ask about the lodge's family-friendly Saturday music nights. Fees vary, from hiking (free) to snowshoeing ($9) to lift tickets ($60/full day). Hours vary by season and condition; check Web site for current info.

Grouse Mountain

6400 Nancy Greene Way; 604-980-9311; *grousemountain.com*
This is how Vancouverites have all other Northwesterners beat. Within five minutes of downtown, Grouse Mountain efficiently whisks skiers to the top of snow-covered Grouse Mountain for alpine skiing. Younger kids can take a motorized sleigh ride (not as cool as it sounds), go ice-skating, walk through trees in snowshoes, or just warm up in the lodge (which serves excellent chili and hamburgers). In summer, families flock here for hiking on the Grouse Grind, to visit grizzlies at the Refuge for Endangered Wildlife, or to go on North America's largest aerial tramway, the Skyride, for spectacular views of Vancouver. Adults/$37.95; youth (13–18)/$22.95; children (5–12)/$13.95; younger than 4/free. The Skyride is open daily, 8:45 a.m.–10 p.m.

Lonsdale Quay Market

123 Carrie Cates Court; 604-985-6261; *lonsdalequay.com*
The less famous cousin market of Granville, Lonsdale is worth visiting on a slow day, if only for the catamaran ride that presents you with deluxe views of downtown Vancouver. Pick up the catamaran ferry Seabus at Waterfront Terminal (*translink.ca*), to take the twelve-minute ride to Lonsdale Quay for lunch. Visit the small Kids Alley, where kids can go in a ball pit, get a haircut, try on clothing, or buy a toy. No car necessary for this little afternoon adventure. Open daily, 9 a.m.–7 p.m.

Lynn Canyon

3663 Park Road; 604-990-3755; *dnv.org/ecology/index.htm*
A shorter and less crowded version of Capilano, without the steep heights or prices. The Lynn Canyon Ecology Centre presents year-round learning opportunities, and if you've got kids who need to run off steam, hiking trails provide ample opportunity. Check the Web site and sign up for naturalist-guided hikes exploring the rainforest's flora and fauna. Suggested donation/$2. Canyon: generally open daily at 7 a.m. Ecology Centre: June–September: open daily, 10 a.m.–5 p.m. October–May: Monday–Friday, 10 a.m.–5 p.m. Saturday and Sunday, noon–4 p.m.

Playland at the PNE

2901 E. Hastings Street; 604-253-2311; *pne.ca/playland*
If you drive past Commercial Avenue, you'll undoubtedly pass by Playland, and your eagle-eyed kids will definitely spot it first. Ride a wooden roller coaster, get wet in a open-air flume ride, climb aboard the sickening "Hellevator," or just drive a mini-car (more my style, but unfortunately only available for little kids). If you won't be going to any of the county fairs this year in your own hometown, or you enjoy stomach-churning rides (goodbye, lunch!), this is a good place to experience the action. More than 48 inches tall/$29.95; less than 48 inches tall/$19.95, 3 years and younger/free; buy online to save. Open late April–late September; hours vary.

PLAY

VanDusen Garden

5251 Oak Street; 604-878-9274; *vandusengarden.org*
An ever-changing garden wonderland of paths that wind through flowers, shrubs, grassy lawns, lakes, and mazes, the garden features impeccable landscaping for appreciative adults and room to roam for implacable kids. Open daily, hours vary (check Web site). Admission April–September: adults/$8.85; youth (13–18)/$6.50; children (6–12)/$4.70; family/$19.50. October–March: adults/$6.50; youth (13–18) $4.70; children (6–12)/$3.40; family/$13.

EAT

Rhizome $-$$

317 E. Broadway; 604-872-3166; *rhizomecafe.ca*
If Ani DiFranco came to Vancouver, she'd eat here. The street outside is rather bleak, but Rhizome's homey interior invites you to stay awhile. Vinyl booths and wooden chairs welcome all comers, whether here to dish into pay-as-you-wish lentil soup, attend an open-mike show, or enjoy a fabulous, healthy meal served by incredibly kind employees. There's even an affordable baby disco party once a month. Open Tuesday–Thursday, 11 a.m.–10 p.m.; Friday, 11 a.m.–midnight; Saturday, 10 a.m.–midnight; Sunday, 10 a.m.–9 p.m. Closed Monday.

getaway
WHISTLER

The name alone inspires thoughts of pure romance; Whistler has been a couples' getaway for decades. In winter, fine powder drifts off dramatic mountains, and gondolas whisk riders up and down the slopes; in summer, wildflowers replace snow, and hiking and biking become warm-weather favorites.

But Whistler is also the perfect winter getaway with kids. After all, once you park your car, the village's family-friendly restaurants, shops, and activities are totally walkable via pedestrian-only streets. Whistler isn't a big-box resort; most of the village's stores and restaurants are independently owned, so you can feel good about supporting the local economy. And there's always something going on; to find kid-friendly fun while you're in town, check out Whistler4Kids (*whistler4kids.com*).

In short, Whistler is a Euro-style escape within driving distance for those of us who can't afford — or mentally cope with — going to Europe with kids.

GETTING THERE

Car: Year-round, you'll travel by the Sea to Sky Highway (B.C. 99), an appropriately named two-and-a-half-hour drive of gorges, islands, and peaks. In fall, winter, and spring, watch for waterfalls and incredible snow-dusted scenery; in summer, admire the jewel-like tones of water, valleys, and mountains. If construction or traffic interfere, the drive may take much longer than two and a half hours.

Train: Families may want to take advantage of the Whistler Mountaineer (*whistlermountaineer.com*), which runs from Vancouver May through October. After all, once you get to Whistler, you may not need a car; almost everything you want to do is within walking distance. The trip takes roughly four or five hours, door to door, and prices start at $200 round trip per adult, $109 round trip per child.

Bus: The Whistler Express Bus (*whistler.com/shuttle*) takes riders from downtown Vancouver hotels or the airport to Whistler. And once you're in town, avoid using a car altogether by using the Whistler Transit System (*busonline.ca/regions/whi*).

SLEEP

Allura Direct $-$$$

604-707-6700 or 866-425-5872; *alluradirect.com/whistler*

Condos and kids are a great combination — you'll get more space than you'll find in a hotel, plus a kitchen and dining facilities. *Alluradirect.com* offers condos for all budgets, with a variety of extras, including fireplaces and hot tubs. On the Web site, there are tips for sifting through your options; once you've decided, you can book directly with the owner. You can also email the site's managers, and they'll provide a personalized response.

Sundial Boutique Hotel $$-$$$

4340 Sundial Crescent; 604-932-2321 or 800-661-2321; *sundialhotel.com*

If I could choose any place to stay (and wasn't limited by my budget), I'd go with one of the Sundial's forty-nine all-suite rooms. Compared to many hotels in the area, Sundial's upscale rooms feel generous, with nearly 700 square feet in most of the one- and two-bedroom suites. Of course, the 27-inch television, DVD player, granite kitchen countertops, fireplace, and new appliances don't hurt. If you can afford it, go for a suite with its own hot tub — the perfect way to unwind, après-ski or -hike.

Tourism Whistler $$-$$$

800-944-7853; *whistler.com*

For deep, deep discounts on exclusive hotels and resorts, use this site's "Suite Secrets," available through the site's "Accommodations Search." As with Priceline, you won't know the name of the place beforehand, but you'll probably be able to deduce it from the location, layout, and room description. Using Suite Secrets, we've stayed at the Westin and the Pan Pacific — gorgeous hotels at great rates.

DO

Blackcomb Base Adventure Zone (summer only)

Whistler Way; 1-800-766-0449;
whistlerblackcomb.com/todo/summer/adventurezone

Feh, who needs snow to enjoy Whistler? At this summer hot spot, kids go down the Westcoaster Luge, up a bungee trampoline, or spin in a human gyroscope. There's also a 25-foot climbing web, mini-golf, and the Great Climbing Wall (and yes, it's huge). The passes are a better deal, because an individual ride costs plenty ($7–$11); $41–$99 day pass, or pay per activity. Open mid-June–September 1; Sunday–Friday, 10 a.m.–6p.m.; Saturday, 10 a.m.–8 p.m.

Coca-Cola Tube Park (winter only)

Base II Zone on Blackcomb Mountain; 800-766-0449;
whistlerblackcomb.com

The Excalibur gondola whisks you from the village to this awesome park. Ride on superhuge tubes on lanes of varying difficulty, then warm up at the Fire Pit with hot chocolate. A nice choice for all-family fun. Adults/$16; youth (13–18)/$12; children (infant–12)/$10 for one hour; discount for second hour. Open December 13–April 26: weekdays, noon–6 p.m.; weekends, 11 a.m.–6 p.m.

The Core Kids Zone

4010 Whistler Way; 604-905-7625; *whistlercore.com*

Looking for an indoor location to blow off steam? The Core Kids Zone has a multilevel, mesh-enclosed "Yeti Land Play Zone," with slides, ladders, and foam padding for younger kids. Older kids can climb on The Core's rock walls. The Core Kids Zone also runs daytime and evening camps (with rock climbing for older kids) during peak seasons, and drop-in child care (days and times vary; get info and sign up at the front desk). The price may seem steep, but you can sit in the giant coin-operated massage chairs and chat with other adults, or go work out. Not bad. $8/hour for first child, $6/hour for second child for parent-supervised play; baby-sitting prices are very fluid, depending upon season and availability — and can run as much as $25/hour when parents are not present. Open Monday–Friday, 6 a.m.–10 p.m.; Saturday, 8 a.m.–10 p.m.; Sunday 8 a.m.–9 p.m.

Cross Country Connection
Next to Lost Lake ticket booth, by Day Skier Lot 5 off Lorimer Road; 604-905-0071; *crosscountryconnection.ca*
Swoosh, whoosh! While Whistler emphasizes downhill skiing, cross-country is sometimes even better for small kids. Toddlers can ride in a Pulk sled, or a converted Chariot Carrier, and baby can take in the views from a backpack-style carrier while you snowshoe. Find out about lessons and rentals at Cross Country Connection, which also provides trail info, maps, and those cool Chariot Carriers. Reserve a Pulk sled with the municipality at 604-935-8248. Lost Lake passes: adults/$18; children (older than 6)/$9; family/$36. Ski rentals range from $12 to $40/day; snowshoes, $12–$20. Open daily 9 a.m.–6 p.m. during winter and summer; 10 a.m.–5 p.m. in fall and spring

Expressions Art Studio
4338 Main Street; 604-932-2822; *expressionsartstudio.com*
Get your craft on at this arts studio, which goes beyond the paint-it-your-self experience. Try sculpting clay, making glass jewelry, creating a mosaic, or painting pottery. Your objet d'art will be ready by the next day. Project availability depends on the age of your child; ask which artsy options are most suitable for your toddler or teen. About $30/person. Open daily, 11 a.m.–6 p.m.

Meadow Park Sports Centre
8625 Highway 99; 604-935-7529; *whistler.ca*
A short five- to ten-minute drive from Whistler, the Meadow Park Sports Centre is the perfect way to spend a few hours. The huge pool offers a lazy whirlpool, a vortex, spouting bears, a slide, hot tubs, and lanes for swimming laps. A deck overlooks the pool, if you'd rather stay out of splashing distance (wear a tee though — it can be hot on that deck!). For a cool alternative, try the ice-skating rink. Finding the current month's online schedule can be a little tricky; it's easiest to call directly and ask when family swim times are available. Adults/$7.25; youth (13–18)/$4.50; children (4–12)/$3.75; family/$14.50. Open daily, 6 a.m.–10 p.m.

River of Golden Dreams
whistler.com/activities/canoe_kayak
With a name like that, how could it not be spectacular? Between June and September, the canoe-able waterway connects Alta Lake to Green Lake and features animal-viewing opportunities, plus awe-inspiring scenery. Go with an outdoor tour organizer, or go by yourself, if you've got the skills. Check the Web site above to navigate your summer canoe and kayak options.

VANCOUVER GETAWAY

Squamish Lilwat Cultural Centre

4584 Blackcomb Way; 866-441-7522; *slcc.ca*
Carved cedar doors welcome you into a world of long ago — and of today. The rich history of the Squamish and Lilwat nations reside inside, from hand-carved canoes to multimedia presentations on modern language. Best for older children, about ten and older (or mature younger kids), who can also enjoy the craft activities, such as weaving and painting. Before visiting, go to the center's Web site to gain some fascinating inside history (e.g., a mother bear and her cub walked through the building before the center was completed, which blessed the site, according to tribal lore). Adults/$18; youth (13–18)/$11; children (6–12)/$8. Open daily, 9:30 a.m.–5 p.m.

Village 8 Cinemas

#100-4394 Blackcomb Way (in Whistler Village); 604-932-5833; *village8.ca*
Vacations are all about escape, and Village 8 provides supersized entertainment on the silver screen. On Cheap Tuesday, all tickets are $10. Adults/$12.50; youth (13–16)/$9.50; child/$7.50. Matinees are shown, but times vary; call or check the Web site for details.

The Whistler Activity and Information Centre

4230 Gateway Drive; 604-938-2769 or 877-991-9988; *tourismwhistler.com*
There's so much more to do in Whistler beyond what's listed here: horseback riding, cross-country skiing, helicopter rides, sleigh rides, and more. Consider making a stop at the Whistler Activity and Information Centre immediately upon arrival. You can look through the brochures and talk with the expert staff at the information desk. They'll tell you what's going on during your stay and can suggest additional family activities. Open daily, 8 a.m.–10 p.m.

Whistler and Blackcomb mountains

866-218-9690 or 604-904-8134; *whistlerblackcomb.com*
The two mountains comprise the largest ski area in North America, and the fine, powdery snow is the stuff of legend. And yes, it's really that fantastic — suited for Olympic athletes, one might say. Grab the skis or your snowboard and head down a mountain — and then back up via more than 20 different lifts.

No skis? No problem. The whole family can take a sightseeing trip up Whistler Mountain, where you'll get heavenly views across the snow-blanketed valley from inside an eight-person gondola. At the top, play in the snow, pose for pictures, or dig into a bowl of hot chili in the lodge. Then, gather your courage and board the enclosed Peak 2 Peak gondola (*peak2peakgondola.com*). You'll be 1,427 feet (436 m) above the ground, suspended in midair across an almost three-mile-long (4.4-km) chasm between Blackcomb and Whistler mountains. Wait for the glass-bottomed gondola, if you're up for additional adrenaline. Bring sunglasses and winter wear, even while sightseeing. The sun and cold can be painful, particularly for small children.

Washington state and Canadian residents benefit from locals-only specials; save by ordering your ticket and/or a package online from *whistlerblack comb.com*; prices range from $49 (sightseeing in winter) to $91 (single-day ski lift ticket in winter's peak season); children are always less, and six and younger are free. Ticket windows open at 8 a.m., but mountain hours vary.

VANCOUVER GETAWAY

Whistler Kids Ski Lessons
Whistler Mountain; 800-766-0449;
whistlerblackcomb.com/rentals/schoolkids/index.htm
It's à la carte at this top-of-the-line ski school: The kids can choose to go a half-day or all day, with a private instructor or a group, or they can decide not to ski at all (the warming hut shows cartoons for those who'd rather stay inside). Many programs offer skiing alongside snacks, crafts, and other fun activities. Hours and prices vary; call for details.

Whistler Public Library
4329 Main Street; 604-935-8433; *whistlerlibrary.ca*
This library offers free drop-in story times for little ones, special programming, and a warm corner for cozying up (or cooling off, depending on the weather). Membership is only $10 for out-of-province visitors, so the library may be the best source of cheap entertainment in Whistler. Anyone with a B.C. public library card can use the Whistler library for free. Open Monday–Saturday, 11 a.m.–7 p.m.; Sunday, 11 a.m.–4 p.m.

PLAY
Whistler Inclusive Playground
At Whistler Medals Plaza
The new 13,000-square-foot facility (to be completed in spring 2010) will include a sheltered play area with swings, a playhouse (ages six and younger only) a tree house (for kids ages seven to twelve) a slide, a sand/water feature and even a bobsled run.

EAT
Avalanche Pizza Corp. $-$$
#109-4295 Blackcomb Way; 604-932-3131; *avalanchepizza.com*
You couldn't get calories faster than at this pizza shop. Order thick-crust slices à la carte or request delivery of whole pies to your hotel room. There's not much space to dine inside, so take your slice away — or eat your pizza on the outdoor piazza. Open daily, 11 a.m.–11 p.m.

Beet Root Café $-$$
#129-4340 Lorimer Road; 604-932-1163
It's a little restaurant known for generous portions, a devoted following, and affordable options. The kids' grilled cheese is only $3.50; the grown-up version (turkey and Brie on ciabatta) runs $7.95. For breakfast, try the popular Belgian waffles with pure maple syrup, or an eggs Benny with smoked salmon and cream cheese. Pick up a chocolate-apricot cookie for après-ski (or -hike) in the hotel. Open daily, 7:30 a.m.–4:30 p.m.

Crepe Montagne $$-$$$
#116-4368 Main Street; 604-905-4444; *crepemontagne.com*
Crêpes aren't particularly special, right? These crêpes beg to differ — they're presented with flair and flavor. Sit on one of the honey-colored benches and

order something off the extensive kids' menu — like the Scoubidou, a crêpe with cheese and tomato. To pass the time, choose an "Asterix" or "Garfield" book (in French) from the restaurant's shelf. It's on the pricey side (around $11–$27 per crêpe), but worth it. Open daily 9 a.m.–2:30 p.m. off-season; during winter (high season) 8 a.m.–10:30 p.m.

Marketplace IGA $-$$$
4330 Northlands Boulevard; 604-938-2850
So, you're sort of at the mercy of local stores, unless you've stopped at the Costco in Vancouver on your way up. But once you're here, a $5 box of Cheerios starts to look pretty cheap. Visit the enormous IGA for family-sized boxes of doughnuts and other baked goodies, plus dairy, bulk trail mix (perfect for hikes), and produce. Open daily, 9 a.m.–9 p.m.

Pasta Lupino $
#121-4368 Main Street; 604-905-0400; *pastalupino.com*
Of course, you could eat at the Old Spaghetti Factory (4145 Village Green Crystal Lodge). But if you're a native Northwesterner, you've already got an OSF near your home. Instead, try Pasta Lupino, a locally owned alternative Italian restaurant serving no-nonsense pasta and sauce. You can pick up your order, then cook it in your kitchen (don't forget to make trolley sounds, if your kids want the OSF ambiance). Open daily, 11 a.m.–9 p.m.

Splitz Grill $
4369 Main Street; 604-938-9300; *splitzgrill.com*
If the ski runs have worked up an animal hunger, head here for immediate carnivorous refueling. Splitz does it right, with burgers that can be loaded from top to bottom with dozens of different condiments, from wild (hummus) to mild (mayo). A second location has opened in Vancouver, but this is the location that put Splitz on the map. Open daily, 11 a.m.–10 p.m.

Sushi Village $-$$$
4272 Mountain Square, R.R. 4; 604-932-3330; *sushivillage.com*
Go early or don't go at all, if you're trying to hit this popular sushi-on-the-square restaurant. And because you're early (right?), ask for a tatami room, where you and the kids have a mini-booth to yourselves. Once tucked in, feast on less-expensive sushi (fish or vegetarian), or more filling chicken teriyaki, or an authentic hot pot dinner. Open daily, 5–10 p.m.; lunch, Friday–Sunday, noon–2:30 p.m.

SHOP

Armchair Books
4205 Village Square; 604-932-5557; *whistlerbooks.com*
Armchair Books has a great selection of local books detailing hikes, wildlife, and history of the Whistler area. But the real reason to head into this well-read shop is to pick up a copy of "Kids Guide to Whistler," a cute little bag of Whistler-centric fun, created by Kerry MacLeod. It contains an activity and fact book, plus a big wooden pencil; it's a great take-home souvenir for kids up to age ten or so. Open daily, 11 a.m.–9 p.m.

VANCOUVER GETAWAY

Fun For Kids Clothing and Accessories
#203-4293 Mountain Square; 604-932-2115
Forget something? Of course you did. Maybe it was a second glove, or hiking socks, or a warm hat. Fun For Kids has what you're looking for, in a variety of silly and fun designs. And the owners have definitely thought of the little things that can make or break a ski vacation, like warm slippers and long-john-style underwear. Open daily, 10 a.m.–6 p.m.

The Great Glass Elevator Candy Shoppe
#115-4350 Lorimer Road; 604-935-1076
A sugary wonderland sure to please, even if Mr. Wonka himself isn't on the premises. Fill a bag with candy from bins, pick up a British chocolate bar, or choose from Scandinavian sweets. Whether the kids want chewy or crunchy, sour or salty (yes, salty!), this sugar shop offers something to suit. Open Sunday–Thursday, 10 a.m.–7 p.m.; Friday and Saturday, 10 a.m.–8 p.m.

Whoola Toys
#105-4359 Main Street; 604-932-2043
Once you've run low on toys, head here to find Playmobil, Legos, cars, trains, and plenty of activity books. Prices are surprisingly reasonable for a tourist destination, perhaps because the store is owned by four local moms. You'll find some good deals, a surprise in such a well-heeled destination. Open Sunday–Thursday, 11 a.m.–6 p.m.; Friday and Saturday, 11 a.m.–7 p.m.

VANCOUVER
GETAWAY

victoria

victoria

One of the Northwest's oldest cities and the capital city of British Columbia, Victoria was founded in 1843 as Fort Victoria by the Hudson's Bay Company. Victoria's dramatic turn-of-the-century architecture is unrivaled.

Here, the new flourishes alongside the old, specifically in the realm of food. Victoria's foodies have invigorated the local dining scene with fresh, local meals cooked in creative ways. Not too fancy, but delicious enough that even the pickiest kids will want to dig in. You could dine out here for a month and still not sample all the great restaurants.

So, go for the old-time fun (tea at the Empress, a walk through the Butchart Gardens, an afternoon at the Royal BC Museum) but, when it comes to dining, look for fresh and new options. Chances are you'll soon be back.

SUGGESTED ITINERARIES

If you're staying for two days: Visit the Royal BC Museum or the Bug Zoo, the Butchart Gardens (or another garden), and do some shopping in downtown Victoria.

If you're staying for three days: Do all of the above, and add a stroll through Oak Bay.

If you're staying for five days: Take in all of the above, plus one of the tacky-cool tourist attractions (the Wax Museum, Butterfly Gardens, or Miniature World).

If you're staying for a week: Put all of the above on your itinerary and add a side trip to Vancouver or Seattle.

MATCH YOUR TRAVEL ITINERARY TO YOUR FAMILY STYLE

Active families: Play in James Bay Park, then bike along the city's lanes or pedal out to Sidney. Stay at the Admiral Inn, where visitors can borrow bikes.

Artsy families: Check out Blue Island Art Supply, explore (Canadian artist and icon) Emily Carr's hometown, and enjoy the Inner Harbour's grand architecture. Stay at the Swan Suites, which offers modern art in every room.

Foodie families: Tea, tea, tea — make it an experience and educate your kids on the history of teatime. Stay at the Royal Scot, where you can cook local goods and warm up leftovers in your pocket-size kitchen.

Retro families: Enjoy the cheesy fun of the Wax Museum and Miniature World before shopping for classic balsawood planes at BC Shaver. Stay at the Fairmont Empress, the grand dame of early-twentieth-century elegance.

Shopping families: Shop in downtown Victoria, in Oak Bay, and along Fort Street's cool collection of antiques and vintage treasures, where the goods are plentiful and distinctive. Stay anywhere you can get a deal (such as Carriage House or Cottage Pirouette), so you can spend a little more money on the town.

FIVE THINGS YOU MUST DO IN VICTORIA:

1. Visit the Royal BC Museum, which offers hands-on natural science and history for kids who typically detest dry subjects (page 140).

2. Check out the Bug Zoo. One of our family's perennial favorites, the zoo's small but fact-packed museum is perfect for kids who love little critters (page 133).

Ladybugs

3. Go out for Bennies. British Columbia has an unusual affinity for eggs Benedict, and few cities do Bennies as well, or in such a diverse manner, as Victoria.

4. Take tea. Go with the traditional at the Empress, or low key at the James Bay Tearoom (page 142) or the White Heather (page 146).

5. Visit gardens. Victoria's microclimate ensures bloomin' goodness almost year-round. Go to the Butchart Gardens (expensive; page 148), or Beacon Hill Park (free; page 142) to commune with nature's showgirls.

WHAT KIDS LIKE BEST, AGE BY AGE

Babies: Bright colors at the Butchart Gardens and shopping at Mothering Touch on Fort Street; visiting a community pool; seeing animals at the Beacon Hill Park.

Toddlers and preschoolers: The sights and sounds of the Royal BC Museum, feeding pigeons and visiting boats along the Inner Harbour, watching the "running of the goats" at Beacon Hill Park, feeding seals at Fisherman's Wharf, and the Bug Zoo.

Elementary-school-age kids: Shop "Comics Row" in downtown Victoria (page 136), try tea at the Fairmont Empress, head to the Butchart Gardens at nighttime for fireworks or Christmas lights. Try on a millipede moustache at the Bug Zoo, and explore history at the Royal BC Museum.

Middle-school-age kids: Enjoy gory sights at the Wax Museum, shop Comics Row, and sample easy-on-the-brain history and natural science at the Royal BC Museum.

Teens: Shop in downtown Victoria, hang out at a Brit-style brewpub or chips shop, enjoy mom-daughter quality time at the Empress, or get kitschy cool at the Wax Museum or Miniature World.

TRAVEL INFORMATION

The Tourist Bureau at the entrance to downtown (812 Wharf Street) presents a wall of pamphlets on hotels and attractions. Open June–August, 8:30 a.m.–8:30 p.m.; September–May, 9 a.m.–5 p.m. *tourismvictoria.com*; 1-800-663-3883.

VICTORIA

VICTORIA IN THE MEDIA

Nelly Furtado, Emily Carr, and Alice Munro have all called Victoria home, as does Colin Firth on a part-time basis. Yes, that might be Mr. Darcy you see in Oak Bay.

Parts of the 1993 film *Little Women* were filmed in Victoria, as were sequels two and three of *X-Men*. For young readers, take a look at picture books *Jessie's Island* and *Waiting for the Whales*, both by Sheryl McFarlane. Both are published by Victoria-based Orca Book Publishers, which releases high-quality books for kids and teens (*orcabook.com*).

VICTORIA NICKNAMES

Little England
The Garden City

SAFETY

Victoria is a calm, small city. Unless you have an overwhelming fear of senior citizens, you'll be fine. The most serious trouble on the island can come from after-hours car break-ins; if you've brought your car, don't leave valuables on the seat.

GETTING THERE

Entry into Victoria by air, land, or sea: U.S. citizens need to present either a passport or an enhanced driver's license (EDL), which will meet the requirements for proof of citizenship to re-enter the U.S. from Canada and Mexico, by land or sea. Check with your state's Department of Licensing to find out more about enhanced driver's licenses.

If you are traveling with your child or children without the other parent (whether because of divorce or other circumstances), bring a notarized letter stating that the child's parent knows you are bringing the kids into Canada. Crossing into Canada can be extremely difficult without such a letter, due to past custody disputes leading to cross-border kidnappings.

Plane: Flights to Victoria leave Seattle via floatplanes operated by Kenmore Air (*kenmoreair.com*) and land directly in Victoria's Inner Harbour. Vancouver-Victoria connections are made by Harbour Air (*harbour-air.com*) or West Coast Air (*westcoastair.com*). Flights take only an hour but are very expensive (prices start at around $200 per seat). Victoria's local airport is Victoria Airport Authority (*victoriaairport.com*), which serves Air Canada, United Express, Horizon Air, and WestJet, among others.

Ferry ride to Victoria: No matter how you go, you'll see impossibly gorgeous landscapes and seascapes of blue, green, and gold as your ferry passes by islands. In fall, winter, and spring, bring binoculars and bird-watch right from your window seat, looking for migratory waterfowl. In summer, eagle-eyed kids might spy splashing orcas or grazing black-tailed deer. Here are your ferry options:

VICTORIA

FUN FACTS

- More than 3,000 lights decorate Victoria's Parliament buildings.

- The narrowest street in North America is Fan Tan Alley (page 136).

- There are eighty-seven steps from the main floor to the tower at Craigdarroch Castle.

- There are 7 million objects in the Royal British Columbia Museum's collection.

- At 451 kilometers (280 miles), Vancouver Island is the largest island on the Pacific coast of North America.

- BC Ferries carries more than 8.1 million vehicles and 20.7 million passengers on 187,000 sailings per year.

- Orcas (killer whales) make Puget Sound and the San Juan Islands their summer home, traveling through Washington state and British Columbia waters.

Seattle-Victoria. The Victoria Clipper's two-and-a-half-hour ride is the way to go from Seattle, if the fare fits into your budget. It's an expensive way to get to Victoria, but is low stress and free of hassle. To cut costs, look into the ferry-hotel deals and the Clipper's free kids' companion fares. Arrive early for check-in and ask for an early boarding pass if you have a younger child in a stroller — you'll move to the front of the line. Seats on board are more like airplane seats, without much room to move around. The best spots are the four-person groupings, next to windows — or at the very front of the boat, where family-friendly movies are screened. *clippervacations.com*

Anacortes-Sidney (car or passenger-only ferry). A longer, and less expensive, route to Victoria — about two and a half hours aboard a Washington state ferry from Anacortes, Washington, to Sidney, B.C., then another half-hour drive down to Victoria. But what a route! Bring card games, board games, or other pastimes for the long trip, and enjoy the calming ride past islands and into San Juan Island harbors. You'll want to bring food for the often-interminable waits at ferry docks. The food offered on board isn't bad, just somewhat expensive. The cheapest way to go? Walk on as passengers, then bus it between Sidney and Victoria, where you'll be on foot the whole way. Make reservations, especially in summer. *wsdot.wa.gov/ferries*

Tsawwassen–Swartz Bay (car or passenger-only ferry). The BC Ferries system goes all out for car commuters on this one-and-a-half-hour trip between Vancouver Island and mainland B.C. On board, you'll find a gift shop, magazine store, luxury buffet, and serve-yourself cafeteria options. For the kids, there's a mini-playground, a video arcade, and short movies. The only downside might be that you're so busy with the ferry activities, you might forget to notice the gorgeous views outside. Make reservations and arrive early, year-round; despite the frequent departures, this is an incredibly popular route and waits can be brutal. *bcferries.com*

Port Angeles–Victoria (car or passenger-only ferry). For Portland and southwest Washington residents, this is probably the quickest way to reach Victoria. The Black Ball Ferry (*cohoferry.com*), operated by a private company, takes you from Port Angeles, Washington, directly into Victoria's downtown. It's also the shortest ride of all water-transportation options (about forty-five minutes). While this boat doesn't offer the little luxuries or languorous ride of the other three, it's fun, fast, and affordable. The Victoria Express (*victoria express.com*) ferries foot passengers between Victoria, B.C., and Port Angeles one to three times per day during peak summer months (late May–late October). Crossing time is fifty-five minutes.

CALENDAR

January/February
VICTORIA TEA FESTIVAL. A one-day event, the festival features tea tastings, workshops, and the chance to purchase hundreds of teas, tea wares, and tea-food selections. *victoriateafestival.com*

February/March
DINE AROUND, STAY IN TOWN. Victoria-area restaurants and accommodations offer special menus and rates to visitors and locals alike. *tourismvictoria.com*

April
VICTORIA HOT JAZZ JUBILEE. Enjoy an exciting weekend of jazz, featuring various jazz bands and styles. *victoria-hot-jazz.com*

May
VANCOUVER ISLAND CHILDREN'S FESTIVAL. Stunning sensory performances, workshops taught by international artists, physically engaging activity centers, and free presentations on an open-air stage will help to inspire creativity. *childrensfestival.com*

June
VICTORIA JAZZFEST INTERNATIONAL. Musicians from around the globe descend on British Columbia's capital city to perform jazz, blues, and world music on multiple stages in downtown Victoria. *jazzvictoria.ca*

July
MOSS STREET PAINT-IN. This free event provides the opportunity for as many as 100 professional and emerging artists to line Moss Street, showcasing their work and meeting visitors. *aggv.bc.ca/moss+ street.aspx*

LUMINARA FESTIVAL. A free, family-friendly event held at St. Ann's Academy and Beacon Hill Park. Come and see the glow of thousands of colorful, handmade lanterns illuminating Victoria. *icavictoria.org/luminara*

ORGANIC ISLANDS FESTIVAL. A celebration of the island's natural, organic, and sustainable products, featuring a children's activity area, music, and food. *organicislands.ca*

August

VICTORIA SYMPHONY SPLASH. A free concert performed by the Victoria Symphony from a barge moored in the Inner Harbour. *victoriasymphony.bc.ca*

VICTORIA DRAGON BOAT FESTIVAL. Almost 100 dragon boat teams from across North America — each with a crew of paddlers — race head to head in a 470-meter (1,540-foot) sprint in full dragon-boat regalia, while timing drums thump away. Fast and colorful, the races are just as exciting for spectators as the crews. *victoriadragonboat.com*

FREE-B FILM FESTIVAL. Classic movies — from the family friendly to the weird and wacky — are shown on select Friday and Saturday nights at 9 p.m. under the stars at the Cameron Bandshell in Beacon Hill Park. Delightful for movie buffs looking to get outdoors on a summer evening, rather than sit inside a theater. *victoriafilmfestival.com*

VICTORIA FRINGE THEATRE FESTIVAL. The Fringe Festival is a nonstop, twelve-day explosion of comedy, improv, drama, performance art, and dance from around the world. *intrepidtheatre.com*

October–November

SALMON RUN AT GOLDSTREAM PARK. Every autumn, millions of Pacific salmon forge their way up the myriad streams of the Pacific Northwest to spawn and die. In Victoria, 60,000 chum salmon appear about mid-October and may be seen for approximately nine weeks. *goldstreampark.com*

GHOST BUS TOURS. The Old Cemeteries Society takes participants on a spooky tour of some of Victoria's most haunted sites. *discoverthepast.com*

ROMP. The Festival of Independent Dance supports the work and development of professional dance artists. *suddenlydance .ca/romp/romp.htm*

December

FESTIVAL OF TREES. The Fairmont Empress hosts this display of trees decorated by local organizations. *fairmont.com/empress*

MAGIC OF CHRISTMAS at the Butchart Gardens. The Butchart Gardens brighten up the darkest nights with thousands of magical, twinkling lights. Traditional holiday carolers, concerts, and warm drinks make an evening at Butchart memorable for all ages. An ice-skating rink is also available. Dress warmly! *butchartgardens.com*

HELMCKEN HOUSE CHRISTMAS. During December, Helmcken, one of the oldest houses in British Columbia, transforms into a scene from a Victorian Christmas story, with handmade decorations and a holiday feast. Admission to Helmcken House is included with paid entry to the Royal BC Museum — just ask for directions to the house once you're finished with the museum.

VICTORIA

ESSENTIALS

Area code: 250

Baby accessories: Wee Travel provides baby cribs, strollers, high chairs, and more. Find more information at *weetravel.ca* or call 604-222-4722.

Emergencies: Call 911 in an emergency. Victoria General Hospital is located at 1 Hospital Way. Call 250-727-4212 for more information.

Mail a postcard: Go to the post office at 704 Yates Street. Open Monday–Friday, 9 a.m.–5 p.m.

Money: U.S. citizens should have no problems taking money out of the ATMs found throughout downtown Victoria or at James Bay Square (a short walk from the ferry terminal at 230 Menzies Street). You can also use your Visa card, just as you do at home. Call the bank before leaving; international spending can sometimes trigger holds, and you'll also want to ask if using your Visa internationally incurs special fees.

News: *The Victoria Times-Colonist* (*timescolonist.com*) presents community news. To discover what local families are doing (including classes and events), check out *Island Parent* (*islandparent.ca*) or *Kids in Victoria* (*kidsinvictoria.com*).

Parks: See a complete list of parks and trails at *crd.bc.ca/parks /location.htm.*

Pharmacy: James Bay Pharmasave is near the Inner Harbour at #113–230 Menzies Street. You can also call 604-383-7196. Open Monday–Friday, 8 a.m.–8 p.m.; Saturday, 9 a.m.–6 p.m.

Taxes: As of mid-2010, the new 12 percent Harmonized Sales Tax will be in effect, which will combine the GST and PST. Read more here: *gov.bc.ca/hst.* Hotel stays and rentals can require additional taxes; ask before you get the bill.

Bellingham-Victoria. A low-key way to turn your trip into a cruise, Victoria–San Juan Cruises provides an all-you-can-eat salmon and chicken buffet to go with your gorgeous views. Tours depart in summer once a day from Bellingham, Washington, and Victoria. A bonus: The Bellingham ferry dock is located in Bellingham's historic Fairview district, with sweet little shops and restaurants. *whales.com/index.php/victoria/schedules-fares*

GETTING AROUND

Navigating Victoria: The downtown core and Inner Harbour are accessible by foot, with the exception of the "Around Victoria" section (page 147) and Oak Bay. Oak Bay can be reached by bus or taxi; the Butchart Gardens and

VICTORIA

other destinations in "Farther Afield" can be accessed by public buses or private tour buses.

Plan on ten–fifteen minutes each way from your Inner Harbour hotel to downtown shopping and eating, especially when walking with children. Most restaurants are located downtown. If staying in the Inner Harbour or downtown (highly recommended), you can walk everywhere you need to go — but bring that umbrella if it's raining. Cabs are also available.

Bring a stroller for younger kids; Victoria's blocks can feel very long to little legs.

Car: Parking at most hotels is free or less than $10; on-street parking or lots in downtown Victoria are usually easy to find, inexpensive, and free on Sundays. Cars make rainy days more bearable, Oak Bay more accessible, and "Farther Afield" destinations easily doable.

Public transportation: If you're heading up without a car, carefully check transit schedules (*bctransit.com/regions/vic*). On Sundays, buses are limited, even to popular tourist attractions like the Butchart Gardens. If arriving in Sidney via the Anacortes ferry, hop on the double-decker no. 71 BC Transit bus for the hour-long ride into downtown Victoria. If landing in Swartz Bay, you'll take the no. 70 bus.

Bike: The sixty-kilometer (about forty-mile) Galloping Goose Trail (*galloping goosetrail.com*) allows you to ride between Victoria and Sooke.

DOWNTOWN

Let's face it, the best things to do in downtown Victoria are shop and eat, eat and shop. Restaurants and stores dot Victoria's pleasant late-nineteenth-century facades. Pedestrian-only alleyways provide a playground for kids pretending to be spies. With older children, don't miss a quick walk through "Comics Row," on Johnson Street. It's a parade of comics, anime, and card stores.

SLEEP
Swans Hotel $$$–$$$$
506 Pandora Avenue; 800-668-7926 or 250-361-3310; *swanshotel.com*

If you'd like to stay downtown, Swans is a good choice. These twenty charm-filled suites offer modern artwork and décor, TV and DVD player, and a full kitchen. If you have a toddler, ask about one-floor suites; the loft suites' floor-to-floor drop may make you nervous. The brewpub at your feet may be good (a parent can pop downstairs for a pint while the kids are with a sitter or the other parent) or bad (noisy bands; ask for a quieter room at the front desk, which may or may not be accommodating). The hotel is located near a facility serving at-risk populations, but the surrounding area is bustling with restaurants and shops.

DO
Victoria Bug Zoo
631 Courtney Street; 250-384-2847; *bugzoo.bc.ca*

Entomologist Carol Maier scours Amazonian jungles and American deserts for kitten-size tarantulas and glow-in-the-dark scorpions. Hold swaying stick insects, watch leaf-cutter ants traverse a wall-size maze, or listen to your bug-tour guide's deadpan repartee. Maier seems to consistently hire employees who've got that knack for entertaining crowds. One of our favorite activities in Victoria. Adults/$8; teens (13–19)/$6; children (3–12)/$5; 2 and younger, free; Summer: Monday–Saturday, 10 a.m.–6 p.m.; Sunday, 11 a.m.–6 p.m. Winter: Monday–Friday, 10:30 a.m.–5 p.m.; Saturday, 10 a.m.–5 p.m.; Sunday, 11 a.m.–5 p.m.

EAT
Green Cuisine $
#5-560 Johnson Street; 250-385-1809; *greencuisine.com*
Vegan cuisine by the pound. Wait — don't run away screaming yet. It's decent, if healthful, food, and Green Cuisine's serve-yourself buffet means that kids can choose literally anything here and it'll be good for 'em, even if it is carob pudding. Open daily, 10 a.m.–8 p.m.; buffet daily, 11:30 a.m.–8 p.m.

Hernande'z $-$$ (cash only)
750 Yates Street; no phone; *hernandezcocina.com*
Incredible food from way south of the border — down El Salvador way. But if the kids love Mexican, they'll appreciate this little, out-of-the-way restaurant serving exquisite, inexpensive, and familiar food. Try the fabulous huarache, a flat, hand-shaped corn tortilla smothered with beans or meat, toppings, and fresh greens. Menu items change with the seasons or ingredients available. Owners Jerson and Tamara love kids — they've got three homeschooled kiddos — and you'll never feel unwelcome. (Read the Web site before you go — it's entertaining.) If you have a car and don't mind a drive, there's a second location at 1600 Bay Street with evening hours (Tuesday–Friday, 5 p.m.–9 p.m.; Saturday, noon–9 p.m.). Yates Street location open Monday–Friday, 11:30 a.m.–8 p.m.

Lady Marmalade $$
608 Johnson Street; 250-381-2872; *ladymarmalade.ca*
Another popular breakfast spot, Lady Marmalade is more of your traditional West Coast eatery with a Canadian twist: Think miso-gravy poutine, or ham, red onion, and chipotle mayo Bennies, or white cheddar waffles. Retro décor (matching puppy salt-and-pepper shakers, '70s-era tables) and great service, as long as you don't ask for substitutions. Sandwiches include baguettes and Mexican-style tortas. No kids' menu, so be prepared to share. Open daily, 8 a.m.–4 p.m.

Mo:Lé $$
554 Pandora Avenue; 250-385-6653; *molerestaurant.ca*
Don't even try to get a seat at this popular restaurant during the weekends, unless you're willing to wait for forty-five minutes to an hour, and for good reason. Mo:Lé's Latin-flavored fusion breakfasts, lunches, and dinners combine divine local ingredients. Pesto-roasted potatoes, huevos rancheros topped with goat feta, and roasted organic apples. The children's menu serves grilled cheese sandwiches, small roasted-yam salad, or organic spelt griddle cakes. Crayons and coloring sheets available. Open daily: weekdays, 8 a.m.–3 p.m.; weekends, 8 a.m.–4 p.m.

The Noodle Box $

818 Douglas Street; 250-384-1314; *thenoodlebox.net*
Lovely, long hokkein noodles, served in the classic take-away box with chopsticks (or forks). Select your noodle meal from a long list of choices, as hot or as mild as you like. The kids' box is made of simple egg noodles with sprouts, soy sauce, and your choice of toppings (chicken, tofu, or veggies). This restaurant is buzzing during peak lunch and dinnertime hours; a better choice with kids is to take your messy meal back to your room to slurp up the goods. Open daily, 11 a.m.–9 p.m.

Paradiso di Stelle $-$$

10 Bastion Square; 250-920-7266
Paradiso di Stelle's mix 'n' match pasta dishes keep everyone content: Just choose your noodle shape, then pair with sauces such as tomato, Alfredo, or smoked salmon. Eat indoors at a window seat or outside with a full view of the harbor. Try Stelle's stellar Italian coffee and gelato for a tasteful finish. Monday–Saturday, 7 a.m.–6 p.m.; Sunday, 9 a.m.–6 p.m.

Rebar $-$$

50 Bastion Square; 250-361-9223; *rebarmodernfood.com*
Visiting families and locals love the Mexican oilcloth-draped tables, the superfriendly service, and the fresh fusion fare (the restaurant often features Thai, Mexican, and Eastern European dishes). Expect long lines in summer; this is one restaurant to get to early or between the rushes at breakfast, lunch, and dinner; best right at opening, between 9:30 and 11:30 a.m. on weekdays, or 1:30–4:30 p.m. any day (as long as it's open). Ask if the kids can play with the giant Godzilla — you'll be glad you did. Summer hours: Monday–Wednesday, 7:30 a.m.–9 p.m.; Thursday–Saturday, 8:30 a.m.–10 p.m.; Sunday, 8:30 a.m.–3:30 p.m. Winter hours: Monday–Saturday, 8:30 a.m.–9 p.m.; closed Sunday.

Rogers' Chocolates Soda Shoppe $

913 Government Street; 800-663-2220; *rogerschocolates.com*
This gorgeous little shop has everything: floats, malts, shakes, and kid-sized bar stools facing a beautiful view of the Inner Harbour. The dark, rich chocolate ice cream sauce is made by the famous Rogers' Chocolates. My kids and I loved the hand-jerked soda syrups you can select or mix (we went with cherry-chocolate soda, topped with whipped cream). Open Monday–Thursday, 9:30 a.m.–8 p.m.; Friday and Saturday, 9:30 a.m.–9 p.m.; Sunday, 10 a.m.–8 p.m.

Solstice Café $

529 Pandora Avenue; 250-475-0477; *solsticecafe.ca*
Organic, wheat-free, and very, very healthy baked goods and coffee in a spacious setting. Some toys and books. Monday, 7:30 a.m.–5 p.m.; Tuesday, 7:30 a.m.–6 p.m.; Wednesday, 7:30 a.m.–9 p.m.; Thursday and Friday, 7:30 a.m.–6 p.m.; Saturday, 9 a.m.–5 p.m.; Sunday 10 a.m.–5 p.m.

Swans Brewpub $-$$

506 Pandora Avenue; 250-361-3310; *swanshotel.com/pub.php*
At this pub, kids can eat in Swans' glassed-in sunroom, which can be pleasant on both sunny and gloomy days. Fairly typical pub fare, with burgers,

VICTORIA DOWNTOWN

flat-bread pizza, soups, salads, and wraps on the menu; kids' menus also available, featuring typical kids' fare (e.g., chicken strips, burgers). But if you want brews and burgers in Victoria, this is definitely a convenient and slightly less spendy stop. Open daily, 7:30 a.m.–2 a.m.

SHOP
Baggins Shoes
#110-561 Johnson Street; 250-388-7022; *bagginsshoes.com*
Do the kids love the low-key cool of Converse or Vans high-tops? Take them here, one of the most complete sneaker stores in North America. Packed from floor to ceiling with Vans, limited-edition Converse, Chuck Taylor All-Stars, and Pumas in candy-store colors and diverse fabrics. Sneakers, sandals, boots, and casual shoes for all ages, depending upon the season. Open Monday–Saturday, 10 a.m.–6 p.m.; Sunday, 11 a.m.–5 p.m.

Beadworld
#63-560 Johnson Street (Market Square); 250-386-5534; *victoriabeadworld.ca*
Beadworld has a welcoming staff, central location, and hundreds of beads glittering like gold. Sweet glass beads, tiny pendants, and a variety of necklace materials make jewelry making easy for any age or gender. Helpful, watchful staff can help kids pick out the right pieces. Open Monday–Saturday, 9:30 a.m.–5:30 p.m.; Sunday, 11 a.m.–5 p.m.

British Candy Shoppe
638 Yates Street; 250-382-2634
Enough enamel-eating candy to make a dentist cry. This store's shelves feature Brit candies in bins, neatly stacked chocolate habits, and even that gooey staple Marmite. Need traditional baked beans for your Victoria in-room breakfast? The British Candy Shoppe can provide. Open Monday–Saturday, 10 a.m.–5 p.m.; Sunday, 11 a.m.–5 p.m. Closed Sunday in winter.

Chinatown Trading Company
551 Fisgard Street; no phone
This store is a microcosm of Victoria's Chinatown: It's full of winding alleys, dead ends, and showy niches. Leave the stroller outside and check out the brocade diaries, paper fans, brilliant porcelain, and quintessential black slippers that fill the store's nooks, while baskets of miniature toys sit in the crannies. Enter on Fisgard, walk through the store, and end up on **Fan Tan Alley** — North America's narrowest alley — in the middle of Canada's oldest Chinatown. The store's hours vary, but is generally open midmorning through late afternoon.

Curious Comics
631 Johnson Street; 250-384-1656; *curious.bc.ca*
Probably the largest and broadest selection along Comics Row in Victoria. Here, you'll find figurines (of everyone from Elvis to Harry Potter), Pokemon cards, all-ages-approved comics racks, comics suitable for teens and older, toddler-size Uglydolls, and of course, *Tintin* books. A great browsing store for all ages. Open Monday–Saturday, 9:30 a.m.–6 p.m.; Sunday, 11 a.m.–5 p.m.

VICTORIA
DOWNTOWN

Kaboodles Toy Store

1320 Government Street; 250-383-0931; *kaboodlestoystore.com*
On the island, it's hard to beat the toy and game selection at Kaboodles. Puzzles, board games, Thomas, Play-Doh, art supplies, tools, and tiny animal figurines abound. On the wall, there are Air Canada and BC Ferry boats. And don't forget to check out the hockey-playing Mr. Potato Head. Open Monday–Thursday, 9:30 a.m.–6 p.m.; Friday, 9:30 a.m.–9 p.m.; Saturday, 9:30 a.m.–6 p.m.; Sunday, 10 a.m.–6 p.m.

Legends Comics and Books

633 Johnson Street (Comics Row); 250-388-3696; *members.shaw.ca/legendscomics*
Remember Comic Book Man from *The Simpsons*? If he had an archenemy, it'd be Gareth Gaudlin, the owner of Legends Comics. He's friendly, funny, and immensely helpful when choosing the perfect vintage or new comic book from his plastic-jacketed stock. Lit-quality graphic novels (new and used) are great reads for older teens. Gaudlin will direct families to the comics section suitable for kids. Open Wednesday–Saturday, 10:30 a.m.–6 pm.; Sunday–Tuesday, noon–5 p.m.

Munro's Books

1108 Government Street; 250-382-2464, 1-888-243-2464 (toll free); *munrobooks.com*
A quiet respite away from Victoria's hustle and bustle, Munro's bookstore is housed in a former 1909 bank building, with soaring 24-foot-high ceilings and gorgeous, intricate details inside. Head to the store's rear and discover a small corner filled with quality children's literature, a sitting area, and genuinely obliging staff. Open Monday–Wednesday, 9 a.m.–7:30 p.m.; Thursday and Friday, 9 a.m.–9 p.m.; Saturday, 9 a.m.–7:30 p.m.; Sunday, 9:30 a.m.–6 p.m.

Murray's Joke and Trick Shop

688 Broughton Street; 250-385-6807; *magictrick.com/store*
A store full of tricks and jokes for petite pranksters and comics-to-be. Open Monday–Saturday, 10 a.m.–5:30 p.m.; Sunday, noon–4 p.m.

Roberta's Hats

1318 Government Street; 250-384-2778
Hats for sale! Hats of every color and size, with adornments of feathers, ribbons, or Che Guevara. Preteens and teens can try on hats in front of mirrors or each other; for babies and toddlers, head to the back, where strawberry-shaped and maple-leaf knit hats fill a small corner, along with more common headgear (think Winnie the Pooh). Monday–Saturday, 10 a.m.–5:30 p.m.; Sunday, 11 a.m.–5 p.m.

Scallywags

624 Fort Street; 250-360-2570; *scallywags-island.ca*
On a rainy day, a stop here can hit the spot. Kids can play in the closet-size play kitchen while you replenish their closets back at home. Choose from Canadian-grown gear from MEXX, B.C.-made woolen booties and girls' clothing, GEOX shoes, and organic baby tees. Clothes for ages newborn–ten years old, plus Melissa & Doug toys. Open Monday–Saturday, 10 a.m.–7 p.m.; Sunday, 11 a.m.–5 p.m.

VICTORIA DOWNTOWN

Smoking Lily

569-A Johnson Street; 250-382-5459; *smokinglily.com*

Smoking Lily showcases local designers, with recycled shirts, jackets, and bags for teens and adults, and screen-printed onesies for babies. Best of all: Bring in a favorite shirt (plain), choose a pattern from their binder full of funky screen-print-style graphics, and they'll put your pick on the shirt and mail it back two weeks later. Open Sunday–Monday, noon–5 p.m.; Tuesday–Saturday, 11 a.m.–5:30 p.m.

Sprouts

202-536 Herald Street; 250-388-9525; *sproutskid.com*

A cool collection of kids' wear, gear, and accessories, with a definite emphasis on products made by local moms. From affordable organic lollipops to high-end strollers, this miniature shop manages to cover all the bases. A sweet little play area in back will keep the monkeys occupied while you ponder purchasing Victoria-created art for the baby's nursery. Open Monday–Saturday, 10 a.m.–5 p.m.; Sunday, 11 a.m.–4 p.m.

Victoria Miniland

#168-560 Johnson Street (Market Square); 250-995-1226; *miniland.ca*

If the kids were inspired by Miniature World, you might want to stop in at Miniland, a tiny shop filled with even-smaller toilets, beds, lamps, and much more for dollhouses. Open Monday–Saturday, 10 a.m.–6 p.m.; Sunday, 11 a.m.–5 p.m.

Yellowjacket Comics & Toys

649 Johnson Street (Comics Row); 250-480-0049

You can practically smell the testosterone at Yellowjacket's door, if the neon-lit Dungeons and Dragons signs didn't tip you off. Individual Magic cards, *Star Wars* figurines, and long tables for impromptu magic games. Open Monday–Saturday, 10 a.m.–6 p.m.; Sunday, 11 a.m.–5 p.m.

Zydeco Gifts

565 Johnson Street; 250-389-1877; *zydecogifts.com*

Zydeco has the usual highbrow oddities available in most West Coast city novelty stores: smartass baby shirts, pirate fridge magnets, barista action figures, and flying spaghetti monster bumper stickers. But those other stores can't compete on the rubber ducky front. Zydeco stocks more than 150 varieties of yellow bathtime friends — from ninja ducks to hippie ducks to cat ducks. Sesame Street's Ernie would love this store. Open Monday–Saturday, 10 a.m.–5:30 p.m.; Sunday, 10 a.m.–5 p.m.

INNER HARBOUR/JAMES BAY

The crescent-shaped Inner Harbour welcomes ships and visitors to its flower-lined shores. This is where you'll disembark from the Victoria Clipper, and Anacortes- and Bellingham-based ferries. Because it's home to the grand Fairmont Empress Hotel, the Parliament Building, Royal Wax Museum, and the Royal BC Museum, you'll undoubtedly end up strolling here at some point. In summer, look for buskers, comedians, and artists along the water's edge; save a few toonies (the Canadian $2 coin) for the shows and wares.

VICTORIA DOWNTOWN

Next to the Inner Harbour, the cozy neighborhood of James Bay includes a petting zoo, lovely parks, a wharf with fish-eating seals, and a wonderful farmers' market. It's my favorite area of town to stay in, though it's farther from Victoria's downtown. But you brought your walking shoes, right?

SLEEP

Admiral Inn $$-$$$
257 Belleville Street; 250-388-6267 or 888-823-6472; *admiral.bc.ca*
The Admiral Inn provides affordable, simple lodging for families. There is a variety of room types, from studio style to larger rooms with full kitchen and a small dining room, but all are located near the Clipper and Black Ball stations, right on Victoria's Inner Harbour. Ask about the bike rentals. The front-desk service is usually impeccable, the rooms are clean, and the location wonderful, but suites can feel a bit drafty at times.

Carriage House Bed & Breakfast $-$$
596 Toronto Street; 250-384-7437 or 877-384-0711 (North America only); *carriagehousebandb.ca*
Here's a very basic, simple stay for families on a budget. Owners Dan Pedrick and Naoko Yamamoto converted a former carriage house (you know, like the kind for horses) into a loft-style stay with a half-kitchen (microwave, mini-fridge, small table, and hot plate), one queen bed on the main floor, and an additional queen accessible by a ladder. Inside the main house's petite rooms, small families are also welcome, if you can squeeze into the triple.

Fairmont Empress Resort Hotel $$$-$$$$
721 Government Street; 250-384-8111 or 866-540-4429; *fairmont.com/empress*
The Empress isn't quite a palace, but it's as close as you'll come in the Pacific Northwest. And the kids will feel like royalty — on check-in, they'll get an activity book and a coupon for popcorn or milk and cookies. There's a pool downstairs, one-bedroom suites, and long hallways filled with portraits of crowned heads. If you can't afford a stay (and let's be clear, it is expensive), just visit the grand sitting rooms. But if you want to go with an upgrade, ask about Fairmont Gold rates, the "hotel within a hotel," with its own concierge service, swanky lobby, appetizer hour, and a family room with a big-screen TV and kids' movies. A wide variety of rooms and layouts is available, so ask questions about your room type to ensure that you're getting what you want.

Royal Scot Hotel and Suites $$-$$$
425 Quebec Street; 250-388-5463 or 800-663-7515; *royalscot.com*
If I have my choice of hotels, I always go for the Royal Scot. In fact, I wish there were a Royal Scot in every city: pool, pool table, game room; affordable, roomy one-bedroom suites with clean rooms and furnishings, kitchens, and cable TV. Just like home. There's a restaurant on site, but you probably won't need it with the small kitchen at your disposal. Elevators and wide hallways mean you won't have a problem navigating the stroller. On-site parking (outdoor or garage) is available for a fee.

DO

Fairmont Empress Resort Hotel
721 Government Street; 250-384-8111 or 866-540-4429; *fairmont.com/empress*
Dignitaries stay at this 1808 hotel when in town, and the graceful, opulent interior perfectly fits the exterior's grandeur. Walk through the glass-ceilinged atrium for free, or make reservations for tea (check under "Eat" section, page 143). While the nearby Parliament building is also gorgeous (and designed by the same architect), the Fairmont is more kid friendly. For a calm moment, go upstairs, above the hotel's main lobby, and take in the harbor view on upscale couches and chairs. And if visiting in winter, the hotel's glittery décor is a must-see. Always open; "true" front doors not open to public — enter through side entrance or Victoria Conference Centre.

Fisherman's Wharf
300 St. Lawrence Street; *fishermanswharfvictoria.com*
Dine on fish 'n' chips at Barb's Place, pick up an ice cream cone, walk among funky houseboats, and feed seals. Resident seal Sammy will look up with huge, pleading eyes, and the kids won't be able to say no. Bring your own fish scraps (raw only) or buy some at the aptly named Fish Store. Hold onto new walkers and rambunctious toddlers: there are no barriers between the boardwalk and icy waters. Many restaurants are closed during the off-season, but you can feed the seals year-round. Walk up the small hill to the Moka House Coffee (110–19 Dallas Road), and get a warm hot chocolate or chilled Italian soda.

James Bay Community Market
Corner of Superior and Menzies streets; 250-381-5323; *jamesbaymarket.com*
Only a few blocks away from the Empress, this market sells a small hodgepodge of handcrafted toys, folk art, kids' clothes, and locally grown foods. From fairy wands to free-range eggs, you'll probably spot something you can't resist. My favorites: fruit-filled muffins, just-picked cherry tomatoes from organic farms, and inexpensive, gourmet drip coffee by the cup. Free concerts on most Saturdays. Open Saturdays, early May–early October, 9 a.m.–3 p.m.

Miniature World
649 Humboldt Street; 250-385-9731; *miniatureworld.com*
Located at the rear of the Fairmont Empress, Miniature Worlds holds tiny dioramas depicting scenes from ancient times to today, accompanied by a tinny soundtrack straight out of 1972. It's a little cheesy, for sure, but it's a cheese that some kids like a lot, with all those mini-battlefields, carnival rides, and nursery rhymes. Faithful re-creations include London Town, Enchanted Valley of Castles, and Space 2201. Explanatory signs are dated and florid; go with the right attitude and it's a fun stop. Adults/$13.05; teens/$10.05; child/$8.05. Open daily, 9 a.m.–5 p.m.; later in summer months. Check Web site for details.

Royal BC Museum
675 Belleville Street; 250-356-7226; *royalbcmuseum.bc.ca*
Three floors of history, science, and nature engage the senses. In the Natural History wing, a kid's senses of sound, smell, and touch are in full force; children

will cower before a thundering woolly mammoth and delight in the fresh, salty air next to a re-created seascape, complete with a miniature tide pool. Kids love running through the Victorian-era Victoria area: climbing stairs into the fanciful hotel, watching a silent-era comedy, or listening for the oncoming chug-chug of a steam train. And before you arrive, see which temporary exhibit is making the rounds (famous past visitors have included RMS *Titanic* mementos and Egyptian mummies). This is one of my favorite museums in the Pacific Northwest. Adults/$15; children (6–18)/$9.50; 5 and younger/free. Summer prices (May 1–September 30): Adults/$27.50; children (6–18)/$18.50; 5 and younger/free. Open daily, 9 a.m.–5 p.m.

Royal London Wax Museum
470 Belleville Street; 877-WAX-FACT; *waxmuseum.bc.ca*

If you've already taken the kids to a wax museum, skip this stop. Otherwise, its sheer novelty will probably interest many kids older than age six or so. Stroll through the museum's glassy-eyed depictions of Queen Elizabeth, George Bush, Charles Dickens, and Pinocchio. The inhabitants are somewhat dated (Goldie Hawn and Bob Hope), but the story area and narrated Northwest Passage area keep interest high. The squeamish might detour around the museum's Chamber of Horrors area — full of bloody torture scenes — or at least mom or dad should vet it first. Adults/$12; military/$10; students/$9; children/$6. Open daily: winter, 10 a.m.–5 p.m.; summer, 9 a.m.–9 p.m.

St. Ann's Schoolhouse and Helmcken House
Located directly behind the Royal BC Museum

Step back into mid-nineteenth-century life at St. Ann's Schoolhouse and the Helmcken House. At St. Ann's, kids can sit in tiny desks and write on slates with chalk, see kids' simple playthings, and check out the old potbellied stove. The Helmcken House was built in 1852 on the same site it sits upon today. Older kids will like the disturbing medical instruments (bone saw, anyone?) belonging to Dr. Helmcken, while younger kids can put on aprons and churn butter or whisk with the house's collection of kitchen implements. Open summer and December only.

Whale watching
From April through October, Vancouver Island's waters host a wide variety of migratory whale life, including humpback whales, orcas, and porpoises. Victoria's whale-watching cruises seek out whale families in the wild, so you won't go home without seeing an iconic Northwest native. Although regulations prohibit watercraft from coming within 100 meters of whales, you'll still be able to get a good look. Parents of younger or seasick-prone children will want to look for an oceangoing vessel like a catamaran or yacht, which also provides bathrooms and indoor/outdoor options. Parents of older or adventure-seeking children will want to hop into an open-air Zodiac inflatable boat, within which you're a little above ocean level and at the mercy of the waves (much to the delight of teens). A catamaran can be the balance between the two. Bring binoculars to help little eyes scout out the whales, and snacks and toys for restless tots, because the tours generally go out for two and a half to four hours at

VICTORIA INNER HARBOUR/JAMES BAY

a time. Prices start at around $90/adult. Outfits providing whale-watching tours include Prince of Whales (*princeofwhales.com*), Eagle Wing Tours (*eaglewingtours.com*), Great Pacific Adventures (*greatpacificadventures.com*) Orca Spirit Adventures (*orcaspirit.com*), and 5 Star Whales (*5starwhales.com*).

PLAY

Beacon Hill Park and Beacon Hill Children's Farm
311 Vancouver Street; 250-381-2532; *beaconhillpark.ca/childrenspark*
The Beacon Hill Children's Farm is a fantastic, toddler-friendly petting zoo, featuring fluffy-headed chickens, dour pigs, noisy donkeys, strutting peacocks, and many other barnyard creatures. The small goat enclosure holds friendly goats and dozens of brushes perfectly sized for little hands, so kids can groom the goats. Don't miss the 10 a.m. or 4 p.m. "running of the goats," when the goats dash between the enclosure and their nighttime pen.

Year-round, the park's playground offers jeep and bulldozer riding toys, a plastic rock-climbing wall, slides, and wild areas to play. And the park's gardens, fountains, and landscaping are a beautiful, low-key alternative to the Butchart Gardens. Free admission to park. Suggested farm donation: adult/$3; children/$2. Park is open year-round from dawn to dusk; Children's Farm is open from end of February to mid-October, 10 a.m.–4 or 5 p.m.; call for exact hours.

Irving Park
Menzies and Michigan streets
More accessible than Beacon Hill Park on less pleasant days, Irving Park features a small playground just a few blocks from the ferry terminal and near a supermarket (Thrifty Foods).

EAT

Cup of Joe Café $
230 Menzies Street; 250-380-2563
Tucked away in the basement of a nondescript business building, employees sling morning meals from a witty menu. Try the "Chuck Berry" pancakes — a heaping stack of buttermilk goodness, served with berry sauce and whipped cream. Open daily, 8 a.m.–3 p.m.

James Bay Tea Room and Restaurant $–$$
332 Menzies Street; 250-382-8282; *jamesbaytearoomandrestaurant.com*
China plates printed with likenesses of Princess Di and Prince Charles line the walls, peeking out from behind teacups with royal faces. James Bay Tearoom serves traditional British food (Welsh rarebit, mmmm!) and classic high teas (egg salad and tuna salad finger sandwiches, toasted crumpets, and tarts). The "kids' tea" consists of peanut butter finger sandwiches and milk. Not the most gourmet of teas in Victoria (the teapot comes with a brightly colored, crocheted tea cozy), but certainly has its own touristy charm and offers a no-stress tea option for the uninitiated. Open Monday–Saturday, 7 a.m.–5 p.m.; Sunday, 8 a.m.–5 p.m.

VICTORIA
INNER HARBOUR/JAMES BAY

Red Fish, Blue Fish $-$$

1006 Wharf Street; 250-298 6877; *redfish-bluefish.com*

Brit-style restaurants abound in Victoria, but few serve the high-quality, innovative fish 'n' chips available at this tiny dockside shed. The enormous portions of sustainable cod, salmon, and halibut are fit for fisherman-size appetites, or perfect for sharing between a child and adult. Not a fish 'n' chips lover? That's OK — try the fish tacones (taco cones), served with Qualicum Bay oysters or barbecued wild salmon. Open daily, 11:30 a.m.–7 p.m.

Tea Lobby at the Fairmont Empress Hotel $$$

721 Government Street; 866-540-4429; *fairmont.com/empress*

Tea at the Fairmont Empress isn't just tea, it's a rite of passage for many Pacific Northwest girls. Many young woman remember the first time they "took tea" at this chateau-style hotel and restaurant with a favorite aunt or grandma. However, it's not just for the preteen girl in your life; the dining room also offers high chairs and free tea for kids younger than two. The tea comes with fusion fare, such as green-tea tarts on a three-tier tea service. The room looks out onto the harbor, and all teatimes are accompanied by a swaying piano player. The prices are luxurious, but how often do you drink tea in a location fit for a queen? Tea seating starts at noon and ends in late afternoon; reservations are required.

Thrifty Foods $

475 Simcoe Street; *thriftyfoods.com*

A small deli, plentiful fruits and vegetables, a bakery, and quick to-go meals (like pizza) are offered here. It's a great place to go when eating on a budget or staying in a room with a kitchenette. Open daily, 8 a.m.–10 p.m.

Willie's Bakery Museum Café $-$$

675 Belleville Street; 250-381-0058; *williesbakery.com*

A cafeteria-style restaurant with soups, salads, pastries, and sandwiches, Willie's is casual and a little on the pricey side, because of its location (think $5 for soup, $8–$9 for basic sandwiches), but there isn't much else nearby if you're having a starving-toddler emergency. Open daily, 9 a.m.–6 p.m.; sandwiches available 11 a.m.–3:30 p.m.

FORT STREET

Within walking distance of Beacon Hill Park (page 142) and downtown, Fort Street has an eclectic mix of independently owned stores, many of which appeal to parents, kids, and teens. And the Euro-style delis provide great foodstuffs for snacks, lunches, or dinners to go; pick up something here and wander back to James Bay Park.

EAT

Blue Fox Café $$

#101-919 Fort Street; 250-380-1683

You might wait in huge lines out the door of this Fort Street favorite, which dishes up large, hearty meals in a small, crowded setting. Stick-to-your-ribs (and arteries) sausage, potatoes, and eggs are some specialties; it's not my first choice for eating out with kids, but if you're in the neighborhood and the wait isn't bad, give it a try. Open Monday–Saturday, 11 a.m.–8 p.m.

Choux Choux Charcuterie $
830 Fort Street; 250-382-7572; *chouxchoux.ca*
Hey, meat lovers: Here's your dream shop. Dark, rich cheeses and meats from France, Germany, Portugal, and Switzerland are featured here, with more than a dozen varieties of salami alone. A good place to pick up picnic-lunch ingredients for the hotel or Beacon Hill Park (page 142). Open Tuesday–Friday, 10 a.m.–5:30 p.m.; Saturday, 10 a.m.–5 p.m.; closed Sunday and Monday.

The Dutch Bakery & Coffee Shop $
718 Fort Street; 250-385-1012; *thedutchbakery.com*
It's a fairy tale come to life — a European treat explosion of cakes, pastries, and Danishes. Kirsch tarts and turkey pies sit next to marzipan cherries and oranges. This is a great place to pick up a special snack for the ferry ride home. Open Tuesday–Saturday, 7:30 a.m.–5:30 p.m.; closed Sunday and Monday.

Sally Bun $
1030 Fort Street; 250-384-1899
Sally Bun sells rolls stuffed with ingredients such as spinach and feta or scrambled eggs and cheese. Perfectly portable and fuss-free, these sandwiches provide an instant dinner en route to anywhere. But get here early, because the best buns sell out by lunchtime. Open Monday–Friday, 8 a.m.–5:30 p.m.; Saturday, 9:30 a.m.–4 p.m. Closed Sunday.

Zambri's $$
110–911 Yates Street; 250-360-1171; *zambris.ca*
This out-of-the-way eatery is tucked behind a London Drugs in a strip mall, so you're not paying for location. Instead, your dollars go toward exquisitely prepared family-style food. Try sides (flour-dusted cauliflower, sautéed broccoli) for $3, hefty meatball sandwiches or pasta with homemade sauces for $7–$10, and fresh fish (such as rockfish with eggplant and soft polenta) for less than $20. No kids' menu, but staff will accommodate your wishes, and the informal dining room isn't stuffy. There's also an outdoor dining area, with a view of . . . a parking lot. Open Tuesday–Saturday, 11:30 a.m.–2:30 p.m. and 5–9 p.m.

SHOP

BC Shaver and Hobbies
742 Fort Street; 250-383-0051; *bcshaver.com*
Like the coolest old-man garage in existence, BC Shaver and Hobbies contains shelves, stacks, and displays full of imported transportation kits (balsa planes, train sets, car models) from the simple (SIKU German-made miniature metal cars) to the sublime (tin antique trucks). Whether you'd like to construct an Eiffel Tower or dinosaur model, or assemble a flatbed trailer, it's all here. Probably one of the best and most complete stores for the transportation-obsessed kid in the Northwest. Monday–Thursday, 9 a.m.– 5:30 p.m.; Friday, 9 a.m.–8:30 p.m.; Saturday, 9 a.m.–5:30 p.m.; closed Sunday and holidays.

VICTORIA
FORT STREET

Island Blue

905 Fort Street; 250-385-9786; *islandblue.com*

If you're in town for a while or live with a little artist, Island Blue provides everything from art kits to drawing instruction books. Drawing materials include paints, chalk, crayons, gel markers, and puffy ink pens; and sticker, origami, and craft sets for younger kids. A special kids' area contains everything you need to keep the kids busy. Open Monday–Friday, 8:30 a.m.–5:30 p.m.; Saturday, 9:30 a.m.–5 p.m.; Sunday, 11 a.m.–4 p.m.

Mothering Touch

975 Fort Street; 250-595-4905; *motheringtouch.ca*

An enormous store stuffed with natural, Canadian-made infant goods. Along with the typical baby books, diapers, and baby carriers, Mothering Touch offers Yukon-made belly-, hand-, foot-, and bum-casting kits, Canadian maplewood teethers, all-weather rain suits, Coquitlam-made skin creams, B.C.-made moccasins, leather bibs with sushi appliqués, and stainless steel feeding bowls. Families staying in Victoria for longer than a few days might be interested in joining a Mothering Touch play group or class; check its Web site for a current schedule. Open Monday–Friday, 10 a.m.–6 p.m.; Saturday and Sunday, 10 a.m.–4 p.m.; closed Friday–Monday on holiday weekends.

OAK BAY

Quaint Oak Bay offers a neighborhood feel, beautiful parks, waterside settings, a mild-mannered tea shop, and toy stores. British accents are in the air (plenty of retired Brits over here) and on the Tudor-style building facades. If you have a car, Oak Street is worth the short drive out.

SLEEP

Oak Bay Guest House $$-$$$$

1052 Newport Avenue; 800-575-3812 or 250-598-3812; *oakbayguesthouse.com*

Oak Bay's Victorian-era eleven-room home will allow children as visitors on a case-by-case basis, and is probably best for older children. The downstairs, richly decorated suite works best for well-behaved small families that want to take advantage of Oak Bay's secluded, village-like atmosphere. A full breakfast is served in the morning, and a small sunroom provides a TV and VCR, tea, puzzles, and paperback books. Talk to owner Egle Vair to see if she can accommodate you.

DO

Oak Bay Recreation Center

1975 Bee Street; 250-595-SWIM (7946); *recreation.oakbaybc.org*

Whether you skate or swim, Oak Bay has an inexpensive option for you. Water fans will enjoy the pool (including toddler pool), tunnel drop slide, and hot tub. The center's Olympic-sized ice rink welcomes everyone during family skate times, and new skaters can get help with skate-assist devices during the rink's Sunday hours. Prices and hours vary; see Web site for details.

VICTORIA OAK BAY

PLAY
Oak Bay Marina and Haynes Park
1327 Beach Drive; 250-598-3369; *oakbaymarina.com*
Haynes Park is a wonderful little green space dotted with benches, views of the Georgia Strait, and a four-person swing. Create a picnic from items purchased at Ottavio (see below) and eat here, or walk down a little farther to find the small dock with boats, and a coffee shop with indoor and outdoor seating. Here's something the kids are sure to love: Buy fish chum indoors at the downstairs fishing supply shop and hand-feed the seals.

EAT
Ottavio $
2272 Oak Bay Ave.; 250-592-4080; *ottaviovictoria.com*
Locals jam the narrow aisles of this Italian deli, trying to decide whether to order a rose or lavender gelato, freshly baked bread, gourmet cheeses, or just a sandwich to go. Save room for BC Gelato or one of Ottavio's ethereal desserts, such as meringue nests and almond tarts. A kids' grilled cheese runs $3, as do the pizzettes. Eat indoors at one of the bakery's tables or outside. The gourmet food area sells imported take-home goodies, including cheeses, chocolates, and chestnut purées. Bakery open Tuesday–Saturday, 9 a.m.–6 p.m. Café open Tuesday–Saturday, 8 a.m.–6 p.m.; closed Sunday.

Serious Coffee $
2060 Oak Bay Avenue; 250-590-8920; *seriouscoffee.com*
A gallery-style coffee shop with leather chairs in a cozy corner and copies of *BC Parent* up on the wall. Nothing fancy — just good coffee, big chairs, and personable service from the coffee shop's owner. Open Monday–Wednesday, 6:30 a.m.–8 p.m.; Thursday and Friday, 6:30 a.m.–10 p.m.; Saturday 8 a.m.–10 p.m.; Sunday 8 a.m.–6 p.m.

White Heather Tea Room $–$$
1885 Oak Bay Avenue; 250-595-8020; *whiteheather-tearoom.com*
Locals love the White Heather's sumptuous Scottish-style, down-to-earth tea. White tablecloths under mismatched cups and saucers provide a homey look, but these green booths get busy — always call to make a reservation. Go for the "Big Muckle" tea, with cream cheese and salmon sandwiches, almond macaroons, hazelnut scones, tarts, clotted cream, and a bottomless pot of tea. Try the Scottish shortbread flecked with ginger. Kids can order a pot of caffeine-free fruit tisane to go with the sugar rush; but this tea shop is best for older kids. Open Tuesday–Saturday, 10 a.m.–5 p.m.; closed Sunday and Monday.

SHOP
Abra-Kid-Abra
2024 Oak Bay Avenue; 250-595-1613; *abra-kid-abra.com*
If you've forgotten something essential for a child younger than seven, Abra-Kid-Abra sells consignment clothing at moderate prices (e.g., $8–$10 for used shirts). Although its prices may seem high, this shop is still your best bet in

Victoria for must-have clothes for less than $10. Open Monday–Saturday, 9:30 a.m.–5 p.m.; Sunday, noon–4 p.m.

Finn & Izzy
2259 Oak Bay Avenue; 250-592-8168
Here's the place to find boy's and girl's clothes from Canadian and imported lines, including MEXX, Kushies, Zutano, and Deux Par Deux. Complete lines of baby layettes, fun jewelry, and modern mobiles are on offer, too. Most items are for the newborn–six set, with some pieces for ages seven to ten. Prices are about what you'd expect at a boutique, but Finn & Izzy offers great seasonal sales. Open Monday–Friday, 10 a.m.–5:30, Saturday 10 a.m.–5 p.m.; closed Sunday.

Lazy Susan's
1974 Oak Bay Avenue; 250-412-1122; *lazysusansonline.com*
Lazy Susan's stocks fun gear with a 1950s twist. Check out the oilcloth bibs, seatbelt bags, baby tees, bird- or robot-shaped bike bells, and pillowcases made into summer-ready shirts. Owner Susan Doyle creates many of the eclectic offerings in both of her stores, in Victoria and Vancouver; definitely worth a stop with crafty kids or teens. Open Monday–Saturday, 10:30 a.m.–5:30 p.m.; closed Sunday.

Science Works
1889 Oak Bay Avenue; 250-595-6033
Geology prodigies unite! Everything your budding biologist- or chemist-to-be might need is here, including experiment kits, microscopes, telescopes, books on B.C. plants and mammals, and even dino tees. And it's right next door to White Heather Tea Room, so you can head here if the kids get antsy. Open Monday–Saturday, 10 a.m.–5:30 p.m.; closed Sunday.

Timeless Toys
117-2187 Oak Bay Avenue; 250-598-8697
The classic playthings kids love in a bedroom-size toy store. If you're going to tea at White Heather, this is a good place to pick up a few quiet-time playthings; merchandise includes Playmobil, Legos, travel-size activity books, puppets, and puzzles. Open Monday–Saturday, 10 a.m.–5 p.m.; Sunday, 11 a.m.–4 p.m.

AROUND VICTORIA

SLEEP

Cottage Pirouette $–$$
401 Lampson Street; 877-386-2166 or 250-386-2166; *cottagepirouette.com*
If you have a car (or patience for bus schedules or a thirty-minute walk to downtown Victoria), you'll realize savings by staying in this small bed-and-breakfast in the Esquimalt neighborhood. It's not near any tourist attractions, but owner Lorraine's en suite rooms and hearty breakfasts welcome those looking for a more home-like stay. She'll pull out board games for fidgety kids and make room for futons on the floor.

DO

The Butchart Gardens

800 Benvenuto Avenue; 250-652-5256; *butchartgardens.com*
Lovely statues, fountains, and steps go through fifty-five acres of sunken gardens, rose gardens, Japanese gardens, and Italian gardens in Canada's largest . . . garden. The landscaping here reflects a tremendous effort, requiring between 250 and 550 staff, depending upon the season. Wonderful in warm weather, Butchart allows families to easily pass a whole afternoon here. In rainy weather, complimentary umbrellas are available. It's a great place for running down paths, identifying flowers (pick up a guide at the entrance), drinking hot chocolate, or reveling in holiday lights. Prices are highest in peak seasons, March–June and in December. Adults/$16.25–$28; teens (13–17)/$8.25–$14; children (5–12)/$2–$3; younger than 5/free; group rates/$14.63–$25.20. Open daily, 9 a.m.–dusk; open evenings during the holiday season for holiday lights — check Web site for times.

Craigdarroch Castle

1050 Joan Crescent Drive; 250-592-5323; *craigdarrochcastle.com*
If your kids enjoyed the historical section of the Royal BC Museum's Victorian-era storefronts, they'll probably appreciate the quaintness of Craigdarroch. Decorated to look as they did more than a hundred years ago, Craigdarroch's sweeping rooms and shining banisters cover four stories. Ask for the child-oriented guide pamphlet at the front desk. Caveat: It's not really a castle, despite the turret. It's more like a creaky antique house; little boys hoping to play "Viking Castle Invader" will be sorely disappointed. Adults/$12; students/$8; children (6–18)/$4; younger than 5/free. Open daily, 10 a.m.–4:30 p.m.; in summer, 9 a.m.–7 p.m.

Gordon Head Recreation Centre

4100 Lambrick Way; 250-475-7100;
gov.saanich.bc.ca/resident/recreation/ghrc.html
Want to do something totally out of the ordinary? Victoria — like many B.C. cities — offers wonderful community centers to their residents and out-of-town visitors. This family-friendly aquatic center boasts numerous features, including three hot tubs, a lazy whirlpool, spray features, slides, and a supershallow toddler pool. Tarzan would love the swinging rope and climbing wall over the big-kid pool. You might be the only out-of-town visitor here, but it's worth swinging by. Family/$11.50; adult/$5.75; students (13–18 with ID card)/$4.50; children(5–12)/$3; 4 and younger/free. Hours vary; call or check Web site.

Save-On-Foods Memorial Centre

1925 Blanshard Street; 250-220-2600; *saveonfoodsmemorialcentre.com*
Home of the Victoria Salmon Kings (*salmonkings.com*), a midlevel professional ice hockey league, it offers a gentle introduction to hockey (if such a thing is possible). You can also catch music performances. See the Web site before visiting, and treat your tween or teen to a surprise concert or a special game (one invites kids out onto the rink with the players). Younger kids will like Marty the Marmot, the Salmon Kings' mascot. $15–$22/single-game hockey tickets; concert prices vary.

Victoria Butterfly Gardens

1461 Benvenuto Avenue; 250-652-3822; *butterflygardens.com*

Feeling chilly? Check out the hot times inside the Victoria Butterfly Gardens. This indoor "jungle" contains hundreds of fluttering butterflies at various stages of the life cycle (eggs, caterpillars, and butterflies), flamingos, South Africa turacos, and koi fish, plus carnivorous vegetation such as Venus flytraps and pitcher plants. Bring a camera to capture the showgirl-worthy pink boa plants and enormous Atlas moths. Adults/$12; students/$11; children (3–12)/$ 6.50; children younger than 3/free. Open daily. Hours vary by season; call or check Web site for details.

getaway
SAN JUAN ISLAND (U.S.)

You'll start to notice a shift on the ferry ride over. It's a decent ferry ride, about two hours from Anacortes, an hour from Victoria. There's no television blaring aboard, just the steady noise of the vessel's engine. You might as well play cards with the kids or let the wind rearrange your hair out on the deck. The ferry passes by dozens of tiny and medium-size islands, many completely uninhabited. Don't be surprised if somewhere on this crossing, you really start to unwind.

Once you're on the 55-square-mile San Juan Island, life slows even more. With enormous expanses of sky, rolling countryside, and dramatic seascapes, we all feel a little smaller (even if we're supposed to be the grownups). Besides the gorgeous scenery, San Juan Island provides wonderful, inexpensive pleasures, such as sunsets, state parks, bowling alleys, farm visits, and movie theaters.

Sticker shock may arrive in the form of your hotel bill, however. This is hardly an undiscovered Eden. Save on expenditures: Bring plenty of snacks with you, or go during the shoulder season (spring or fall), when many attractions, restaurants, and stores are still open — just not as late.

GETTING THERE AND GETTING AROUND

The Washington State Ferries system (*wsdot.wa.gov/ferries*) pinballs from Anacortes, Washington, through the U.S. and Canadian San Juan Islands, to Sidney, B.C., 30 minutes north of Victoria. If you prefer to leave your car behind, you can park your car, for a fee, at the Anacortes ferry terminal. Prices vary by season and day of week, but round-trip passenger fares are around $22/adult and $17.60/child for the ride between Anacortes and Friday Harbor, San Juan Island's port town. Bring your car along, and the fare bumps up to $55.75–$81.20 for a car and driver (plus extra for passengers in the car). Sailing times vary, depending the season; check the Web site for a current schedule and fares.

Warning: There is no service between Sidney, B.C., and Washington state during winter (early January–late March).

VICTORIA GETAWAY

From Seattle, you can board the passenger-only Clipper (*clippervacations.com*), which sails once daily, May through September. From Seattle to Friday Harbor, journey time is three and a half hours, with additional whale and sealife searches added for a fee. Adults/$85–$155; kids/$42.50–$77.50, or in some cases, free.

If you're a foot passenger, once on the island, you'll be staying in and around Friday Harbor, unless you brought (or plan to rent) a bike, use the San Juan Island Transit (*sanjuantransit.com*), available May– September, take a taxi, or rent a car. If the latter, bring your child's car seat.

Read more about what's going on during your stay at the *San Juan Islander* (*sanjuanislander.com*).

SLEEP
Bed and Breakfasts
Bed and Breakfast Association of San Juan Island; *san-juan-island.net*
If you're bringing a car, you have more choices. Visit this site to find an island bed-and-breakfast that welcomes children. Choose between rustic, suite-style, or farm-stay options.

Earthbox Motel & Spa $$–$$$
410 Spring Street; 360-378-4000 or 800-793-4756; *earthboxmotel.com*
A rehabbed motor inn, Earthbox has been classed up with muted tones and dark wood furnishings. Your top choice may be the suite-style rooms, but the downside is that there are only two, and they book quickly. The "Sun" wing is good for families, with large rooms and two queen beds, but the walls are thin. The "Sky" rooms offer one large king bed, which may work for small (and snuggly) families.

Roche Harbor Resort $$$–$$$$
248 Reuben Memorial Drive; 360-378-2155 or 800-451-8910;
rocheharbor.com
This is the place to go if you want family-style luxury; it's a four-star act in a lush, waterside setting. Family-ready options include stand-alone cottages, suites, and rooms. Most of the larger options are outfitted with flat-screen televisions, microwaves, mini-fridges, and other amenities. The real attraction of Roche Harbor is location; it's isolated, yet close enough to Friday Harbor (twenty-minute drive) to still go into town for a movie. Several restaurants, gift shops, artist's kiosks, and a grocery store are scattered around the property, but there's not much for kids. Thankfully, though, in summer, it offers family programs.

DO
Farm tours at Pelindaba Lavender Farm and Krystal Acres Alpaca Farm & Country Store
Pelindaba Lavender Farm: 33 Hawthorne Lane; 360-378-4248; *pelindabalavender.com*. April–October, open daily, 9:30 a.m.–5:30 p.m. Closed November–March. **Krystal Acres Alpaca Farm & Country Store:** 152 Blazing Tree Road; 360-378-6125; *krystalacres.com*. April–December: open daily, 10 a.m.–5 p.m. January–March: open Friday–Monday, 11 a.m.–5 p.m.

Stop by these two visitor-welcoming farms, and stroll through fragrant lavender fields, pat an alpaca, or browse the stores at either one. Alternately, try another farm along San Juan Island's country roads to pick up fresh eggs, veggies, or fruits.

Island Bicycles
380 Argyle Avenue; 360-378-4941; *islandbicycles.com*
Rent a one-speed, mountain, or touring bike here, along with Burley or BOB bike trailers for toddlers and trail-a-bikes for older children who can't yet keep a steady pace. Prices start at adults/$5; children/$2.50. Open June–September, daily 9 a.m.–6 p.m. Winter hours vary.

Lime Kiln Point State Park
1567 Westside Road; 360-378-2044; *parks.wa.gov*
Truly one of the more spectacular parks in the Pacific Northwest, Lime Kiln offers the recipe for a perfect late-afternoon picnic. Take in spectacular views from west-facing, easy hiking trails next to stands of madrona and fir; mix with the possibility of spotting a migrating whale; and add picnic tables. The decommissioned lighthouse serves as a whale-watching station today, and provides information on spotting and identifying pods. While your chance of seeing a whale is only about one in five, you'll be glad you made the trek out here.

Palace Theatre
209 Spring Street; 360-370-5666
First-run movies on two screens. Check what's playing when you're in town; depending on your age of child, it may or may not be suitable.

Paradise Lanes
365 Spring Street; 360-370-5667; *paradiselanes.net*
Don't let a rainy day get you down. Instead, roll yourself a good time at San Juan's classic bowling lanes, conveniently situated downtown. Get a lucky strike on one of Paradise's lanes, play video games in the adjoining room, or eat a midpriced breakfast, lunch, or dinner in Paradise's restaurant. Adults/$3.75–$4.25; children/$3.25–3.75. Shoes extra, 10 percent discount for emergency and public safety personnel including firefighters, police, and EMTs. Open Monday–Thursday, noon–9:30 p.m.; Friday and Saturday, 11 a.m.–11 p.m.; Sunday, 11 a.m.–8 p.m.

Roche Harbor Village
Off Roche Harbor Road, at entrance to Roche Harbor Resort; 800-451-8910 or 360-378-2155; *rocheharbor.com*
On the north end of San Juan Island is another port of entry known as Roche Harbor Village. Not just any resort, this area is listed on the National Register of Historic Places and is approximately ten miles from Friday Harbor. Roche Harbor has beautiful Victorian gardens, an airstrip, marina, lodging, grocery store, restaurants, sculpture park, shopping, water activities, and local artists' booths.

VICTORIA GETAWAY

San Juan Island Marine Center
4 Front Street, Suite C; 360-378-6202; *sjimarine.com*
Rent family Hobie pedal kayaks, small boats, electric-powered dinghies, or radio-control tugboats. Explore the port, Brown Island, and the protected harbor from the water, take a short ride to the Turn Island State Park for a hike and a picnic, or go fishing or crabbing. Prices start at $18/hour.

San Juan Island National Historic Park: English Camp and American Camp
American Camp off of Cattle Point Road, English Camp off of West Valley Road; 360-378-2902; *nps.gov/sajh*
These two camps are a mere thirteen miles apart, but travel time requires about twenty-five to forty minutes on slowly winding country roads. English camp (only open in summer) is halfway up the island, while the year-round American Camp is at the island's southeastern tip. Both ranger stations offer a free children's guide, which helps explain the island's infamous Pig War, as well as the natural flora and fauna. If you can only go to one, I'd suggest American Camp. It's a fifteen-minute drive from Friday Harbor and contains artifacts and a ranger station with a nice selection of Victorian-era (read: simple) toys and books on island nature.

San Juan Island Trails
Cross-island; *sanjuanislandtrails.org*
San Juan's gently rolling hills and pastoral landscapes make a prime location for family hiking or biking trips. But be forewarned: The trail shoulders are slim, so bike rides are best for older children who are steady on two wheels and fully grasp safety rules. To get in the right gear, check out the island's hiking and biking routes at San Juan Island Trails' Web site.

Sculpture Park at Westcott Bay Reserve
Off Roche Harbor Road, at entrance to Roche Harbor Resort; 360-370-5050; *westcottbay.org*
Ten miles from Friday Harbor, the Westcott Bay Sculpture Park holds more than one hundred works of modern art on nineteen acres of land. Kids will enjoy the quirky table-and-chairs, crocodile, and deer sculptures, among others. The fenced-in park's not big, but it's large enough to roam around in, as long as you keep a close eye on the little ones when near the small lake (which, of course, also features its own sculpture).

The Whale Museum
62 First Street N.; 360-378-4790; *whalemuseum.org*
This funky little museum provides educational, hands-on exhibits on Puget Sound whale life. Kids enjoy the whale telephone booth, where they can eavesdrop on whale squeaks and whistles, and the mock whale observation station. Don't miss the gory worm display in the museum's rear, which includes a 27-foot-long parasitic worm found in a porpoise. Ew. The kids' area offers orca suits for dress-up, coloring books, a movie, and picture books about whale life. Adults/$6; children (5–18)/$3; younger than 5/free. Open daily, 10 a.m.–6 p.m.; winter hours vary.

EAT

Backdoor Kitchen & Catering $$-$$$
400-B A Street; 360-378-9540; *backdoorkitchen.com*
One of San Juan's most coveted restaurants, with a focus on fresh, local fare. It's spendy though, and the atmosphere is more for canoodling couples than families. If the kids are already asleep, and you're staying at Earthbox, you can request a meal to go, and Backdoor will deliver it to the hotel. Generally open Wednesday–Monday, 5–9 p.m., but hours vary, so call first.

Café Demeter $
80 Nichols Street; 360-370-5443; *cafedemeter.food.officelive.com*
Pick up hand-shaped ciabatta, veggie pizzas, savory or sweet croissants, or just get a steaming bowl of carrot-ginger soup, served with a hearty chunk of bread. The homemade soups and freshly baked breads change daily. However, you can always count on the signature bagels and olive-oil-enriched ciabatta. Open Tuesday–Friday, 7:30 a.m.–3:30 p.m.; Saturday, 7:30–whenever (closing time varies).

The Doctor's Office $
85 Front Street; 360-378-8865
Located right across from the ferry dock, this tiny deli offers breakfast and lunch sandwiches, homemade soups, pastries, and smoothies. Inside, there are a few games, a paperback library, and about four tables. Huge portions, so don't over-order. Open daily 4:30 a.m.–8 or 10 p.m. (depending on the last ferry).

Downriggers $$-$$$
10 Front Street; 360-378-2700; *downriggerssanjuan.com*
Come dinnertime, everyone flocks to this San Juan favorite for gorgeous food in a gorgeous setting. Large windows face out onto the harbor; ask for a seat by the window or a raised booth. The children's menu offers classic kids' fare, and the appetizers are large enough for two kids to share. Standout adult dishes are tinged with Mexican flair. Also open for breakfast on Saturdays and Sundays at 9 a.m. Open daily, 11 a.m.–9 p.m.

Lime Kiln Café $
Roche Harbor Pier; 800-451-8910; *rocheharbor.com/dining_limekiln.html*
This is a low-key cafe with views of Roche Harbor, offering options like burgers, sandwiches, and fish. During the off-season, head here for a hot cup of coffee or hot chocolate. Year-round, trying a fresh doughnut (vanilla, chocolate, or plain) made on site is essential. Open 7 a.m.–8 p.m. in summer; 7 a.m.–4 p.m. in off-season.

The Market Chef $$
225 A Street; 360-378-4546
Casual yet upscale, The Market Chef offers an ever-changing array of bistro-style meals (salads, soups, sandwiches) using local ingredients. The owners have kids, so they understand your needs. Open Monday–Friday, 10 a.m.–4 p.m. Closed on weekends.

VICTORIA GETAWAY

Mi Casita $
95 Nichols Street; 360-378-6103
Locals flock to this little Mexican restaurant, off the main thoroughfare (check your map before setting out, or just ask a resident to steer you in the right direction). You'll find Mexican-American food that children typically enjoy and outdoor seating on sunny days. Open Monday–Saturday at 4 p.m. with the last seating at 8 p.m. Closed Sunday.

Sweet Retreat & Espresso $
264 Spring Street; 360-378-1957
Locals recommend this small, well-priced stop, particularly if you're looking for a quick and early breakfast before you hop on the ferry. Check out the bagels, English muffin egg sandwiches, or muffins to go; kids crowd the place for ice cream on nice afternoons. Open daily, 8 a.m.–4 p.m.

SHOP
Griffin Bay Bookstore
155 Spring Street; 360-378-5511; *griffinbaybook.com*
A corner of Griffin Bay is devoted to high-quality children's classics, picture books, and middle-school-grade readers. Sit on one of the store's air-filled beanbag chairs and share a book together. Or pick out one of your childhood favorites — Griffin Bay is likely to carry it. Open daily, 9 a.m.–6 p.m.

King's Market, Marine and Clothing
160 Spring Street W.; 360-378-4505; *kings-market.com*
Forgot something? Probably. Will King's have it? Maybe. This one-stop-shopping solution is the biggest grocery game in town, so hopefully it'll be able to come to your aid. Open daily, 7:30 a.m.–9 p.m.

Osito's
120 S. First Street; 360-378-4320
Stop into San Juan's deluxe toy store to check out their two stories of dolls, educational playthings, clothes, and toddler toys. A fun loft inside holds some-times-necessary rain gear, in case you left yours at home. Play at the train table or browse the sale racks. Open Monday–Saturday, 10 a.m.–5 p.m.; Sunday, 11 a.m.–4 p.m.

Pelindaba Lavender
150 First Street; 360-378-6900, 866-819-1911; *pelindabalavender.com*
This shop isn't great for grabby kids; it's full of breakables and bath goodies. But dash in for one of Pelindaba's delightful (and spendy — around $6 for six) cookie packages, like coconut-cranberry-lavender cookies or lavender short-breads. Savor slowly. Open daily, 9:30 a.m.–5 p.m.; hours vary during off season.

index

INDEX

INDEX

Lora Shinn is a writer specializing in family travel for local, regional, and national publications. Lora has lived in the Pacific Northwest since age four, and has long enjoyed the region's cities, slopes, and seashore. She currently lives in Seattle with her husband and two children.